Student Companion

Grade 6

Acknowledgments for illustrations and composition: Rory Hensley, David Jackson, Jim Mariano, Rich McMahon, Lorie Park, Ted Smykal, Ralph Voltz, and Laserwords

ISBN-13: 978-0-13-327625-1
ISBN-10: 0-13-327625-2
2 3 4 5 6 7 8 9 10 V016 17 16 15 14 13

digits™ System Requirements

▶ Supported System Configurations

	Operating System (32-bit only)	Web Browser* (32-bit only)	Java® Version**
PC	Windows® XP (SP3) Windows Vista (SP1) Windows 7	Internet Explorer® 7 Internet Explorer 8 Internet Explorer 9 Mozilla Firefox® 11 Google Chrome™	1.4.2 1.5 [5.0 Update 11 or higher] 1.6 [6.0 through Update 18]
Mac	Macintosh® OS 10.6.x, 10.7.x	Safari® 5.0 Safari 5.1 Google Chrome™	1.5 [5.0 Update 16 or higher]

* Pop-up blockers must be disabled in the browser.
** Java (JRE) plug-in must be installed and JavaScript® must be enabled in the browser.

▶ Additional Requirements

Software	Version
Adobe® Flash®	Version 10.4 or higher
Adobe Reader® (required for PC*)	Version 8 or higher
Word processing software	Microsoft® Word®, Open Office, or similar application to open ".doc" files

* Macintosh® OS 10.6 has a built-in PDF reader, Preview.

Screen Resolution
PC
Minimum: 1024 x 768*
Maximum: 1280 x 1024
Mac
Minimum: 1024 x 768*
Maximum: 1280 x 960
*recommended for interactive whiteboards

Internet Connection
Broadband (cable/DSL) or greater is recommended.

AOL® and AT&T™ Yahoo!® Users
You cannot use the AOL or AT&T Yahoo! browsers. However, you can use AOL or AT&T as your Internet Service Provider to access the Internet, and then open a supported browser.

The trademarks referred to above are the property of their respective owners, none of whom have authorized, approved, or otherwise sponsored this product.

▶ For *digits*™ Support

go to **http://support.pearsonschool.com/index.cfm/digits**

digits™ Learning Team

My Name: _____

My Teacher's Name: _____

My School: _____

Kala

Xiao

Lisa

Jay

Francis (Skip) Fennell
digits Author

Approaches to mathematics content and curriculum, educational policy, and support for intervention

Eric Milou
digits Author

Approaches to mathematical content and the use of technology in middle grades classrooms

Art Johnson
digits Author

Approaches to mathematical content and support for English language learners

William F. Tate
digits Author

Approaches to intervention, and use of efficacy and research

Helene Sherman
digits Author

Teacher education and support for struggling students

Grant Wiggins
digits Consulting Author

Understanding by Design

Stuart J. Murphy
digits Author

Visual learning and student engagement

Randall I. Charles
digits Advisor

Janie Schielack
digits Author

Approaches to mathematical content, building problem solvers, and support for intervention

Jim Cummins
digits Advisor

Supporting English Language Learners

Jacquie Moen
digits Advisor

Digital Technology

Log into **MyMathUniverse**

Be sure to save all of your your log-in information by writing it here.

Class URL: _____

My Username: _____

My Password: _____

1 First, go to MyMathUniverse.com.

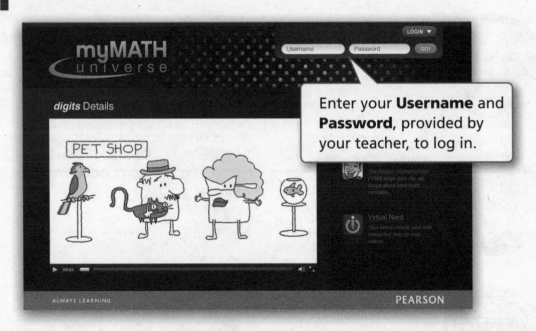

Enter your **Username** and **Password**, provided by your teacher, to log in.

2 After you've logged in, choose your class from the **home page**.

Choose **your class** from the list.

3 When you have chosen your class, this is your **Overview page.**

Click **To Do** to view your due items.

Click **Practice** to explore *digits* lessons on your own.

Click **Done** to view your past due and completed items.

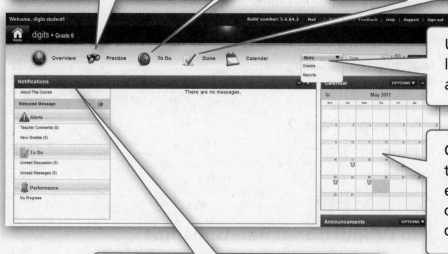

Under **More** you can link to your **Grades** and **Reports**.

Click the **Calendar** to view items due each day. Red alarm clocks are for past due assignments!

Check your **Notifications**, including:
- Teacher Comments
- Grades posted
- Messages from your teacher
- Your progress in *digits*

As you work online, make sure to hit "Save" so you don't lose your work!

Save

Welcome to digits.

Using the Student Companion

digits is designed to help you master mathematics skills and concepts in a way that's relevant to you. As the title **digits** suggests, this program takes a digital approach. The Student Companion supports your work on **digits** by providing a place to demonstrate your understanding of lesson skills and concepts in writing.

Your companion supports your work on **digits** in so many ways!

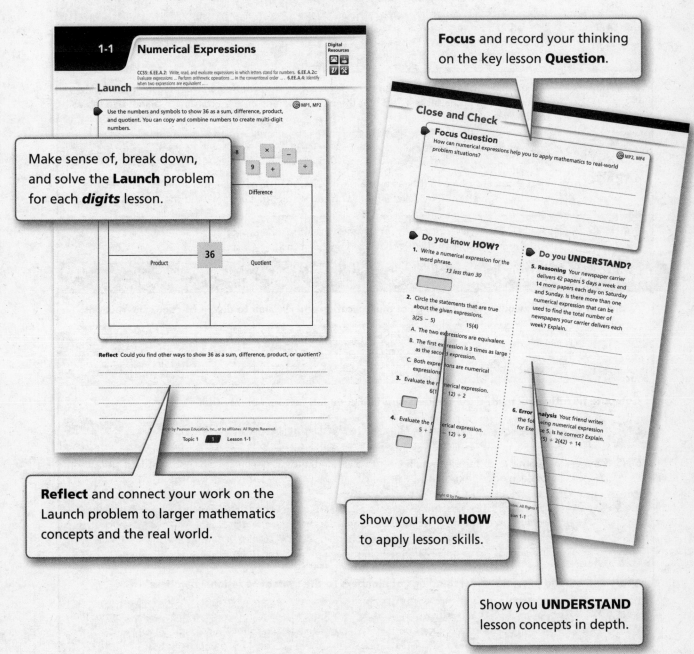

Focus and record your thinking on the key lesson **Question**.

Make sense of, break down, and solve the **Launch** problem for each **digits** lesson.

Reflect and connect your work on the Launch problem to larger mathematics concepts and the real world.

Show you know **HOW** to apply lesson skills.

Show you **UNDERSTAND** lesson concepts in depth.

Gr 6 | Common Core State Standards

Number	Standard for Mathematical Content
6.RP	**Ratios and Proportional Relationships**

Understand ratio concepts and use ratio reasoning to solve problems.

Number	Standard for Mathematical Content
6.RP.A.1	Understand the concept of a ratio and use ratio language to describe a ratio relationship between two quantities.
6.RP.A.2	Understand the concept of a unit rate $\frac{a}{b}$ associated with a ratio $a : b$ with $b \neq 0$, and use rate language in the context of a ratio relationship.
6.RP.A.3	Use ratio and rate reasoning to solve real-world and mathematical problems, e.g., by reasoning about tables of equivalent ratios, tape diagrams, double number line diagrams, or equations.
6.RP.A.3a	Make tables of equivalent ratios relating quantities with whole number measurements, find missing values in the tables, and plot the pairs of values on the coordinate plane. Use tables to compare ratios.
6.RP.A.3b	Solve unit rate problems including those involving unit pricing and constant speed.
6.RP.A.3c	Find a percent of a quantity as a rate per 100 (e.g., 30% of a quantity means $\frac{30}{100}$ times the quantity); solve problems involving finding the whole, given a part and the percent.
6.RP.A.3d	Use ratio reasoning to convert measurement units; manipulate and transform units appropriately when multiplying or dividing quantities.

Number	Standard for Mathematical Content
6.NS	**The Number System**

Apply and extend previous understandings of multiplication and division to divide fractions by fractions.

Number	Standard for Mathematical Content
6.NS.A.1	Interpret and compute quotients of fractions, and solve word problems involving division of fractions by fractions, e.g., by using visual fraction models and equations to represent the problem.

Compute fluently with multi-digit numbers and find common factors and multiples.

Number	Standard for Mathematical Content
6.NS.B.2	Fluently divide multi-digit numbers using the standard algorithm.
6.NS.B.3	Fluently add, subtract, multiply, and divide multi-digit decimals using the standard algorithm for each operation.
6.NS.B.4	Find the greatest common factor of two whole numbers less than or equal to 100 and the least common multiple of two whole numbers less than or equal to 12. Use the distributive property to express a sum of two whole numbers 1–100 with a common factor as a multiple of a sum of two whole numbers with no common factor.

Apply and extend previous understandings of numbers to the system of rational numbers.

Number	Standard for Mathematical Content
6.NS.C.5	Understand that positive and negative numbers are used together to describe quantities having opposite directions or values; use positive and negative numbers to represent quantities in real-world contexts, explaining the meaning of 0 in each situation.

Number	Standard for Mathematical Content

6.NS The Number System (continued)

Apply and extend previous understandings of numbers to the system of rational numbers.

Number	Standard for Mathematical Content
6.NS.C.6	Understand a rational number as a point on the number line. Extend number line diagrams and coordinate axes familiar from previous grades to represent points on the line and in the plane with negative number coordinates.
6.NS.C.6a	Recognize opposite signs of numbers as indicating locations on opposite sides of 0 on the number line; recognize that the opposite of the opposite of a number is the number itself.
6.NS.C.6b	Understand signs of numbers in ordered pairs as indicating locations in quadrants of the coordinate plane; recognize that when two ordered pairs differ only by signs, the locations of the points are related by reflections across one or both axes.
6.NS.C.6c	Find and position integers and other rational numbers on a horizontal or vertical number line diagram; find and position pairs of integers and other rational numbers on a coordinate plane.
6.NS.C.7	Understand ordering and absolute value of rational numbers.
6.NS.C.7a	Interpret statements of inequality as statements about the relative position of two numbers on a number line diagram.
6.NS.C.7b	Write, interpret, and explain statements of order for rational numbers in real-world contexts.
6.NS.C.7c	Understand the absolute value of a rational number as its distance from 0 on the number line; interpret absolute value as magnitude for a positive or negative quantity in a real-world situation.
6.NS.C.7d	Distinguish comparisons of absolute value from statements about order.
6.NS.C.8	Solve real-world and mathematical problems by graphing points in all four quadrants of the coordinate plane. Include use of coordinates and absolute value to find distances between points with the same first coordinate or the same second coordinate.

6.EE Expressions and Equations

Apply and extend previous understandings of arithmetic to algebraic expressions.

Number	Standard for Mathematical Content
6.EE.A.1	Write and evaluate numerical expressions involving whole-number exponents.
6.EE.A.2	Write, read, and evaluate expressions in which letters stand for numbers.
6.EE.A.2a	Write expressions that record operations with numbers and with letters standing for numbers.
6.EE.A.2b	Identify parts of an expression using mathematical terms (sum, term, product, factor, quotient, coefficient); view one or more parts of an expression as a single entity.
6.EE.A.2c	Evaluate expressions at specific values of their variables. Include expressions that arise from formulas used in real-world problems. Perform arithmetic operations, including those involving whole number exponents, in the conventional order when there are no parentheses to specify a particular order (Order of Operations).

Grade 6 **Common Core State Standards** *continued*

Number	Standard for Mathematical Content

6.EE Expressions and Equations *(continued)*

Apply and extend previous understandings of arithmetic to algebraic expressions.

6.EE.A.3	Apply the properties of operations to generate equivalent expressions.
6.EE.A.4	Identify when two expressions are equivalent (i.e., when the two expressions name the same number regardless of which value is substituted into them).

Reason about and solve one-variable equations and inequalities.

6.EE.B.5	Understand solving an equation or inequality as a process of answering a question: which values from a specified set, if any, make the equation or inequality true? Use substitution to determine whether a given number in a specified set makes an equation or inequality true.
6.EE.B.6	Use variables to represent numbers and write expressions when solving a real-world or mathematical problem; understand that a variable can represent an unknown number, or, depending on the purpose at hand, any number in a specified set.
6.EE.B.7	Solve real-world and mathematical problems by writing and solving equations of the form $x + p = q$ and $px = q$ for cases in which p, q, and x are all nonnegative rational numbers.
6.EE.B.8	Write an inequality of the form $x > c$ or $x < c$ to represent a constraint or condition in a real-world or mathematical problem. Recognize that inequalities of the form $x > c$ or $x < c$ have infinitely many solutions; represent solutions of such inequalities on number line diagrams.

Represent and analyze quantitative relationships between dependent and independent variables.

6.EE.C.9	Use variables to represent two quantities in a real-world problem that change in relationship to one another; write an equation to express one quantity, thought of as the dependent variable, in terms of the other quantity, thought of as the independent variable. Analyze the relationship between the dependent and independent variables using graphs and tables, and relate these to the equation.

6.G Geometry

Solve real-world and mathematical problems involving area, surface area, and volume.

6.G.A.1	Find the area of right triangles, other triangles, special quadrilaterals, and polygons by composing into rectangles or decomposing into triangles and other shapes; apply these techniques in the context of solving real-world and mathematical problems.
6.G.A.2	Find the volume of a right rectangular prism with fractional edge lengths by packing it with unit cubes of the appropriate unit fraction edge lengths, and show that the volume is the same as would be found by multiplying the edge lengths of the prism. Apply the formulas $V = lwh$ and $V = bh$ to find volumes of right rectangular prisms with fractional edge lengths in the context of solving real-world and mathematical problems.
6.G.A.3	Draw polygons in the coordinate plane given coordinates for the vertices; use coordinates to find the length of a side joining points with the same first coordinate or the same second coordinate. Apply these techniques in the context of solving real-world and mathematical problems.
6.G.A.4	Represent three-dimensional figures using nets made up of rectangles and triangles, and use the nets to find the surface area of these figures. Apply these techniques in the context of solving real-world and mathematical problems.

Number	Standard for Mathematical Content

6.SP Statistics and Probability

Develop understanding of statistical variability.

6.SP.A.1	Recognize a statistical question as one that anticipates variability in the data related to the question and accounts for it in the answers.
6.SP.A.2	Understand that a set of data collected to answer a statistical question has a distribution which can be described by its center, spread, and overall shape.
6.SP.A.3	Recognize that a measure of center for a numerical data set summarizes all of its values with a single number, while a measure of variation describes how its values vary with a single number.

Summarize and describe distributions.

6.SP.B.4	Display numerical data in plots on a number line, including dot plots, histograms, and box plots.
6.SP.B.5	Summarize numerical data sets in relation to their context, such as by:
6.SP.B.5a	Reporting the number of observations.
6.SP.B.5b	Describing the nature of the attribute under investigation, including how it was measured and its units of measurement.
6.SP.B.5c	Giving quantitative measures of center (median and/or mean) and variability (interquartile range and/or mean absolute deviation), as well as describing any overall pattern and any striking deviations from the overall pattern with reference to the context in which the data were gathered.
6.SP.B.5d	Summarize numerical data sets in relation to their context, such as by: Relating the choice of measures of center and variability to the shape of the data distribution and the context in which the data were gathered.

Number	Standard for Mathematical Practice
MP1	Make sense of problems and persevere in solving them.
MP2	Reason abstractly and quantitatively.
MP3	Construct viable arguments and critique the reasoning of others.
MP4	Model with mathematics.
MP5	Use appropriate tools strategically.
MP6	Attend to precision.
MP7	Look for and make use of structure.
MP8	Look for and express regularity in repeated reasoning.

Vocabulary

Language of Math for Topic 1

Lesson	Vocabulary	
	New	**Review**
Readiness 1 Rating Music Artists		whole number
1-1 Numerical Expressions	equivalent expressions evaluate a numerical expression numerical expression	order of operations
1-2 Algebraic Expressions	algebraic expression	numerical expression
1-3 Writing Algebraic Expressions		algebraic expression
1-4 Evaluating Algebraic Expressions	evaluate an algebraic expression	algebraic expression
1-5 Expressions with Exponents	base exponent power	order of operations
1-6 Problem Solving		algebraic expression
Topic 1 Topic Review	algebraic expression base equivalent expressions exponent numerical expression power	order of operations

Vocabulary

Language of Math for Topic 2

Lesson	Vocabulary	
	New	**Review**
Readiness 2 Renting Movies		expressions
2-1 The Identity and Zero Properties	Identity Property of Addition Identity Property of Multiplication Zero Property of Multiplication	illustrate
2-2 The Commutative Properties	Commutative Property of Addition Commutative Property of Multiplication	addend equivalent expressions
2-3 The Associative Properties	Associative Property of Addition Associative Property of Multiplication	addend equivalent expressions
2-4 Greatest Common Factor	common factor composite number factors greatest common factor prime factorization prime number	whole number
2-5 The Distributive Property	Distributive Property	greatest common factor
2-6 Least Common Multiple	least common multiple common multiple multiple	prime factorization
2-7 Problem Solving		equivalent expressions greatest common factor
Topic 2 Topic Review	common multiple composite number Distributive Property greatest common factor least common multiple prime factorization prime number	addend equivalent expressions whole number

Vocabulary

Language of Math for Topic 3

Lesson	Vocabulary	
	New	Review
Readiness 3 Video Game Economics		expressions
3-1 Expressions to Equations	equation false equation open sentence solution of an equation true equation	equivalent expressions
3-2 Balancing Equations	equivalent equations	equation
3-3 Solving Addition and Subtraction Equations	inverse operations	equivalent equations solution of an equation
3-4 Solving Multiplication and Division Equations		inverse operations
3-5 Equations to Inequalities	inequality solution of an inequality	inequality
3-6 Solving Inequalities	equivalent inequalities solution of an inequality	equivalent equations solution of an inequality
3-7 Problem Solving		solution of an equation solution of an inequality
Topic 3 Topic Review	equation equivalent equations equivalent inequalities false equation inequality open sentence true equation	equivalent expressions

Vocabulary

Language of Math for Topic 4

Lesson	Vocabulary	
	New	**Review**
Readiness 4 Working at an Amusement Park		coordinate plane expression
4-1 Using Two Variables to Represent a Relationship	dependent variable independent variable	variable
4-2 Analyzing Patterns Using Tables and Graphs		dependent variable independent variable
4-3 Relating Tables and Graphs to Equations		dependent variable independent variable
4-4 Problem Solving		exponent
Topic 4 Topic Review	dependent variable independent variable	variable

Vocabulary

Language of Math for Topic 5

Lesson	Vocabulary	
	New	**Review**
Readiness 5 Math in Music		fraction whole number
5-1 Multiplying Fractions and Whole Numbers		denominator equation fraction improper fraction mixed number numerator simplest form whole number
5-2 Multiplying Two Fractions		denominator factor fraction numerator product simplest form
5-3 Multiplying Fractions and Mixed Numbers		mixed number
5-4 Multiplying Mixed Numbers		Distributive Property
5-5 Problem Solving		expression
Topic 5 Topic Review		denominator Distributive Property fraction improper fraction mixed number numerator simplest form whole number

Vocabulary

Language of Math for Topic 6

Lesson	Vocabulary	
	New	**Review**
Readiness 6 Making Pizzas		fraction whole number
6-1 Dividing Fractions and Whole Numbers	reciprocals	denominator fraction numerator quotient
6-2 Dividing Unit Fractions by Unit Fractions		area of a rectangle divisor reciprocal unit fractions
6-3 Dividing Fractions by Fractions		divisor reciprocal
6-4 Dividing Mixed Numbers		divisor improper fractions mixed numbers reciprocal
6-5 Problem Solving		equation reciprocal
Topic 6 Topic Review	reciprocals	denominator divisor fraction improper fractions mixed numbers numerator quotient

Vocabulary

Language of Math for Topic 7

Lesson	Vocabulary	
	New	Review
Readiness 7 Fast Food Nutrition		whole number
7-1 Adding and Subtracting Decimals		decimal whole number
7-2 Multiplying Decimals		rounding
7-3 Dividing Multi-Digit Numbers	compatible numbers	quotient
7-4 Dividing Decimals		decimal whole number
7-5 Decimals and Fractions		rounding word form of a number
7-6 Comparing and Ordering Decimals and Fractions		compare order
7-7 Problem Solving		equation equivalent
Topic 7 Topic Review	compatible numbers	decimal rounding whole number

Vocabulary

Language of Math for Topic 8

Lesson	Vocabulary	
	New	**Review**
Readiness 8 Comparing the Planets		coordinate plan decimal whole numbers
8-1 Integers and the Number Line	integers opposites	negative numbers positive numbers
8-2 Comparing and Ordering Integers		compare order
8-3 Absolute Value	absolute value	distance
8-4 Integers and the Coordinate Plane	coordinate plane image line of reflection ordered pair origin quadrant reflection transformation *x*-axis *x*-coordinate *y*-axis *y*-coordinate	negative numbers positive numbers
8-5 Distance		distance
8-6 Problem Solving		distance image quadrant reflection
Topic 8 Topic Review	absolute value coordinate plane image integers line of reflection opposites ordered pair quadrant reflection transformation	distance negative numbers positive numbers

Vocabulary

Language of Math for Topic 9

Lesson	Vocabulary	
	New	**Review**
Readiness 9 Baseball Stats		decimal fraction
9-1 Rational Numbers and the Number Line	rational numbers	opposites
9-2 Comparing Rational Numbers		absolute value rational numbers
9-3 Ordering Rational Numbers		order
9-4 Rational Numbers and the Coordinate Plane		ordered pair
9-5 Polygons in the Coordinate Plane	polygon vertex of a polygon	segment
9-6 Problem Solving		vertex of a polygon
Topic 9 Topic Review	polygon rational numbers vertex of a polygon	absolute value opposites ordered pair segment

Vocabulary

Language of Math for Topic 10

Lesson	Vocabulary	
	New	**Review**
Readiness 10 Working with Playlists		fraction whole number
10-1 Ratios	ratio terms of a ratio	compare describe
10-2 Exploring Equivalent Ratios	equivalent ratios	ratio
10-3 Equivalent Ratios		equivalent ratios
10-4 Ratios as Fractions		greatest common factor simplest form
10-5 Ratios as Decimals		decimal
10-6 Problem Solving		ratio
Topic 10 Topic Review	equivalent ratios ratio terms of a ratio	decimal greatest common factor simplest form

Vocabulary

Language of Math for Topic 11

Lesson	Vocabulary	
	New	**Review**
Readiness 11 School Fundraisers		equation fraction whole number
11-1 Unit Rates	rate unit rate	ratio
11-2 Unit Prices	unit price	unit rate
11-3 Constant Speed		constant speed
11-4 Measurements and Ratios	conversion factor	rate
11-5 Choosing the Appropriate Rate		reciprocals
11-6 Problem Solving		rate
Topic 11 Topic Review	conversion factor rate unit rate unit price	constant speed ratio reciprocals

Vocabulary

Language of Math for Topic 12

Lesson	Vocabulary	
	New	**Review**
Readiness 12 Recycling		coordinate plan expression ratio
12-1 Plotting Ratios and Rates		ratio
12-2 Recognizing Proportionality		equivalent ratios proportional relationship
12-3 Introducing Percents	percent	ratio
12-4 Using Percents	circle graph	percent
12-5 Problem Solving		ratio
Topic 12 Topic Review	circle graph percent	equivalent ratios proportional relationship ratio

Vocabulary

Language of Math for Topic 13

Lesson	Vocabulary	
	New	**Review**
Readiness 13 Designing a Playground		expression rectangle square
13-1 Rectangles and Squares	area area of a rectangle area of a square	rectangle square
13-2 Right Triangles	area of a right triangle base of a triangle compose a shape height of a triangle	diagonal right triangle
13-3 Parallelograms	area of a parallelogram base of a parallelogram decompose a shape height of a parallelogram	parallelogram
13-4 Other Triangles		acute triangle obtuse triangle
13-5 Polygons	polygon regular polygon	hexagon octagon trapezoid
13-6 Problem Solving		polygon regular polygon
Topic 13 Topic Review	area compose a shape decompose a shape polygon regular polygon	acute triangle diagonal obtuse triangle parallelogram rectangle right triangle square

Vocabulary

Language of Math for Topic 14

Lesson	Vocabulary	
	New	**Review**
Readiness 14 Planning a Birthday Party		area rectangle square volume
14-1 Analyzing Three-Dimensional Figures	base of a prism base of a pyramid edge of a three-dimensional figure face of a three-dimensional figure height of a prism height of a pyramid lateral face of a prism lateral face of a pyramid prism pyramid three-dimensional figure vertex of a three-dimensional figure	center
14-2 Nets	net	regular polygon
14-3 Surface Areas of Prisms	surface area of a three-dimensional figure	cube net prism
14-4 Surface Areas of Pyramids		net pyramid
14-5 Volumes of Rectangular Prisms	volume of a prism	cubic unit
14-6 Problem Solving		cube rectangular prism pyramid
Topic 14 Topic Review	net prism pyramid surface area of a three-dimensional figure three-dimensional figure volume of a prism	center cube cubic unit regular polygon

Vocabulary

Language of Math for Topic 15

Lesson	Vocabulary	
	New	Review
Readiness 15 Organizing a Book Fair		bar graph line plot
15-1 Statistical Questions	data statistical question	explain justify
15-2 Dot Plots	dot plot frequency	data
15-3 Histograms	histogram	frequency
15-4 Box Plots	box plot	maximum minimum
15-5 Choosing an Appropriate Display		box plot dot plot histogram
15-6 Problem Solving		histogram
Topic 15 Topic Review	box plot data dot plot frequency histogram statistical question	maximum minimum

Vocabulary

Language of Math for Topic 16

Lesson	Vocabulary	
	New	**Review**
Readiness 16 Planning a Camping Trip		absolute value rational number whole number
16-1 Median	measures of center median	box plot cluster gap
16-2 Mean	mean	measure of center
16-3 Variability	measure of variability range variability	mean median
16-4 Interquartile Range	first quartile interquartile range third quartile	maximum measure of variability median minimum range
16-5 Mean Absolute Deviation	absolute deviation from the mean deviation from the mean mean absolute deviation	mean
16-6 Problem Solving		mean absolute deviation median range
Topic 16 Topic Review	absolute deviation from the mean deviation from the mean interquartile range mean absolute deviation measure of variability measures of center median range	box plot cluster gap maximum minimum

This page intentionally left blank.

Numerical Expressions

Digital
Resources

CCSS: 6.EE.A.2: Write, read, and evaluate expressions in which letters stand for numbers. **6.EE.A.2c:** Evaluate expressions ... Perform arithmetic operations ... in the conventional order ... . **6.EE.A.4:** Identify when two expressions are equivalent ... .

Launch

MP1, MP2

Use the numbers and symbols to show 36 as a sum, difference, product, and quotient. You can copy and combine numbers to create multi-digit numbers.

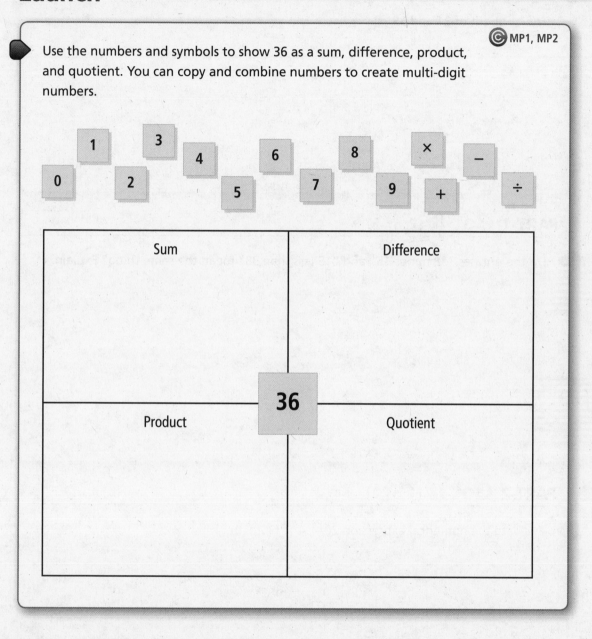

Reflect Could you find other ways to show 36 as a sum, difference, product, or quotient?

_____

_____

_____

_____

Got It?

What is a numerical expression for the word phrase?

The quotient of 21 and 55

Do the phrases "38 minus 15" and "15 less than 38" mean the same thing? Explain.

Evaluate the numerical expression $20 - 4 \times (36 \div 9)$.

Got It?

How much greater is the value of (18 + 6) × 2 than 18 + (6 × 2)?

PART 3 Got It

Which of the following statements are true about the given expressions?

450 + 150 and 2 × (450 + 150)

I. The two expressions are equivalent.

II. The second expression is two times as large as the first expression.

III. Both expressions are numerical expressions.

Close and Check

▶ Focus Question

How can numerical expressions help you to apply mathematics to real-world problem situations?

_____

_____

_____

_____

▶ Do you know HOW?

1. Write a numerical expression for the word phrase.

   13 less than 30

2. Circle the statements that are true about the given expressions.

   $3(25 - 5)$ $15(4)$

   A. The two expressions are equivalent.

   B. The first expression is 3 times as large as the second expression.

   C. Both expressions are numerical expressions.

3. Evaluate the numerical expression.

   $6(15 - 12) \div 2$

4. Evaluate the numerical expression.

   $5 + 3(42 - 12) \div 9$

▶ Do you UNDERSTAND?

5. **Reasoning** Your newspaper carrier delivers 42 papers 5 days a week and 14 more papers each day on Saturday and Sunday. Is there more than one numerical expression that can be used to find the total number of newspapers your carrier delivers each week? Explain.

   _____

   _____

   _____

   _____

   _____

6. **Error Analysis** Your friend writes the following numerical expression for Exercise 5. Is he correct? Explain.

   $42(5) + 2(42) + 14$

   _____

   _____

   _____

   _____

Algebraic Expressions

CCSS: 6.EE.A.2a: Write expressions ... with numbers and with letters standing for numbers ... .
6.EE.A.2b: Identify parts of an expression using mathematical terms ... . **6.EE.B.6:** Use variables to ... write expressions when solving a real-world ... problem ... . Also, **6.EE.A.2**.

Launch

Ⓒ MP2, MP8

Sort the five tiles into two groups. Describe each group.

Then, sort the five tiles into two groups again but in a different way. Describe each group.

| $a + 2$ | $9 - 2$ | 4×5 | $6 + y$ | $3 + 2$ |

Way 1

Group 1	Group 2

Way 2

Group 1	Group 2

Reflect What could the letters a and y mean?

_____

_____

_____

Got It?

PART 1 Got It

Which expressions are algebraic expressions?

I. $100 \div 25$ **II.** $80y - 35$ **III.** $9(15x)$ **IV.** $16xy + 20$

PART 2 Got It

Suppose you rent a bicycle to ride around a park. The rental fee is $12 for each hour the bike is rented and $5 for a helmet. Which quantity is *not* a variable quantity?

I.   The length of time you rent the bike
II.   The total cost of renting the bike
III. The rental fee of the helmet
IV. The distance you travel

PART 3 Got It

Describe the circled part of the expression using an appropriate term or phrase.

$5x - \underbrace{2(10x \div 5)} \div (2x + 3)$

Close and Check

> ## Focus Question MP2, MP4
> What does a variable allow you to do that you couldn't do before?
>
> _____
>
> _____
>
> _____
>
> _____

▶ Do you know HOW?

1. Circle the algebraic expressions. Underline the numerical expressions.

   $9 + (15 - 7)$ $10c - 4$

   $14(13 - d)$ $6 \div (r + 2)$

2. You walk dogs in your neighborhood. You charge $5 for each dog you walk. Sometimes you walk more than one dog a day. Sometimes you walk the same dog several days a week. Circle the variable quantities.

   A. The number of dogs you walk each day.

   B. The amount you charge for each dog.

   C. The number of times you walk each dog every week.

3. Which part of the expression represents a quotient of two terms?

   $3(4d - 8) + (7 - d) \div 5$

▶ Do you UNDERSTAND?

4. **Vocabulary** What makes a constant term different from a term with a variable?

   _____

   _____

   _____

   _____

5. **Reasoning** To convert a temperature from degrees Celsius C to degrees Fahrenheit F, you can use the formula $F = C\left(\frac{9}{5}\right) + 32$. How do variables make this formula useful?

   _____

   _____

   _____

   _____

   _____

   _____

This page intentionally left blank.

Writing Algebraic Expressions

Digital Resources

CCSS: **6.EE.A.2:** Write, read, and evaluate expressions in which letters stand for numbers. **6.EE.B.6:** Use variables to represent numbers and write expressions when solving a real-world or mathematical problem ... . Also, **6.EE.A.2a.**

Launch

The city's second-best scientist invents a new and improved dog washing machine to sell to animal shelters. He charts the machine's performance.

How can he quickly figure out how many minutes it will take to wash any number of dogs? Use pictures, words, or symbols to tell how.

MP4, MP7

Dog Washing Machine Times

Dogs	Minutes to Wash
1	6
2	12
3	18
4	24
?	?

Reflect Think about the pictures, words, or symbols you used. Which part represents what you know and which part represents what you don't know?

_____

_____

_____

_____

Got It?

PART 1 Got It

What is an algebraic expression for "18 more than *a*?"

Discuss with a classmate.

Use a diagram, such as a bar diagram, to explain your answer.

PART 2 Got It

Spring Lake is 3 miles shorter than Grand Lake. Write an expression that represents the length of Spring Lake, where ℓ is the length of Grand Lake.

PART 3 Got It

A national park charges $26 per adult and $16 per child for rafting down one of their two rivers. What algebraic expression can be used to represent the total cost for *a* adults and *c* children to raft down the Wild River?

Close and Check

▶ Focus Question

Algebraic expressions allow you to describe situations where you don't know all of the information. How can you use algebraic expressions to help you make decisions?

_____

_____

_____

▶ Do you know HOW?

1. What is an algebraic expression for the product of 12 and a number?

2. You are 4 inches taller than your friend. Write an algebraic expression to represent how tall you are.

3. A satellite television provider charges $39.95 per month for service. On-demand movies can be rented for $3.99 each. Broadcasts of special events can be rented for $49.95 each. Write an algebraic expression to represent the total monthly cost if you rent m movies and s special events.

4. The movie shop sells posters for $7, DVDs for $15, and CDs for $9. Write an algebraic expression to represent the total cost for 2 posters, d DVDs, and c CDs.

▶ Do you UNDERSTAND?

5. Writing Explain why two different variables, m and s, are needed in Exercise 3.

_____

_____

_____

_____

6. Reasoning How can the algebraic expression in Exercise 3 help you make a decision about how many on-demand movies and special events you can rent?

_____

_____

_____

_____

_____

This page intentionally left blank.

Evaluating Algebraic Expressions

CCSS: 6.EE.A.2: ... evaluate expressions in which letters stand for numbers. 6.EE.A.2c: Evaluate expressions at specific values of their variables. Include expressions that arise from formulas used in real-world problems ... .

Launch

© MP1, MP2

Your friend collects antique transit tokens. He likes to imagine what it was like to ride different buses and trains around the world. He records the value of each token in different ways.

Tell what you need to know to find the value of each token.

Token 1

$$\$45 \div 3$$

Token 2

$$\$12 \times g$$

Reflect Which token could have any value based on the expression attached to it? Explain.

_____

_____

_____

_____

_____

Got It?

PART 1 Got It

Evaluate $150 + 3p$ for $p = 30$.

PART 2 Got It

Evaluate $10(a + b) - 6c$ for $a = 12$, $b = 5$, and $c = 9$.

PART 3 Got It

A dog walker charges $10 to walk a large dog and $6 to walk a small dog.

a. Write an expression to represent how much the dog walker earns for walking b large dogs and s small dogs.

b. How much will the dog walker earn for walking 8 large dogs and 3 small dogs?

Close and Check

Focus Question

Algebraic expressions allow you to describe situations where you don't know all of the information. How can you use algebraic expressions to help you make decisions?

_____

_____

_____

_____

Do you know HOW?

1. Evaluate $117 - 5r$ for $r = 9$.

2. Evaluate $12x - (4y + 7z)$ for $x = 9$, $y = 4$, and $z = 2$.

3. Admission to an amusement park costs $35 for children, $52 for adults, and $29 for senior citizens. Write an expression to represent the cost of admission for any number of people.

4. Which would be less expensive: admission for 3 children and 3 senior citizens to the amusement park, or admission for 2 children and 3 adults? Write and evaluate the expression for the less expensive admission price.

Do you UNDERSTAND?

5. **Error Analysis** Your friend wrote an algebraic expression using only one variable for Exercise 3. Why is this incorrect?

_____

_____

_____

_____

6. **Vocabulary** What does it mean to evaluate an algebraic expression?

_____

_____

_____

_____

_____

_____

This page intentionally left blank.

Expressions with Exponents

Digital Resources

CCSS: 6.EE.A.1: Write and evaluate numerical expressions involving whole-number exponents.
6.EE.A.2c: Evaluate expressions at specific values of their variables. Include expressions that arise from formulas used in real-world problems ... .

Launch

Solve the riddle.

© MP4, MP8

On day 1, you get 3 coins.
For each of the next 3 days,
your number of coins triples.
Write a numerical expression to show the
number of coins you will have in the end.
Then write the total number of coins.

Reflect Suppose the tripling continues for 100 days. How would the numerical expression change? Explain.

_____

_____

_____

_____

_____

Got It?

PART 1 Got It (1 of 2)

What is the value of $4^3 + 6$?

PART 1 Got It (2 of 2)

Your friend says that 2^3 and 3^2 are equivalent because they both contain 2 and 3. Do you agree? Justify your answer.

Got It?

PART 2 Got It (1 of 2)

What is the value of $2x^2 - z^2$ for $x = 12$ and $z = 8$?

PART 2 Got It (2 of 2)

A student gives ab^3 as an answer when asked to write the expression $ab \cdot ab \cdot ab$ using exponents. What is the student's error?

PART 3 Got It

You want to buy new carpet for another room. The room measures 12 feet by 12 feet. If the carpet cost $8 per square foot, how much would the new carpet cost?

Close and Check

Focus Question

How do exponents allow you to communicate more precisely to others?

_____

_____

_____

_____

Do you know HOW?

1. What is the value of $6^3 - 100$?

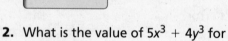

2. What is the value of $5x^3 + 4y^3$ for $x = 4$ and $y = 3$?

3. A storage company uses boxes that have the same length, width, and height. Write and simplify an expression to show how much a box with side lengths that measure 4 ft can hold.

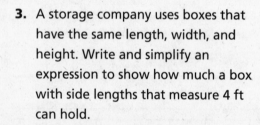

4. Write an equivalent expression using exponents.

$a \cdot 2 \cdot b \cdot a + b \cdot 2 \cdot a \cdot 2 \cdot b \cdot a$

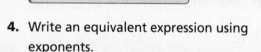

Do you UNDERSTAND?

5. Writing You earn an allowance for chores you finish each week. You earn $2 on Monday. For the next 6 days, your daily earnings are twice what you earned the day before. Is this a reasonable weekly allowance? Explain.

_____

_____

_____

_____

6. Vocabulary You write an expression using exponents to show 4 multiplied by itself 6 times. Which number is the base and which number is the exponent? Explain.

_____

_____

_____

_____

_____

Problem Solving

Digital Resources

CCSS: 6.EE.A.2: Write, read, and evaluate expressions in which letters stand for numbers. **6.EE.A.2a:** Write expressions that record operations with numbers and with letters standing for numbers ... .

Launch

ⓒ MP3, MP6

Pick one of the situations modeled below. Write an algebraic expression for it and tell how it matches the picture.

Algebraic Expression:

What It Means:

Reflect What makes the situation you describe an algebraic expression instead of a numerical expression?

_____

_____

_____

_____

_____

Got It?

PART 1 Got It (1 of 2)

The library also has 465 fiction books, and an unknown number, *y*, of these books are mystery stories. Which algebraic expression best represents the number of fiction books that are not mysteries that the library has?

Discuss with a classmate

Read the problem statement together.
How many different kinds of books are described in the problem?
Which phrase is the key to identifying the operation you need for the algebraic expression?

PART 1 Got It (2 of 2)

Why do you think that the bar diagram models for addition and subtraction look a lot alike?

PART 2 Got It

What expression can be used to describe the missing label in this bar diagram?

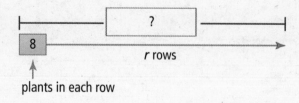

plants in each row

Close and Check

Focus Question

Algebraic expressions allow you to describe situations where you don't know all of the information. How can you use algebraic expressions to help you analyze relationships and simplify complicated situations?

_____

_____

_____

Do you know HOW?

1. There are 432 students attending North Middle School. *s* number of them are sixth graders. Complete the bar diagram to model the expression for the number of students that are not sixth graders.

```
|------------------    ------------------|
|                  |                       |
|                  |                       |
|                  |                       |
```

2. Boxes of fruit are delivered to a market. Each box holds 36 pieces of fruit. There are *b* number of boxes delivered each week. Complete the bar diagram to model the expression representing the total number of pieces of fruit delivered each week.

```
|------------    ------------|
|          |  ─────────────────────────▶
|          |
```

Do you UNDERSTAND?

3. **Writing** How do you know whether the variable in a bar diagram for a multiplication or division word problem goes above the diagram or in a section below?

_____

_____

_____

_____

4. **Error Analysis** Your friend wants to raise $235 by washing cars. He uses a bar diagram to decide how much to charge for each car. What error did he make?

```
|------------- p price -------------|
| $235 |  ─────────────────────────▶
|      |        total cars
```

_____

_____

_____

_____

This page intentionally left blank.

New Vocabulary: algebraic expression, base, equivalent expressions, exponent, numerical expression, power
Review Vocabulary: order of operations

Vocabulary Review

Identify two challenging vocabulary terms from this topic. Write one vocabulary term in the center oval, and fill in the surrounding boxes with details that will help you better understand the term.

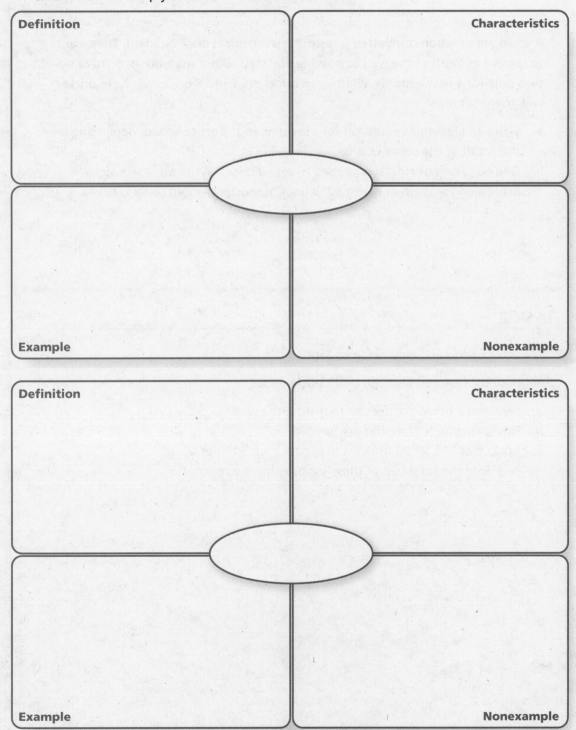

Definition	Characteristics

Example	Nonexample

Definition	Characteristics

Example	Nonexample

Pull It All Together

TASK 1

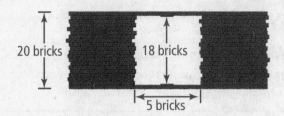

20 bricks

18 bricks

5 bricks

A town preservation committee is restoring a historical brick building. They want to replace as much of the wall as possible and stay within their budget. There will be a hole for a new window, which is 18 bricks high and 5 bricks wide. No bricks will go in that area.

a. Write an algebraic expression for the number of bricks needed, depending on the width of the restored area.

b. One 60-lb bag of mortar is needed to set 60 bricks. Write an algebraic expression for the number of 60-lb bags of mortar needed to set b bricks.

TASK 2

Use information and answers from Task 1.

Suppose the restored wall will be 15 bricks wide.

a. How many bricks are needed to restore the wall?

b. How many bags of mortar are needed?

c. Bricks cost $15 for 30 bricks, and mortar costs $14 per 60-lb bag. Find the total cost of these supplies for the restoration.

2-1

The Identity and Zero Properties

Digital Resources

CCSS: 6.EE.A.2c: Evaluate expressions at specific values of their variables. Include ... real-world problems ... . **6.EE.A.3:** Apply the properties of operations to generate equivalent expressions ... . **6.EE.A.4:** Identify when two expressions are equivalent ... .

Launch

Ⓒ MP1, MP2

Your friend eats *c* number of carrots each week. Each carrot has 0 grams of fat.

Write an expression to show how many grams of fat are in *c* number of carrots. Then evaluate the expression for three different numbers of carrots. Explain your results.

Reflect How would the problem change if a carrot had 1 gram of fat? Explain.

_____

_____

_____

_____

Got It?

PART 1 Got It

Which statements illustrate the Identity Property of Addition?

I. $0 + x = x$ **II.** $x + y + 0 = x + y$ **III.** Zero plus five is five.

PART 2 Got It (1 of 2)

Which statements illustrate the Identity Property of Multiplication?

I. $c \cdot 0 = 0$ **II.** $w \cdot 1 = w$ **III.** $1 \cdot bc = bc$

PART 2 Got It (2 of 2)

What property or properties are illustrated by the statement $0 \cdot 1 = 0$?

Got It?

PART 3 Got It (1 of 2)

Hockey teams earn 3 points for a win, 0 points for a loss, and 1 point for a tie. Use the expression below to find the total number of points Team B has earned.

Which part of the expression below would you simplify using the Zero Property of Multiplication?

$(3 \cdot W) + (0 \cdot L) + (1 \cdot T)$

Hockey Records

Team	W	L	T
A	6	2	4
B	7	5	0

PART 3 Got It (2 of 2)

Which team has more points? Is that the team with the better record? Explain.

Hockey Records

Team	W	L	T
A	6	2	4
B	7	5	0

Close and Check

Focus Question

Certain numbers are special. For example, 10 is special because our number system is based on it. How are 0 and 1 special?

_____

_____

_____

_____

Do you know HOW?

1. Circle the statements that illustrate the Zero Property of Multiplication.

   $0a = 0$ $\qquad$ $0 + (3d) = 3d$

   $(3b + 4c)0 = 0$ $\quad$ $(c \cdot 12) + 0 = 12c$

2. Circle the property or properties illustrated by the statement $0 + (3d) = 1(3d)$.

   Zero Property of Multiplication

   Identity Property of Addition

   Identity Property of Multiplication

3. In a certain game, some moves earn 3 points, some earn 1 point, and others earn 0 points. Use the expression $3e + 1c + 0i$ to find the total points scored by Player A.

   Game Moves

	e	c	i
Player A	5	3	8
Player B	7	2	3

    points

Do you UNDERSTAND?

4. **Reasoning** In Exercise 3, did the player who made more moves score the most points? Explain. Use the Zero Property of Multiplication in your answer.

   _____

   _____

   _____

   _____

   _____

5. **Compare and Contrast** How are the Identity Properties of Multiplication and Addition alike? How are they different?

   _____

   _____

   _____

   _____

   _____

The Commutative Properties

Digital Resources

CCSS: 6.EE.A.3: Apply the properties of operations to generate equivalent expressions... . **6.EE.A.4:** Identify when two expressions are equivalent (i.e., when the two expressions name the same number regardless of which value is substituted into them) ... .

Launch

© MP4, MP8

Use the tiles to show three different algebraic expressions that describe the relationship between your age and your friend's age. Explain what each expression means.

Your Age	7	9	11
Your Friend's Age	5	7	9

0	1	2	3	4
5	6	7	8	9

a   +   −

Expression   **Explanation**

Reflect Was it easy or hard to think of three different expressions about the ages of you and your friend? Explain.

___

Got It?

PART 1 Got It (1 of 2)

Use the Commutative Property of Addition to find an expression equivalent to the one represented by the diagram below.

$$20 + x$$

20	x

PART 1 Got It (2 of 2)

Does the Commutative Property of Addition apply to addition expressions with more than two addends? Explain your reasoning.

Discuss with a classmate

Read each other's explanation for the problem.
Is the explanation clear?
Are there any words or phrases that you do not understand? If so, ask your classmate to explain them to you.

Got It?

PART 2 Got It (1 of 2)

While on a dig, the archaeologists write their initial beneath the meals they will prepare for the team.

Use the Commutative Property of Multiplication to write two equivalent expressions that show the total number of meals prepared each week.

	Meal 1	Meal 2	Meal 3
Sun.	S	C	P
Mon.	J	C	M
Tues.	S	P	J
Wed.	P	M	C
Thurs.	P	J	M
Fri.	S	P	M
Sat.	J	C	S

PART 2 Got It (2 of 2)

Does the statement "3 · 8 = 4 · 6" illustrate the Commutative Property of Multiplication?

PART 3 Got It

Which statements are true about algebraic expressions that are equivalent because of the Commutative Properties?

I.   The expressions have the same numbers and variables.

II. The expressions involve addition or multiplication.

III. The expressions involve subtraction or division.

Close and Check

▶ Do you know **HOW?**

1. Use the Commutative Property of Addition to write an expression equivalent to the one represented by the diagram.

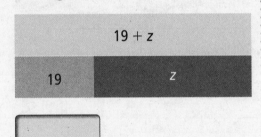

[_____]

2. A car gets 27 miles per gallon of gas. Write two equivalent expressions that show the total number of miles the car can travel on any number of gallons of gas.

3. Draw lines to match the equivalent expressions in the two columns.

$7 + 2 + 9$	$8 \cdot 6 \cdot 3$
$1c \cdot 4r$	$ab + bc + cd$
$3 \cdot 6 \cdot 8$	$r \cdot 4 \cdot c$
$cb + dc + ba$	$9 + 2 + 7$

▶ Do you **UNDERSTAND?**

4. Writing Clerk 1 uses the expression $4a + 3g - 2$ to find the total. Clerk 2 uses $3g + 4a - 2$. Will the totals be the same? Explain.

> **Apples:** $4/bag
>
> **Grapes:** $3/bag
>
> > Get $2 off today!

_____

_____

_____

5. Reasoning Can an equation show both the Identity Property of Addition and the Commutative Property of Addition? Explain.

_____

_____

_____

The Associative Properties

CCSS: 6.EE.A.3: Apply the properties of operations to generate equivalent expressions ... . **6.EE.A.4:** Identify when two expressions are equivalent (i.e., when the two expressions name the same number regardless of which value is substituted into them) ... .

Launch

MP2, MP7

Evaluate the expression $t + 89 + 11$, for $t = 38$. Show each step that you take.

Then evaluate the expression again for $t = 38$ but use different steps. Tell whether your first or second way was easier and explain why.

Way 1	Way 2
$t + 89 + 11$	$t + 89 + 11$

Reflect Does it matter what steps you take when adding numbers?

_____

_____

_____

_____

_____

Got It?

PART 1 Got It (1 of 2)

 Use the Associative Property of Addition to write an expression equivalent to $(x + 2) + 3$.

PART 1 Got It (2 of 2)

Evaluate the expressions to determine whether you can apply the Associative Property to subtraction. Explain.

$(10 - 5) - 3$ and $10 - (5 - 3)$

PART 2 Got It (1 of 2)

 Use the Associative Property of Multiplication to write an expression equivalent to $(18 \cdot 7) \cdot y$.

Got It?

PART 2 Got It (2 of 2)

Determine whether you can use the Associative Property to regroup numbers in a division expression. Use the expressions below to explain your answer.

(8 ÷ 4) ÷ 2 and 8 ÷ (4 ÷ 2)

PART 3 Got It

Use the Associative Property of Addition to write two equivalent expressions.

Close and Check

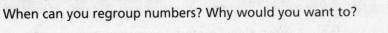

▶ Focus Question

MP3, MP6

When can you regroup numbers? Why would you want to?

_____

_____

_____

_____

_____

▶ Do you know **HOW?**

1. Use the Associative Property of Addition to write an expression equivalent to $(7 + 2) + t$.

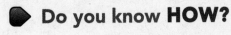

2. There are 60 minutes in an hour and 24 hours in a day. How many minutes are in d days? Use the Associative Property of Multiplication to write two equivalent expressions.

3. Identify the property of addition or multiplication each expression models. Write **I** for Identity, **C** for Commutative, or **A** for Associative.

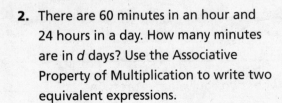

$c + 8 + r = r + c + 8$

$(wx) \cdot (yz) = w \cdot (xy) \cdot z$

$abc = cba$

$1c = c$

▶ Do you UNDERSTAND?

4. Error Analysis Your friend uses the Associative Property to rewrite the expression $(6 \cdot 18) + 2$ as $6 \cdot (18 + 2)$ to make it easier to evaluate. Is he correct? Explain.

_____

_____

_____

_____

5. Reasoning Rewrite the expression using the Commutative and Associative Properties of Addition so that it can be evaluated using mental math. Then solve and explain your reasoning.

$$13 + 16 + 27 + 24$$

_____

_____

_____

_____

Greatest Common Factor

Digital Resources

CCSS: 6.NS.B.4: Find the greatest common factor of two whole numbers less than or equal to 100 and the least common multiple of two whole numbers less than or equal to 12 ... .

Launch

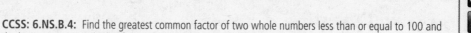

© MP3, MP4, MP8

A florist wants to use up all the flower shop's remaining roses and daisies to make several centerpieces. All the centerpieces need to be the same. What could each centerpiece look like? Describe the florist's options.

16 Roses

24 Daisies

Reflect How did you determine if a centerpiece would match the florist's criteria?

_____

_____

_____

Got It?

What is the greatest common factor of 30 and 75?

Find the prime factorization of 90.

Got It?

PART 3 Got It (1 of 2)

Use prime factorization to find the GCF of 60 and 88.

PART 3 Got It (2 of 2)

What is the GCF of any two distinct prime numbers? Explain.

Close and Check

Focus Question

How does the greatest common factor relate two or more whole numbers?

_____

_____

_____

_____

Do you know HOW?

1. What is the greatest common factor of 64 and 72?

[ ]

2. Write the prime factorization of 76.

[ ]

3. Complete the factor trees below. Then use prime factorization to find the GCF of 45 and 60.

```
      45                    60
   /    \               /     \
  5    [ ]             5      [ ]
        / \                    / \
     [ ]  [ ]              [ ]  [ ]
                                 / \
                              [ ]  [ ]
```

GCF: [ ]

Do you UNDERSTAND?

4. Writing To find the GCF of two numbers that have many factors, is it easier to list the factors of each number and compare or to find the prime factorization of each number and multiply common factors? Explain.

_____

_____

_____

_____

_____

5. Reasoning Do all composite numbers share a GCF that is greater than 1? Explain.

_____

_____

_____

_____

The Distributive Properties

CCSS: 6.NS.B.4: ... Use the distributive property to express a sum of two whole numbers 1–100 with a common factor as a multiple of a sum of two whole numbers with no common factor ... . **6.EE.A.3:** Apply the properties of operations to generate equivalent expressions ... . Also, **6.EE.A.4.**

Launch

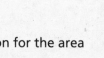 MP1, MP7

Three friends agree to paint parts of a background for a play. They know the width of each part but only agree that the height (*h*) of each part should be the same.

Write an expression for the area of each part. Then write an expression for the area of the whole background.

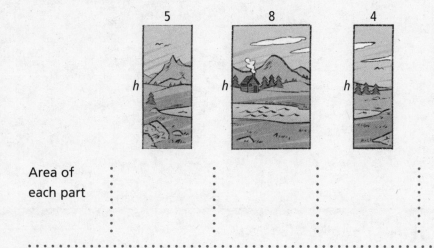

Area of each part

Area of whole background

Reflect When they put the parts together, will the height of the background be *h* or 3 · *h*? Explain.

_____

_____

_____

Got It?

PART 1 Got It

Use the Distributive Property and common factors to write an expression equivalent to $15 + 35$.

PART 2 Got It (1 of 2)

Use the Distributive Property to write an expression equivalent to $5(3x + 10)$.

Got It?

Use the Distributive Property to write an expression equivalent to $3(x^2 + 5x + 9)$.

PART 3 Got It

A camper canoes for 2 hours and hikes for 3 hours each day. The number of hours she hikes and canoes in d days is represented by the expression $d(2 + 3)$.

Use the Distributive Property to write an equivalent expression that also shows the number of hours the camper canoes and hikes in d days.

Close and Check

► Focus Question

How does a common factor help you rewrite an expression? How does this help you think about a situation in a new way?

_____

_____

_____

_____

► Do you know **HOW?**

1. Use the Distributive Property and GCF to write an expression equivalent to $24 - 18$.

2. Use the Distributive Property to write an expression equivalent to $7(2x^2 - 4x + 7)$.

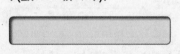

3. Each day, a toy factory worker assembles 216 toys before his lunch break. After lunch, he assembles 168 more. Write 2 equivalent expressions to show how many toys the worker assembles in d days.

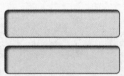

► Do you **UNDERSTAND?**

4. **Compare and Contrast** You and a friend each rewrite the expression $45f - 24f$ using common factors. How are these expressions alike? How are they different?

   $f(45 - 24)$ $3f(15 - 8)$

   _____

   _____

   _____

   _____

   _____

5. **Writing** Which of the three expressions in Exercise 4 do you think is the easiest to evaluate? Explain.

   _____

   _____

   _____

   _____

   _____

Least Common Multiple

Digital Resources

CCSS: 6.NS.B.4: Find the greatest common factor of two whole numbers less than or equal to 100 and the least common multiple of two whole numbers less than or equal to 12 ... .

Launch

MP3, MP8

A sports arena coordinator is scheduling games for November. The arena can host one game each day. So the coordinator schedules a basketball game every three days and a hockey game every four days. Will this schedule work? Explain your reasoning.

November						
Sun	Mon	Tues	Wed	Thurs	Fri	Sat
		1	2	3 [B]	4 [H]	5
6	7	8	9	10	11	12
13	14	15	16	17	18	19
20	21	22	23	24	25	26
27	28	29	30			

Reflect Can you solve the problem without a calendar? Explain.

_____

_____

_____

_____

_____

Got It?

PART 1 Got It

What is the least common multiple of 6 and 24?

PART 2 Got It

Use prime factorization to find the LCM of 14 and 21.

Got It?

PART 3 Got It

Hot dogs come 10 per package. Hot dog buns come 8 per package. You are having a party and serving hot dogs with hot dog buns. When you start grilling, you open a package of each. When is the next time you will open a new package of each at the same time?

Close and Check

Focus Question

What does it mean for a number to be the least common multiple of two numbers?

Do you know HOW?

1. Find the least common multiple (LCM) of 6 and 8.

2. Write and simplify an expression using the prime factorization of 16 and 20 to find the LCM.

3. A page in a stamp album holds 18 stamps. A page in a photo album holds 8 photos. What is the least number of stamps and photos you need so that each album has the same number of items and only full pages?

4. At a grand opening, every 15th customer to enter the bookstore receives a bookmark. Every 25th customer receives a $5 gift certificate. Which customer is the first to receive both gifts?

Do you UNDERSTAND?

5. **Reasoning** A caterer orders table decorations for an event. One kind of decoration is sold in packs of 12. Another is sold in packs of 18. He finds the LCM before placing his order. Why might he have done this?

6. **Compare and Contrast** Explain what is the same about how you use prime factorization to find the greatest common factor and the least common multiple. What is different?

Additional Problem Solving

Digital Resources

CCSS: 6.NS.B.4: Find the greatest common factor of two whole numbers less than or equal to 100 and the least common multiple of two whole numbers less than or equal to 12... . **6.EE.A.3:** Apply the properties of operations to generate equivalent expressions... .

Launch

ⓒ MP3, MP6

Use the symbols, numbers, and variable to create three equivalent expressions. Tell which of the Topic's properties (Zero, Identity, Commutative, Associative, and Distributive) you use to create the expressions. You can use multiple copies of each tile if you wish.

| (|) | · | + | 2 | 3 | 6 | s |

Reflect Can you model an expression using the Identity Property in this problem? Why or why not?

_____

_____

_____

_____

_____

Got It?

PART 1 Got It

A theater owner is purchasing three packs of bunting and three pink flamingos to decorate for the movie theater's 10th anniversary. Determine whether there is enough money in the $75 budget.

$18

$12

PART 2 Got It

A teacher needs to cut construction paper into equal-sized squares. The paper measures 24 in. by 36 in. and she doesn't want to waste any of it. What is the greatest possible side length for each square piece?

Got It?

PART 3 Got It

Describe and correct the error in reasoning.

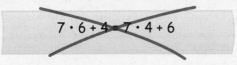

Discuss with a classmate

Did you describe the error in the reasoning? Review your descriptions and ask for definitions of any unfamiliar words.

Did you correct the error in the reasoning? If you were unable to correct the error, try the problem again now that you have discussed any unfamiliar words.

Close and Check

Focus Question MP2, MP7

How do the properties of operations help you solve problems?

_____

_____

_____

_____

Do you know HOW?

1. You have 33 party invitations to deliver. When you meet your friend, you have delivered 27 invitations. Your friend gives you 13 more to deliver. Use the Distributive Property to complete the equation to find how many invitations you still have to deliver.

$$3(\boxed{} - \boxed{}) + 13 = \boxed{}$$

2. A jewelry kit contains 126 beads and 96 charms. What is the greatest number of identical necklaces that can be made using all of the beads and charms?

3. Rewrite the expression using the Distributive Property.

$$21d + 27d + 15d$$

Do you UNDERSTAND?

4. **Error Analysis** Your friend tries to simplify the following expression but incorrectly applies a property. Explain his error and write the correct expression.

$$7 \cdot (6 - 3) = (7 - 6) \cdot (7 - 3)$$

_____

_____

_____

_____

5. **Reasoning** One dog goes to the dog park every 6 days. Another dog goes to the park every 9 days. Today, both dogs are at the park. Should you use the GCF or LCM to find when both dogs will be at the park together again? Explain.

_____

_____

_____

New Vocabulary: common multiple, composite number, Distributive Property, greatest common factor, least common multiple, prime factorization, prime number
Review Vocabulary: addend, equivalent expressions, whole number

Vocabulary Review

Identify two challenging vocabulary terms from this topic. Write one vocabulary term in the center oval, and fill in the surrounding boxes with details that will help you better understand the term.

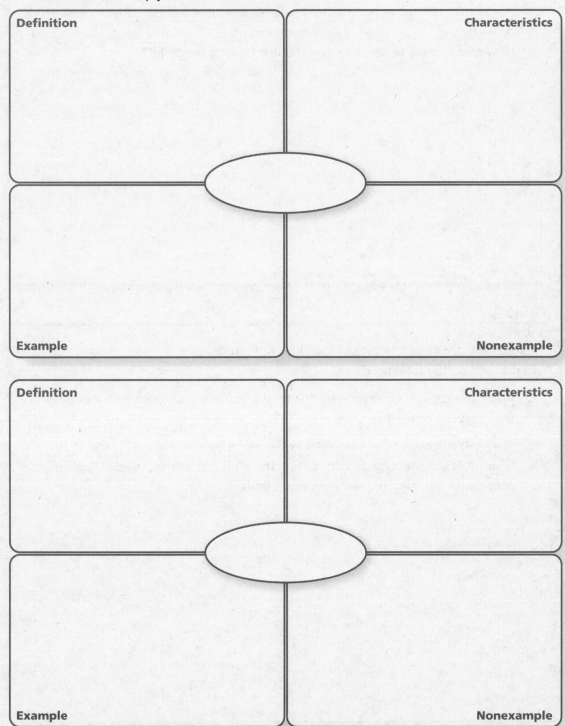

| Definition | Characteristics |
| Example | Nonexample |

| Definition | Characteristics |
| Example | Nonexample |

Pull It All Together

TASK 1

A company is performing quality checks for their sparkling water. They are testing every 8th bottle for how well it is sealed, and every 6th bottle for carbonation.

a. Which bottle will be the first tested for both how well it is sealed, and for carbonation?

b. The bottles are packed into square boxes. These are packed onto large rectangular (96 inches by 56 inches) pallets. How large can the square boxes be?

c. How many square boxes will cover the first layer of the pallet?

TASK 2

A customer who buys 7 bottles of sparkling water receives a $5 discount on the total purchase.

a. Write an algebraic expression for the total amount a restaurant customer pays for 21 bottles of sparkling water.

b. The same customer buys four other items, which cost $75, $47, $25, and $13. How could you use mental math to find the total cost of these items? Explain your reasoning using properties of operations.

Expressions to Equations

CCSS: 6.EE.A.2: Write, read, and evaluate expressions in which letters stand for numbers.
6.EE.B.5: ... Use substitution to determine whether a given number in a specified set makes an equation or inequality true.

Launch

© MP2, MP5

Shuffle the expressions in the top row of scales so that all of the scales in the bottom row balance.

This scale is balanced.

| 7 + 9 | 2 • 9 | a + 11 | 4 • 4 | 26 − 8 | 64 ÷ 4 |

Reflect What does it mean for two sides of the scale to be balanced?

_____

_____

_____

_____

Got It?

PART 1 Got It

Which are equations?

I. $t + 5 = 17$ II. $3c$ III. $10y = 13d$

PART 2 Got It (1 of 2)

Which expressions are equal?

I. 16×2 II. $24 + 8$ III. 4×4

Got It?

Are the expressions $12a + (6 + 3a)$ and $3(5a + 2)$ equivalent? Explain.

PART 3 Got It

Which equation(s) have a solution of 12?

I. $17 - m = 5$ II. $k - 12 = 0$ III. $12 + z = 24$

Close and Check

Focus Question

What is an equation? How is an equation with variables different from the equations you've seen in the past?

_____

_____

_____

Do you know HOW?

1. Complete the equation.

   $x(17 - 8) =$ ☐ $x - 8$ ☐

2. Match each expression with an equivalent expression.

   A. $\dfrac{18w}{6}$ ☐ $7w + 8w$

   B. $20w + 12w$ ☐ $10w \cdot 2$

   C. $10w + 10w$ ☐ $4w(5 + 3)$

   D. $10w + 5w$ ☐ $50w - 25w$

   E. $25(2w - w)$ ☐ $18w \div 6$

3. Circle the equations for which 5 is a solution.

   $3x = 15$

   $12 - a = 6$

   $35 \div 7 = r$

   $f + 9 = 14$

Do you UNDERSTAND?

4. **Vocabulary** Tell which of the following is an *expression* and which is an *equation*. Explain.

   $4t = 28$ $8c + 7$

   _____

   _____

   _____

   _____

5. **Error Analysis** Your friend applied the Distributive Property to conclude that $8(x + 2)$ is equivalent to $8x + 2$. Describe your friend's error and give an expression that is equivalent.

   _____

   _____

   _____

   _____

   _____

   _____

   _____

Balancing Equations

CCSS: 6.EE.A.2: Write, read, and evaluate expressions in which letters stand for numbers.

Launch

Ⓒ MP3, MP5

This scale is balanced. How could you keep the scale balanced if the left side changes to Box X and 5 pennies?

Reflect How can you change the sides of a balanced scale and keep it balanced?

_____

_____

_____

_____

_____

Got It?

The scale balances with 4x on one side and 20 on the other. What must you do to the scale below to make it balanced?

Got It?

PART 2 Got It

The scale balanced with 24 on the left and 6*b* on the right. What must you do to rebalance the scale?

PART 3 Got It

The solution of $17 + t = 25$ is $t = 8$. Which equation is equivalent to $17 + t = 25$?

I. $17 + t = 25 + t$ **II.** $3 + 17 + t = 3 + 25$ **III.** $17 + t + t = 25 + 25$

Discuss with a classmate

Choose one of the equations that you did NOT select as equivalent.
Explain to your classmate what part(s) of that equation failed to make it equivalent to the original equation $17 + t = 25$.

Close and Check

Focus Question

MP1, MP3, MP8

How is it possible for two different equations to describe the same situation? What does it mean for two equations to be equivalent?

_____

_____

_____

_____

Do you know HOW?

1. A scale is balanced with 3a on one side and 9 on the other. What must you do to keep the scale balanced?

$$3a - 5 = 9 - \boxed{}$$

2. Use the information on the scale to complete the equivalent equation.

$$\boxed{}\, b = 77$$

3. Which equation is equivalent to $5c + 2 = 12$?

I. $5c + 2 = 12 + 2$

II. $5c + 2 - c = 12 - c$

III. $2(5c + 2) = 2(12)$

A. I and II

B. I and III

C. II and III

D. all of them

Do you UNDERSTAND?

4. Reasoning Why is it important to do the same thing to both sides when balancing an equation?

_____

_____

_____

_____

5. Error Analysis Describe and correct the error in writing an equivalent equation.

$$r + 6 = 16$$
$$r + 6 - 5 = 16 + 5$$

_____

_____

_____

_____

_____

Solving Addition and Subtraction Equations

CCSS: 6.EE.B.7: Solve real-world and mathematical problems by writing and solving equations of the form $x + p = q$ and $px = q$ for cases in which p, q and x are all nonnegative rational numbers.

Launch

Ⓒ MP1, MP7

Each row, column, and diagonal in the number square has the same sum.

a	7	2
1	5	b
8	c	4

2 1 5

8 0 3 6

9 4 7

Find the values of a, b, and c.

$a = \boxed{}$ $b = \boxed{}$ $c = \boxed{}$

Explain.

Reflect Did you use addition or subtraction to find each missing value? Could you use either operation?

_____

_____

_____

_____

Got It?

PART 1 Got It

Solve the equation $8 + x = 36$.

PART 2 Got It

Each equation shows an operation. For which equation(s) is addition the inverse operation?

I. $b + 27 = 78$ **II.** $25 = g - 19$ **III.** $18 + v = 19$

PART 3 Got It

Write a simpler, equivalent equation to solve $d - 29 = 85$.

Close and Check

Focus Question

MP2, MP7

How do you use addition and subtraction to undo each other? Why might this be helpful in balancing equations?

_____

_____

_____

Do you know HOW?

1. Solve the equation.

$$7 + w = 23$$

$$w = \boxed{}$$

2. Write the inverse operation for each equation shown in the table below. Use **S** for subtraction and **A** for addition.

Equation	Inverse Operation
$12 + r = 47$	
$d - 15 = 4$	
$14 - s = 10$	
$t + 7 = 23$	
$56 + w = 92$	
$y - 8 = 61$	

3. Circle the equation that has a solution of 16.

$$x + 6 = 22 \qquad x - 6 = 22$$

Do you UNDERSTAND?

4. Vocabulary What are inverse operations? Give an example.

_____

_____

_____

_____

_____

5. Error Analysis Identify the error in solving the equation and give the correct answer.

$$5 + 7 + z = 33$$
$$12 + z = 33$$
$$12 + 12 + z = 33 + 12$$
$$z = 45$$

_____

_____

_____

_____

_____

This page intentionally left blank.

Solving Multiplication and Division Equations

Digital Resources

CCSS: 6.EE.B.7: Solve real-world and mathematical problems by writing and solving equations of the form $x + p = q$ and $px = q$ for cases in which p, q and x are all nonnegative rational numbers.

Launch

© MP4, MP6

Some students sign up for summer swim classes. The swim coach splits them evenly to form 13 classes with 8 students in each class. How many students sign up for swim class?

Show how to solve the problem using division and multiplication.

Division	Multiplication

Reflect Could you have solved the problem using only division and not any multiplication? How?

_____

_____

_____

Got It?

PART 1 Got It

Solve the equation $5s = 30$.

PART 2 Got It

Each equation shows an operation. For which equation(s) is division the inverse operation?

I. $m \div 3 = 27$ **II.** $39 = h \cdot 13$ **III.** $10 \cdot z = 120$

PART 3 Got It

Solve the equation $m \div 15 = 25$.

Close and Check

Focus Question

©MP2, MP7

How do you use multiplication and division to undo each other? Why might this be helpful in balancing equations?

_____

_____

_____

Do you know HOW?

1. Write and solve the modeled equation.

42

x	x	x	x	x	x	x

$\boxed{}\ x = \boxed{}$

$x = \boxed{}$

2. Write the inverse operation for each equation shown in the table below. Use **A** for addition, **S** for subtraction, **M** for multiplication and **D** for division.

Equation	Inverse Operation
$36 = 12r$	
$d \div 15 = 4$	
$5 + f = 13$	
$56 = 7t$	
$14 \div s = 2$	
$63 - p = 46$	

Do you UNDERSTAND?

3. **Writing** Draw and explain a model of the equation $3x = 18$.

_____

_____

_____

_____

_____

4. **Reasoning** A teacher has 72 pencils to split among 24 students. She asks the class to write an equation to figure out how many each gets.
Student A writes: $72 \div 24 = x$
Student B writes: $24x = 72$
Who is correct? Explain.

_____

_____

_____

This page intentionally left blank.

Equations to Inequalities

CCSS: 6.EE.B.8: Write an inequality ... to represent a constraint or condition in a real-world or mathematical problem. Recognize that inequalities of the form $x > c$ or $x < c$ have infinitely many solutions; represent solutions of such inequalities on number line diagrams.

Launch

MP1, MP4, MP5

The long jump record at the local school is 18 feet. Describe a jump that could break the record in three different ways—using a picture, using words, and using symbols.

Picture	Words	Symbols

Reflect How many jumps could tie the record? How many jumps could break the record?

_____

_____

_____

Got It?

PART 1 Got It

Which situation(s) could be modeled by inequalities?

I. You must be 13 or older to buy a certain DVD.

II. You should not drive over the speed limit of 70 mi/h.

PART 2 Got It

What inequality models the situation?

Got It?

PART 3 Got It (1 of 2)

Which is the graph of $x \geq 16$?

I.
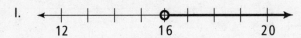

II.

III.
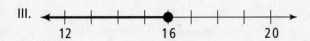

PART 3 Got It (2 of 2)

Are the graphs of $x < 3$ and $x \leq 3$ the same? Explain.

Close and Check

Focus Question

MP2, MP4

How does the concept of inequality help you describe situations?

_____

_____

_____

_____

Do you know HOW?

1. Tell whether each statement can be written as an equality or an inequality. Write **E** for equality and **I** for inequality.

Statement	Equality or Inequality
The temperature will reach at least 72° today.	
My puppy is six months old today.	
There are no more than 31 days in any given month.	
There are less than 28 students in each classroom.	
There are the same number of boys as there are girls in my family.	

2. Use the number line to graph the inequality.

$$x \leq 6$$

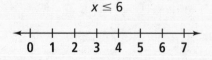

Do you UNDERSTAND?

3. Writing Which of the following graphs includes 4 in its solution set? Explain.

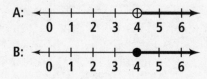

_____

_____

_____

4. Reasoning For safety, riders of an amusement park roller coaster must be at least 4 ft 6 in. tall. Write the inequality to show this. Then describe why an inequality represents this situation better than an equation.

_____

_____

_____

_____

_____

Solving Inequalities

Digital Resources

CCSS: 6.EE.B.5: ... Use substitution to determine whether a given number in a specified set makes an equation or inequality true. **6.EE.B.8:** ... Recognize that inequalities of the form $x > c$ or $x < c$ have infinitely many solutions; represent solutions ... on number line diagrams.

Launch

 MP1, MP6

You have $27 and want to invite the most friends possible to go to a concert. What is the greatest number of people, including you, that can go? Explain.

Reflect Could fewer friends go with you to the concert?

_____

_____

_____

Got It?

Which numbers are solutions of the inequality $3k < 21$?

I. 4   **II.** 7   **III.** 12

The balance in the account is $290. Suppose your aunt writes a check for $59.
Could she write a second check for $60 and keep the balance above $150?
Explain.

Discuss with a classmate

Read each other's explanation for the problem.
Is the explanation clear?
Underline any key vocabulary terms that were used in the explanation.
Discuss each of the words you underlined.
Revise the explanation if your original explanation did not use vocabulary correctly.

Got It?

PART 2 Got It

What is the solution of $x + 5 \geq 13$?

I. $x \geq 8$

II.

PART 3 Got It

Decide which statements are *true*.

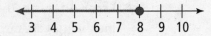

I.   The graph shows the solution of $2x \leq 8$.

II. The graph shows the solution of $24 \geq 3x$.

III. The graph shows the solution of both $x - 3 \leq 5$ and $x + 4 \leq 12$.

Close and Check

Focus Question

How is it possible for two different inequalities to describe the same situation? What does it mean for two inequalities to be equivalent?

_____

_____

_____

_____

Do you know HOW?

1. Circle the inequalities that have 25 as a solution.

$72 + x < 100$ $216 \geq 4x$ $x + 13 < 38$

$45 - x > 131$ $x \div 7 \leq 9$

2. Complete the steps to solve the inequality.

$$h \div 4 > 6$$

$$h \div 4 \cdot \boxed{} > 6 \cdot \boxed{}$$

$$h > \boxed{}$$

3. Graph the inequalities on the number lines.

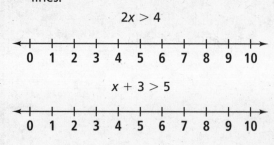

$2x > 4$

$x + 3 > 5$

Do you UNDERSTAND?

4. **Reasoning** Are the inequalities in Exercise 3 equivalent? How do you know?

_____

_____

_____

_____

5. **Error Analysis** The following inequalities are displayed in your class.

$$y > 4 \qquad g < 8$$

Your classmate says that the inequalities are equivalent because 5 is a solution of both. Is she correct? Explain your reasoning.

_____

_____

_____

_____

_____

Additional Problem Solving

CCSS: 6.EE.B.7: Solve real-world and mathematical problems by writing and solving equations of the form $x + p = q$ and $px = q$ for cases in which p, q and x are all nonnegative rational numbers. Also, 6.EE.B.5.

Launch

© MP1, MP2

Use the clues to find the value of each gemstone. Match the gemstone values to the lock numbers to open the treasure chest.

Reflect How would the problem change if the clues had letters instead of shapes?

_____

_____

_____

_____

Got It?

PART 1 Got It

Draw a model and write an equation to represent the problem.

Students working the concession stand at a school play sold a total of 64 juice boxes and energy bars during intermission. They sold 21 energy bars. How many juice boxes j did they sell?

PART 2 Got It

Draw a model and write an equation to represent the problem.

One hiking trail is 9 km long. A longer trail is c km long. Together the trails are 20 km long. How long is the longer trail?

Got It?

PART 3 Got It

A truck driving on an interstate highway can weigh at most 80,000 pounds. When empty, a dump truck weighs 32,000 pounds. How much can a load in the truck weigh, *w*, for the truck to be able to travel on the interstate?

Write an inequality to model the situation. Then solve the inequality to find the weight of the load.

Close and Check

Focus Question

What can equations and inequalities show better than words can?

_____

_____

_____

_____

Do you know HOW?

1. A food bank needs donations of 1,275 cans of food each month. This month, 729 more cans of food are needed. How many cans of food have already been donated? Complete the model and write an equation to represent the problem.

2. A dragonfly can fly up to 7 meters per second. It travels 56 meters to catch a mosquito. What is the time t it takes the dragonfly to catch it? Write and solve an inequality to model the situation.

Do you UNDERSTAND?

3. Writing What clues can you use to determine whether a problem represents an equality or an inequality?

_____

_____

_____

_____

_____

4. Reasoning The inequality $x > 8$ is displayed on chart paper. Your teacher asks you to list all of the solutions to this inequality. Can you list all of the solutions? Explain why or why not.

_____

_____

_____

_____

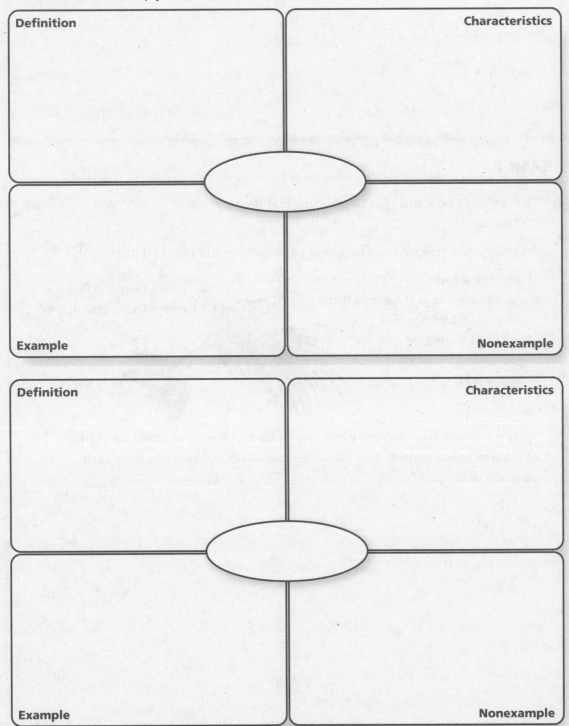

3-R Topic Review

New Vocabulary: equation, equivalent equations, equivalent inequalities, false equation, inequality, inverse operations, open sentence, true equation

Review Vocabulary: equivalent expressions

Vocabulary Review

Identify two challenging vocabulary terms from this topic. Write one vocabulary term in the center oval, and fill in the surrounding boxes with details that will help you better understand the term.

Definition	Characteristics
Example	Nonexample

Definition	Characteristics
Example	Nonexample

Pull It All Together

TASK 1

Write a word problem that can be described by the equation $h + 19 = 72$.

TASK 2

The Loblolly Pine is one type of pine tree that grows in the United States.

A Loblolly Pine tree sold to a customer has an information card attached to it.

Loblolly Pine Facts
- A mature tree is at least 60 ft tall.
- A mature tree has a straight trunk that contains no knots for up to 30 ft.

Current height: 8 ft
Current trunk length: 6 ft

Write an equation or inequality that relates each of the current measurements of the tree to the general facts about the Loblolly Pine tree. Then solve each equation or inequality.

Using Two Variables to Represent a Relationship

CCSS: 6.EE.C.9: Use variables to represent two quantities in a real-world problem that change in relationship to one another; write an equation to express one quantity … in terms of the other quantity … .

Launch

MP1, MP3

Think inside and outside the box. Inside the box, write three things that relate to the weight of the box. Outside the box, write three things about the box that do not relate to its weight.

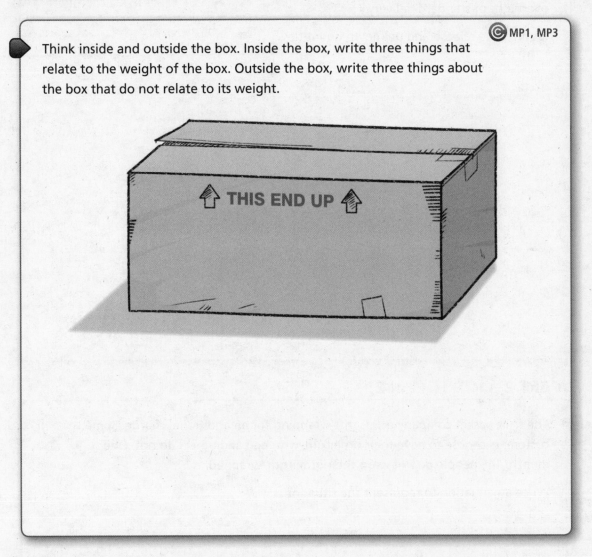

Reflect Why does it matter what things relate to the weight of the box?

_____

_____

_____

_____

_____

Got It?

PART 1 Got It

The fruit basket business takes 312 orders in one month. Orders can be shipped overnight or standard delivery.

Identify the related and unknown quantities.

PART 2 Got It (1 of 2)

The fruit basket company offers gift wrapping for an additional charge. Some customers choose to have their order gift-wrapped and others do not. One month, 145 people do *not* want their order gift-wrapped.

Write an equation to represent the situation.

Got It?

Is there more than one correct answer when you are writing an equation?

PART 3 Got It

The number of flowers in a bouquet determines the cost.

Identify the dependent variable.

Discuss with a classmate

What do you know about buying flowers that helped you with this problem? Which action, picking out the flowers or finding the cost of the flowers, happens first? How does this help you determine the dependent variable?

Close and Check

▶ Focus Question

What does it mean for one quantity to depend on another? How do you represent such a relationship?

_____

_____

_____

_____

▶ Do you know HOW?

1. Circle the related and unknown quantities in the word problem.

   > A conservation program plants 756 trees to reforest an area of land. A number of the trees are coniferous and a number of the trees are deciduous.

2. Write an equation to represent the situation above.

   [   ]

3. In each situation, underline the independent variable, and then circle the dependent variable.

   A. The wind chill factor is related to the wind speed.

   B. The amount of merchandise bought determines the amount of sales tax charged.

   C. You earned d dollars for working h hours.

▶ Do you UNDERSTAND?

4. **Vocabulary** How can you determine which variable is dependent and which variable is independent? Give an example.

   _____

   _____

   _____

   _____

5. **Error Analysis** A classmate writes an equation to determine how many boys b she can invite to her party after she invites her girlfriends g. She is allowed to have 25 guests. Explain her mistake, and then write the correct equation.

   $$g - b = 25$$

   _____

   _____

   _____

   _____

Analyzing Patterns Using Tables and Graphs

CCSS: 6.NS.C.8: Solve real-world and mathematical problems by graphing points in ... the coordinate plane ... . **6.EE.C.9:** ... Analyze the relationship between the dependent and independent variables using graphs and tables ... .

Launch

© MP4, MP7

Each time you open a box, you see two more boxes. There are seven boxes in all.

What is the minimum number of boxes you need to open to see all seven boxes? Explain your reasoning.

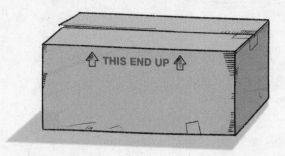

Reflect What are the dependent and independent variables in the problem?

_____

_____

_____

_____

Got It?

PART 1 Got It (1 of 2)

Draw the fourth figure in the pattern. After you draw the fourth figure, complete the table.

Number of Triangles	Number of Circles
1	3
2	4
3	5

PART 1 Got It (2 of 2)

Figures 1, 2, and 3 show a pattern. Describe why Figure 4 is *not* the fourth tree in the pattern.

 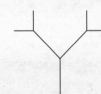 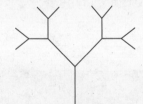 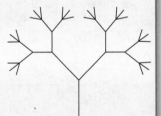

Figure 1   **Figure 2**   **Figure 3**   **Figure 4**

Got It?

PART 2 Got It

Use the table to graph the relationship between the x-column and the y-column.

x	y
0	4
1	5
2	6
3	7
4	8

PART 3 Got It

The graph shows the relationship between the speed of a car and the car's fuel economy. Name a point that falls on the graph.

Got It?

A kapok tree is a very tall rainforest tree. Assume that a kapok tree grows 12 feet each year. Complete the table and use the points to graph the growth of the kapok tree.

Year	Height (ft)
0	0
1	12
2	24
3	
4	
5	

Use the graph to predict how tall a kapok tree will be in Year 8.

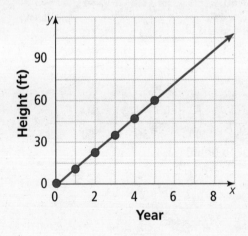

Close and Check

Focus Question

How do you find a pattern in a table?

_____

_____

_____

_____

Do you know HOW?

1. Toys are shipped to a store by the box. Determine the pattern and complete the table to show how many toys are delivered for each number of boxes shipped.

Boxes	0	2		
Toys	0	20		

2. Use the table above to graph the relationship between the number of boxes shipped and the number of toys delivered.

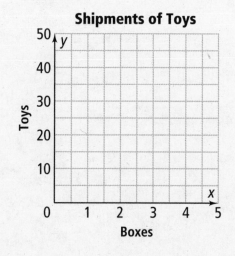

Shipments of Toys

Do you UNDERSTAND?

3. Writing The data for each 10-year census for the past 100 years is graphed. How can the graph be used to estimate the population between each census?

_____

_____

_____

_____

4. Error Analysis A classmate says the y column increases by 12 each time, so the next point (x, y) is (6, 42). Explain his mistake and tell what he should have written.

x	1	3	5	6
y	6	18	30	**42**

_____

_____

_____

_____

This page intentionally left blank.

Relating Tables and Graphs to Equations

CCSS: 6.EE.C.9: Use variables to represent two quantities in a real-world problem ... write an equation to express one quantity ... in terms of the other quantity ... Analyze the relationship between the variables using graphs and tables, and relate these to the equation.

Digital Resources

Launch

© MP3, MP8

Label each column in the table to reflect the pattern in the shapes.
Then describe at least three patterns you see, within or across columns, using those label names.

1	1	4
2	4	8
3	9	12

Pattern 1 ⋮ Pattern 2 ⋮ Pattern 3

Reflect Where have you seen the patterns in this problem before? Explain.

Got It?

PART 1 Got It

Use the table to relate the independent variable x to the dependent variable y. Write an equation that shows the relationship.

x	y
0	0
2	8
4	16
6	24
8	32
10	40

PART 2 Got It (1 of 2)

Use the graph to write an equation that represents the relationship between x and y.

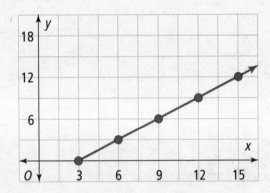

Got It?

PART 2 Got It (2 of 2)

To the right is a graph showing five different lines. Four of the lines are labeled with the equation that represents the relationship between *x* and *y*. What is the missing equation? Start by looking for a pattern among the lines that are already labeled.

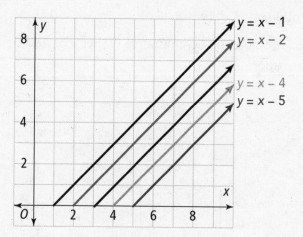

PART 3 Got It (1 of 2)

For a Saturday night show, a local band is paid $200 plus $5 for each ticket sold.

Write an equation that shows the relationship between the number of tickets sold and the total pay that the band receives.

Discuss with a classmate

Compare the equations that you wrote for this problem.
How did you choose the variable(s) to assign?
How did you determine how many variables you would need in order to write the equation?
Explain how you determined the expression for each side of the equation you wrote.
Relate the expression to the words in the problem statement.

Got It?

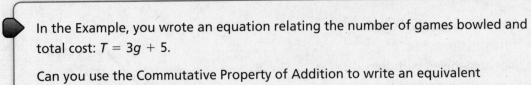

In the Example, you wrote an equation relating the number of games bowled and total cost: $T = 3g + 5$.

Can you use the Commutative Property of Addition to write an equivalent equation?

Close and Check

Focus Question

©MP1, MP8

How are graphs, tables, and equations related?

_____

_____

_____

_____

Do you know HOW?

1. Use the table to relate the independent variable x to the dependent variable y. Write an equation that shows the relationship.

x	y
3	12
5	14
7	16
9	18

_____

2. Use the graph to write an equation that represents the relationship between x and y.

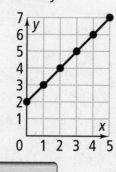

_____

Do you UNDERSTAND?

3. Reasoning Is it easier to write an equation based on a graph or a table? Explain.

_____

_____

_____

_____

_____

4. Error Analysis A classmate says the graph in Exercise 2 could represent the number of tokens won at an arcade. Explain the error in her suggestion.

_____

_____

_____

_____

_____

_____

This page intentionally left blank.

Problem Solving

CCSS: 6.EE.A.2c: Evaluate expressions at specific values of their variables … . **6.EE.C.9:** Use variables to represent two quantities in a real-world problem … write an equation to express one quantity … in terms of the other quantity … .

Launch

© MP3, MP4

Two friends need to save more money for a $300 trip. They decide to mow lawns. Each friend picks a different method to determine how many lawns they need to mow to save enough money.

Describe why each method works. Which method would you use? Explain your reasoning.

Method 1

Lawns Mowed	Future Savings
1	$23
2	$38
3	$53
4	$68

Method 2

$$T = 15\ell + 8$$

Reflect How much money do the friends have before mowing lawns? Explain.

_____

_____

_____

Got It?

PART 1 Got It

Suppose you open a bank account and deposit $1. At the end of each year, the bank will pay you $200. Write an equation that relates the year and the amount of money in the account.

PART 2 Got It

Suppose you open a bank account and deposit $1. At the end of each year, the bank will triple your money. Write an equation that relates the year and the amount of money in the account.

Got It?

PART 3 Got It

You will deposit $1. Which bank should you choose if you are going to withdraw your money in 7 years?

$$T = 1 + 200y$$

$$T = 3^y$$

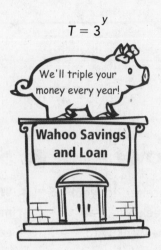

Close and Check

Focus Question

What types of problems are best solved using tables?

Do you know HOW?

1. You save the $50 you received for your birthday and $5 each week. Write an equation that relates the week w to the amount of money m saved.

2. Three friends share a secret. Every day after that, the number of people who know the secret triples. Write an equation that relates the day d to the number of people p who know the secret.

3. A job has 2 pay options. Option 1 pays $25 each day. Option 2 pays $2 the first day and doubles the amount for each day worked. Write an equation for each option that relates the days worked d to the total earned t.

   Option 1   Option 2

Do you UNDERSTAND?

4. **Writing** Based on Exercise 3, how many days would you have to work to earn more in one day on Option 2 than you would in one day on Option 1? Explain how you made your decision.

5. **Error Analysis** Every week there are 5 times as many fruit flies in a colony as the week before. The colony begins with 5 fruit flies. Your friend writes the equation $f = w^5$ to relate the week w to the number of flies f. Explain his mistake and write the correct equation.

New Vocabulary: dependent variable, independent variable
Review Vocabulary: variable

Vocabulary Review

Identify two challenging vocabulary terms from this topic. Write one vocabulary term in the center oval, and fill in the surrounding boxes with details that will help you better understand the term.

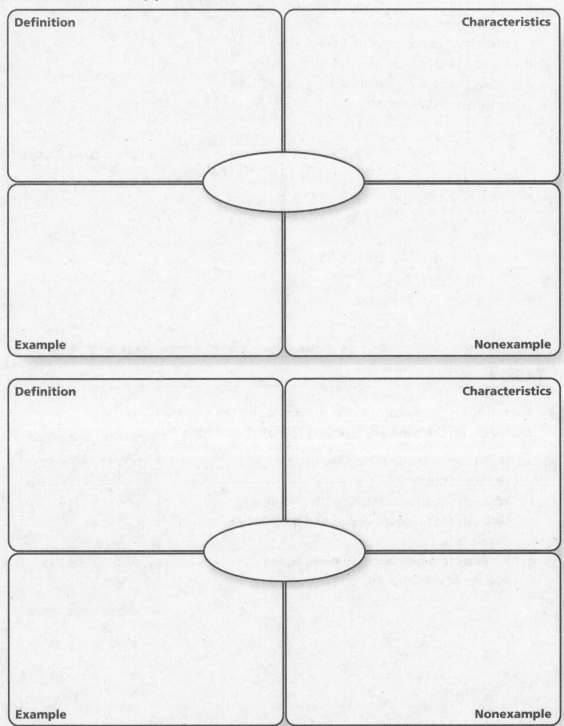

Pull It All Together

TASK 1

Eating causes a person's blood sugar level to change. Here is a graph of a person's blood sugar level one morning.

a. What is the independent variable?

b. What is the dependent variable?

c. What time did the person eat breakfast? Explain your reasoning.

d. Name a point on the graph that shows the person's blood sugar has risen since breakfast.

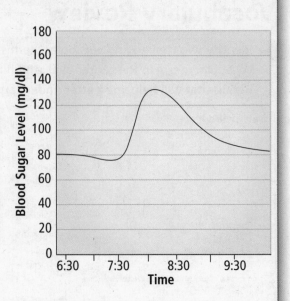

TASK 2

A scientist is growing bacteria for an experiment. She makes a table showing the number of bacteria cells after each hour.

a. Write a sentence describing the pattern you see in the table.

b. Write an equation that shows the relationship between the number of hours and the number of cells.

c. If this pattern continues, what will be the number of cells after 10 hours?

Hours	Number of cells
0	1
1	2
2	4
3	8
4	16

Multiplying Fractions and Whole Numbers

CCSS: 6.NS.A.1: Interpret and compute quotients of fractions, and solve word problems involving division of fractions by fractions, e.g., by using visual fraction models and equations to represent the problem.

Launch

MP2, MP4

Compare $\frac{1}{3} \cdot 5$ and $\frac{1}{5} \cdot 3$. Without finding the product of each expression, tell which expression has the greater product. Use pictures and words to support your argument.

Reflect How many copies of a unit fraction like $\frac{1}{4}$ do you need to have a product equal to 1? Greater than 1? Explain.

_____

_____

_____

_____

_____

Got It?

PART 1 Got It

Which multiplication equation matches the model?

I. $2 \times \frac{5}{8} = \frac{10}{8}$, or $1\frac{2}{8}$

II. $5 \times \frac{2}{8} = \frac{10}{8}$, or $1\frac{2}{8}$

PART 2 Got It (1 of 2)

Which multiplication matches the model?

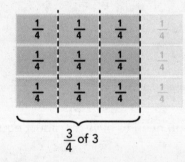

$\frac{3}{4}$ of 3

I. $\frac{3}{4} \times 3 = \frac{6}{4}$, or $1\frac{2}{4}$

II. $\frac{3}{4} \times 3 = \frac{9}{4}$, or $2\frac{1}{4}$

Got It?

Since $\frac{3}{4} \times 3 = \frac{9}{4}$, or $2\frac{1}{4}$ what does $3 \times \frac{3}{4}$ equal? Explain.

PART 3 Got It

Find the product $\frac{4}{7} \times 3$

Close and Check

Focus Question

Is multiplying a whole number and a fraction different from multiplying a fraction and a whole number? Explain.

_____

_____

_____

_____

Do you know HOW?

1. Write the multiplication equation that matches the model.

2. Use the diagram to show $3 \cdot \frac{3}{4}$. Then write the product in simplest form.

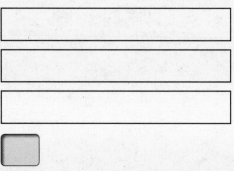

3. Find the product of $\frac{5}{6} \cdot 7$ and write it in simplest form.

Do you UNDERSTAND?

4. Error Analysis A student draws this diagram to model $2 \cdot \frac{1}{4}$. Describe the error and draw a correct model.

$\frac{1}{4}$	$\frac{1}{4}$

_____

_____

_____

5. Reasoning A recipe calls for $3\frac{3}{4}$ cups of berries. You need to make 5 batches of the recipe for a party. You have 18 cups of berries. Do you have enough berries? Explain.

_____

_____

_____

_____

Multiplying Two Fractions

Digital Resources

CCSS: 6.NS.A.1: Interpret and compute quotients of fractions, and solve word problems involving division of fractions by fractions, e.g., by using visual fraction models and equations to represent the problem.

Launch

Ⓒ MP1, MP4

Your favorite museum is $\frac{3}{4}$ mile from your home. You walk $\frac{1}{2}$ of the way there and ride the bus $\frac{1}{2}$ of the way there.

Tell how far you walk. Include a picture in your response.

Reflect How can you find $\frac{1}{2}$ of a whole number like 1? Do you do something different to find $\frac{1}{2}$ of a fraction like $\frac{3}{4}$? Explain.

_____

_____

_____

_____

_____

Got It?

PART 1 Got It (1 of 2)

The square represents 1 whole. Which multiplication matches the model?

I. $\frac{2}{3} \times \frac{1}{3} = \frac{2}{9}$

II. $\frac{2}{2} \times \frac{2}{3} = \frac{4}{6}$

III. $\frac{2}{3} \times \frac{2}{3} = \frac{4}{9}$

PART 1 Got It (2 of 2)

If you multiply two fractions that are both less than 1, can the product ever be greater than 1?

Got It?

PART 2 Got It

Find the product $\frac{2}{5} \times \frac{4}{5}$.

PART 3 Got It

Find the area of the piece of grass sod modeled in the diagram. Write your answer in simplest form.

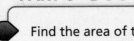

$\frac{5}{6}$ m

$\frac{3}{5}$ m

Close and Check

Focus Question

Is the product of two proper fractions greater than the fractions being multiplied? Explain.

_____

_____

_____

_____

Do you know HOW?

1. Use the unit square to show $\frac{3}{4}$ of $\frac{1}{3}$. Write the product in simplest form.

2. Find the product of $\frac{7}{12} \cdot \frac{4}{5}$. Write the product in simplest form.

3. Find the area of the postage stamp in simplest form.

$\frac{5}{9}$ in.

$\frac{3}{10}$ in.

44

Do you UNDERSTAND?

4. **Compare and Contrast** How is the product of a proper fraction and a whole number similar to and different from the product of two proper fractions?

_____

_____

_____

_____

_____

_____

5. **Reasoning** How does predicting the range of the product help in problem solving?

_____

_____

_____

Multiplying Fractions and Mixed Numbers

CCSS: 6.NS.A.1: Interpret and compute quotients of fractions, and solve word problems involving division of fractions by fractions, e.g., by using visual fraction models and equations to represent the problem.

Launch

© MP4, MP7

Your neighbor plans a rectangular garden 3 yards long by $3\frac{1}{2}$ yards wide.

What will the area of the garden be? Show how you found out.

3 yd

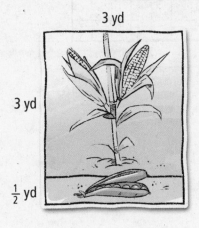

3 yd

$\frac{1}{2}$ yd

Reflect Think about the different properties you studied: Identity Properties, Commutative Properties, Distributive Property, and Associative Property. Explain how you could use one of the properties in this problem.

_____

_____

_____

_____

Got It?

PART 1 Got It

 A hummingbird feeder holds $2\frac{1}{4}$ cups of sugar water. The feeder is half full. Use the model to find how much sugar water is in the bird feeder.

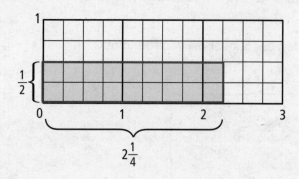

PART 2 Got It (1 of 2)

 A track is $\frac{1}{3}$ mile around. If you jog $4\frac{1}{2}$ times around the track, how far will you jog?

Got It?

PART 2 Got It (2 of 2)

When you multiply a proper fraction by a mixed number, is the product greater than or less than the proper fraction? Explain.

PART 3 Got It (1 of 2)

A school marching band practices for $2\frac{1}{3}$ hours after school on Friday. The band spent $\frac{3}{4}$ of the time practicing the routine they will perform in a parade on Saturday. For how long did the band practice the routine?

PART 3 Got It (2 of 2)

When you multiply a mixed number by a proper fraction, is the product *greater than* or *less than* the mixed number? Explain.

Close and Check

Focus Question

How can you compare the product of a proper fraction and a mixed number to the fraction? How can you compare the product of a proper fraction and a mixed number to the mixed number?

_____

_____

_____

Do you know HOW?

1. A water cooler holds $4\frac{1}{2}$ gallons of water. The container is $\frac{2}{3}$ full. Use the grid to show how many gallons of water are in the cooler.

[ ] gallons

2. A gas tank holds $9\frac{1}{2}$ gallons of gas. The tank is $\frac{8}{9}$ full. How many gallons of gas are in the tank?

 gallons

3. Find the area of the bookmark below.

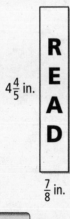

$4\frac{4}{5}$ in.

$\frac{7}{8}$ in.

Do you UNDERSTAND?

4. Reasoning Explain how you know that finding a fractional part of a whole number is the same as multiplying that fraction by a whole number.

_____

_____

_____

5. Compare and Contrast Show two ways to model $2\frac{1}{2} \cdot \frac{1}{2}$. Explain which way you prefer.

_____

_____

_____

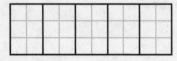

Multiplying Mixed Numbers

Digital Resources

CCSS: 6.NS.A.1: Interpret and compute quotients of fractions, and solve word problems involving division of fractions by fractions, e.g., by using visual fraction models and equations to represent the problem.

Launch

© MP4, MP7

Your neighbor's garden plan grows to include tomatoes and pumpkins. The garden is now $4\frac{1}{2}$ yd long and $3\frac{1}{2}$ yd wide. What is the area of the garden now? Show how you found out.

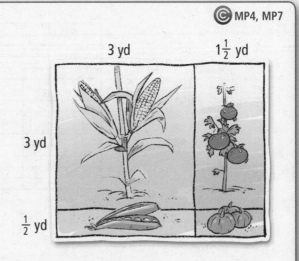

3 yd $1\frac{1}{2}$ yd

3 yd

$\frac{1}{2}$ yd

Reflect Your neighbor plans a $4\frac{1}{2}$ yd by $3\frac{1}{2}$ yd garden. Would the area change if the plan changed to a $3\frac{1}{2}$ yd by $4\frac{1}{2}$ yd garden? Explain.

Got It?

PART 1 Got It

Write a multiplication equation involving mixed numbers that matches the model.

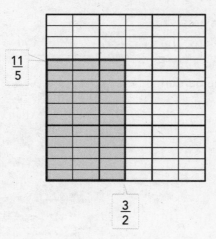

$\frac{11}{5}$

$\frac{3}{2}$

PART 2 Got It (1 of 2)

The diagram shows the length and width of a math bulletin board. Find the area of the bulletin board.

$4\frac{1}{3}$ ft

Pentominoes

F   I   L   N   P

T   U   V   W   X   Y   Z

$2\frac{2}{5}$ ft

Got It?

PART 2 Got It (2 of 2)

When you estimate the product $4\frac{1}{3} \times 2\frac{2}{5}$ using rounding, why is your estimate less than the actual value?

PART 3 Got It (1 of 2)

Use the Distributive Property to find $4 \times 9\frac{2}{9}$.

Got It?

If you use the Distributive Property to multiply $4 \times 2\frac{2}{5}$, what additional step do you need to take before you can add the products of the two parts? Explain.

Close and Check

MP2, MP8

> ## Focus Question
> How is multiplying two mixed numbers like multiplying two proper fractions? How is it different?
>
> _____
>
> _____
>
> _____
>
> _____

Do you know HOW?

1. Write and solve an equation using mixed numbers to represent the model.

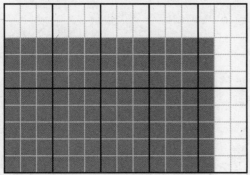

2. Find the area of the drawing.

$4\frac{1}{3}$ in.

$2\frac{3}{5}$ in.

3. Use the Distributive Property to rewrite the expression $5 \cdot 4\frac{11}{12}$.

Do you UNDERSTAND?

4. Writing How might the Distributive Property make multiplying a whole number and a mixed number easier?

_____

_____

_____

_____

5. Error Analysis Each sandwich uses $3\frac{7}{8}$ ounces of turkey. There is enough turkey for $4\frac{1}{2}$ sandwiches. You estimate that there is about 16 ounces of turkey. Your friend estimates the weight to be about 12 ounces. Which estimate is better? Explain.

_____

_____

_____

_____

This page intentionally left blank.

Problem Solving

CCSS: 6.NS.A.1: Interpret and compute quotients of fractions, and solve word problems involving division of fractions by fractions, e.g., by using visual fraction models and equations to represent the problem.

Launch

Ⓒ MP2, MP6

The length of a United States flag must be $1\frac{9}{10}$ times its width. A flag company plans a large flag with a width of $8\frac{1}{2}$ feet. What must the length be? Explain.

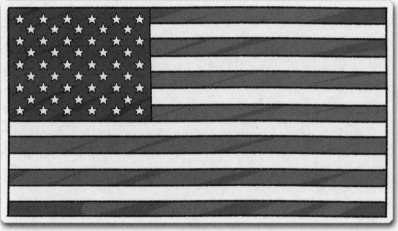

$8\frac{1}{2}$ ft

? ft

Reflect You used estimation to check reasonableness when multiplying whole numbers. Can you do the same when multiplying mixed numbers? What would you estimate for this problem?

_____

_____

_____

_____

_____

Got It?

PART 1 Got It

$3\frac{1}{4} \cdot m$ is always greater than $3\frac{1}{4}$ if:

I. $m > 1$ **II.** $m < 1$ **III.** $m = 1$

PART 2 Got It

A recipe for rice says to use $1\frac{1}{2}$ cups of water for each cup of rice. If a chef uses $3\frac{5}{6}$ cups of rice, how much water should she use?

Got It?

A dog walker charges $10 to walk a large dog and $6 to walk a small dog.

a. Write an expression to represent how much the dog walker earns for walking *b* large dogs and *s* small dogs.

b. How much will the dog walker earn for walking 8 large dogs and 3 small dogs?

Close and Check

Focus Question ⒸMP1, MP4

What real-world problems can be solved by multiplying fractions or mixed numbers?

_____

_____

_____

_____

Do you know HOW?

1. Use >, <, or = to compare each expression to the given fraction.

$3\frac{5}{6} \cdot 2\frac{1}{3}$ $3\frac{5}{6}$

$2\frac{4}{9} \cdot \frac{3}{3}$ $2\frac{4}{9}$

$1\frac{1}{10} \cdot \frac{1}{10}$ $1\frac{1}{10}$

2. A contractor needs $3\frac{3}{5}$ gallons of water for each batch of cement. How many gallons water will he need to make $9\frac{1}{2}$ batches of cement?

[ ] gallons

3. On the first day, a bird feeder is $\frac{9}{10}$ full of seeds. Each following day, the feeder contains $\frac{2}{3}$ of the amount from the day before. How full will the bird feeder be on the fourth day?

[ ]

Do you UNDERSTAND?

4. Reasoning How can multiplying fractions and mixed numbers be useful when making more or less than one full batch of the pretzel recipe?

Soft Pretzels

1¼ cup water
½ cup sugar
1½ teaspoon salt
½ cup baking soda

_____

_____

_____

_____

5. Writing Write a word problem that you could use the expression to solve.

$$2\frac{1}{2} \cdot 4\frac{1}{4}$$

_____

_____

_____

_____

Topic Review

Review Vocabulary: denominator, Distributive Property, fraction, improper fraction, mixed number, numerator, simplest form, whole number

Vocabulary Review

Identify two challenging vocabulary terms from this topic. Write one vocabulary term in the center oval, and fill in the surrounding boxes with details that will help you better understand the term.

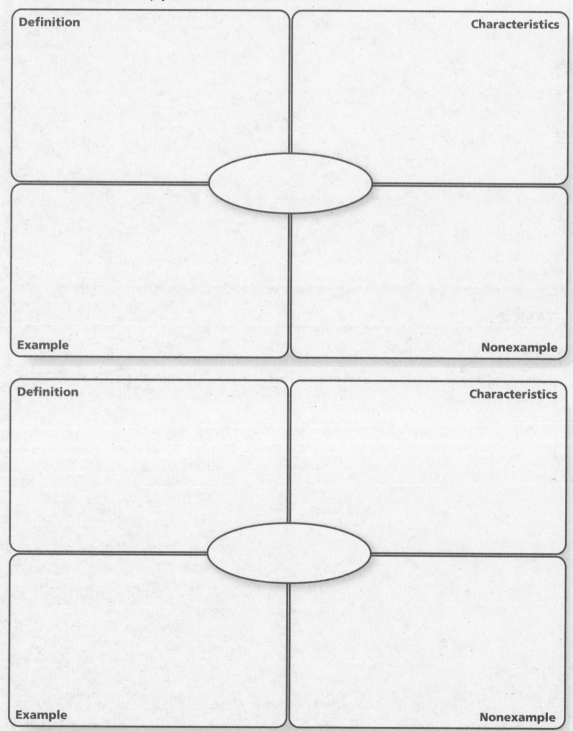

Definition

Characteristics

Example

Nonexample

Definition

Characteristics

Example

Nonexample

Pull It All Together

TASK 1

A baseball team played 55 day games and 35 night games during its season. The team won $\frac{7}{11}$ of its day games and $\frac{2}{5}$ of its night games. What is the total number of games the team won?

TASK 2

You are installing rectangular solar panels on a roof. The panels are $4\frac{1}{3}$ ft by $\frac{7}{8}$ ft. You need a total of at least 45 ft^2 of panel area to generate enough power. Will 12 panels be enough?

6-1

Dividing Fractions and Whole Numbers

CCSS: 6.NS.A.1: Interpret and compute quotients of fractions, and solve word problems involving division of fractions by fractions, e.g., by using visual fraction models and equations to represent the problem.

Launch

Find each quotient. Use a picture to represent each problem.

© MP1, MP4

4 ÷ 4

4 ÷ 2

4 ÷ 1

$4 \div \frac{1}{2}$

Reflect Which problem resulted in a quotient greater than 4? Why do you think that happened?

_____

_____

_____

_____

Got It?

What division equation does this number line model show?

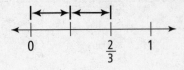

When you divide a fraction by a whole number greater than one, how does the quotient compare to the fraction? Explain your reasoning.

Got It?

PART 2 Got It (1 of 2)

What division equation does this number line model show?

PART 2 Got It (2 of 2)

When you divide a nonzero whole number by a proper fraction, how does the quotient compare to the whole number? Explain your reasoning.

PART 3 Got It

A factory's pipe-cutting machine cuts pieces of pipe to be threaded. The standard length of pipe used for cutting is 8 feet. How many $\frac{2}{3}$ ft long pieces of pipe can be cut from a standard length of pipe?

Close and Check

Focus Question

How does the relationship between multiplication and division help you to divide fractions and whole numbers?

_____

_____

_____

_____

Do you know **HOW?**

1. Use the number line to model $\frac{4}{5} \div 2$. Then write the solution.

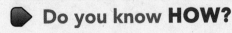

2. Circle the division equation modeled by the number line.

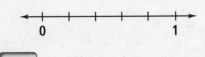

   A. $3 \div \frac{1}{4}$

   B. $12 \div \frac{1}{3}$

   C. $4 \div \frac{1}{3}$

3. A fabric store donates 15 yards of fabric for a community quilt project. Each piece of fabric measures $\frac{5}{8}$ yard. How many $\frac{5}{8}$-yard pieces of fabric is the store donating?

Do you **UNDERSTAND?**

4. **Reasoning** Will the quotient of a proper fraction divided by a whole number ever result in a whole number? Explain.

_____

_____

_____

_____

_____

5. **Writing** Explain why the first expression can be rewritten as the second expression.

$$5 \div \frac{2}{3} \qquad 5 \cdot \frac{3}{2}$$

_____

_____

_____

_____

_____

Dividing Unit Fractions by Unit Fractions

CCSS: 6.NS.A.1: Interpret and compute quotients of fractions, and solve word problems involving division of fractions by fractions, e.g., by using visual fraction models and equations to represent the problem.

Launch

© MP4, MP6

A customer orders $\frac{1}{2}$ pound of tuna for a special treat for his cats. He asks the deli worker to divide the tuna into $\frac{1}{10}$-pound pieces so each cat gets the same treat.

How many cats does the customer have? Show how you know.

Reflect Suppose the customer ordered 20 pounds of tuna and asked for it to be divided into 5-pound pieces. Would you have solved the problem differently working with whole numbers compared to working with unit fractions? Explain.

_____

_____

_____

Got It?

A carrot cake is cut into twelfths. If you buy half of the carrot cake how many pieces will you have?

Use a number line to find $\frac{1}{2} \div \frac{1}{12}$.

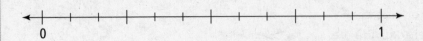

Got It?

PART 2 Got It

The area of a rectangular hayfield is $\frac{1}{72}$ square mile. If the field is $\frac{1}{12}$ mile wide, how long, in miles, is the hayfield?

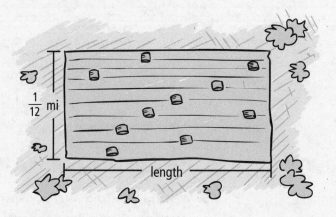

PART 3 Got It

Which story problem could be answered by finding $\frac{1}{2} \div \frac{1}{16}$?

I.   How much is $\frac{1}{2}$ of $\frac{1}{16}$ pound of trail mix?

II. How many $\frac{1}{16}$-pound snacks can be made from $\frac{1}{2}$ pound of trail mix?

Close and Check

Focus Question

Using models can help you divide unit fractions. Using reciprocals can also help you divide unit fractions. Which method is best in which situations?

_____

_____

_____

_____

Do you know HOW?

1. Use the number line to model $\frac{1}{2} \div \frac{1}{10}$. Then write the solution.

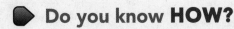

2. A community garden is being plotted on a $\frac{1}{60}$-square-mile site. The length of the garden is $\frac{1}{12}$ mile. How wide, in miles, is the garden plot?

 mile

3. How many $\frac{1}{21}$-yard pieces can be cut from a $\frac{1}{3}$-yard piece of string? Write and solve an equation.

4. A farmer needs to replace $\frac{3}{4}$ mi of fence. The first corner post does not need replaced. If he places a post every $\frac{1}{12}$ mi, how many fence posts will he need?

Do you UNDERSTAND?

5. Writing How did you decide which fraction is the dividend and which fraction is the divisor in Exercise 3?

_____

_____

_____

_____

6. Error Analysis A man purchases $\frac{1}{2}$ pound of seeds to make bird feeders. Each feeder requires $\frac{1}{16}$ pound of seeds. He sets up an equation to find how many bird feeders he can make. Explain his error and find the number of feeders he can make.

$$\frac{1}{16} \div \frac{1}{2} = \frac{1}{8}$$

_____

_____

_____

_____

Dividing Fractions by Fractions

Digital Resources

CCSS: 6.NS.A.1: Interpret and compute quotients of fractions, and solve word problems involving division of fractions by fractions, e.g., by using visual fraction models and equations to represent the problem.

Launch

MP6, MP7

Find the fraction that makes this number sentence true.
Explain how you know you are right.

$$\frac{\square}{\square} \div \frac{2}{9} = 3$$

Reflect How are multiplication and division related? Does it matter if the numbers involved are whole numbers or fractions?

_____

_____

_____

_____

Got It?

PART 1 Got It

Which division does this number line show?

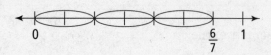

I. $\frac{6}{7} \div 3 = 1$ II. $\frac{6}{7} \div 3 = 3$ III. $\frac{6}{7} \div \frac{2}{7} = 3$ IV. $1 \div \frac{6}{7} = \frac{7}{6}$

PART 2 Got It

Find $\frac{5}{14} \div \frac{4}{7}$.

Got It?

Which story problem could be answered by finding $\frac{2}{3} \div \frac{9}{10}$?

I. How many $\frac{9}{10}$-quart pitchers can be filled with $\frac{2}{3}$ quart of water?

II. How many $\frac{2}{3}$-quart pitchers can be filled with $\frac{9}{10}$ quart of water?

Close and Check

Focus Question

How can using models or reciprocals help you divide fractions?

_____

_____

_____

_____

Do you know HOW?

1. One lap of a running track is $\frac{7}{8}$ mile. Each member of the relay team sprints $\frac{7}{16}$ mile before handing the baton to the next runner. Use the number line to find how many team members must run to complete one lap of the track.

0   1

[ ] team members

2. Find $\frac{9}{11} \div \frac{3}{8}$. Simplify the quotient.

[ ]

3. How many $\frac{3}{16}$-pound servings of fish there are in a package containing $\frac{9}{14}$ pound of fish? Write and solve an equation. Simplify the quotient.

[ ]

4. A baker has $\frac{15}{16}$ pound of flour. Each dinner roll recipe calls for $\frac{1}{11}$ pound of flour. How many full recipes can the baker make?

[ ]

Do you UNDERSTAND?

5. Writing Write and solve a fraction story problem using the following expression: $\frac{11}{12} \div \frac{2}{9} = 4\frac{1}{8}$.

_____

_____

_____

_____

_____

6. Error Analysis A classmate says $\frac{15}{16} \div \frac{3}{4} = \frac{3}{4} \div \frac{15}{16}$. Is your classmate correct? Explain.

_____

_____

_____

_____

_____

_____

Dividing Fractions and Mixed Numbers

CCSS: 6.NS.A.1: Interpret and compute quotients of fractions, and solve word problems involving division of fractions by fractions, e.g., by using visual fraction models and equations to represent the problem.

Digital Resources

Launch

MP2, MP3, MP8

Without dividing, tell which expression will result in a quotient greater than $\frac{1}{2}$ and which will result in a quotient less than $\frac{1}{2}$. Explain how you know.

Expression 1

$$\frac{1}{2} \div \frac{4}{3}$$

Expression 2

$$\frac{1}{2} \div \frac{3}{4}$$

Expression 3

$$\frac{1}{2} \div 1\frac{1}{4}$$

Reflect Does dividing by a fraction always result in a quotient greater than the dividend? Explain.

_____

_____

_____

_____

Got It?

PART 1 Got It

▶ Find $2 \div 2\frac{3}{4}$

PART 2 Got It

▶ The net weight of the baseballs in the box shown below is $60\frac{3}{4}$ ounces. If the weight of each baseball is the same, how much does each baseball weigh?

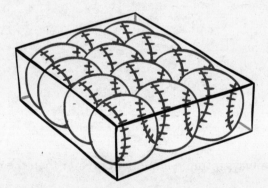

Got It?

PART 3 Got It

You're getting low on dog food, so you buy a new bag that has 40 cups of food. Your old bag still has 8 cups in it. Each day you feed your dog $2\frac{2}{3}$ cups of food. For how many days can you feed your dog with the food you have?

Close and Check

► Focus Question

How is dividing with mixed numbers related to dividing with whole numbers? How is it related to dividing with fractions?

_____

_____

_____

_____

► Do you know HOW?

1. Find $2\frac{2}{5} \div 1\frac{3}{5}$. Simplify the solution.

2. Each DVD is in a case. There are 12 cases in a box that is shipped to a video store. The contents of the box weigh $51\frac{3}{5}$ ounces. The weight of each DVD in its case is the same. How much does each DVD in its case weigh?

3. A carpenter is building sets of two picture frames. The first frame uses $7\frac{3}{5}$ inches of wood trim. The second frame uses $9\frac{1}{3}$ inches of trim. How many sets of picture frames can be made from 72 inches of trim? Simplify the quotient.

 sets

► Do you UNDERSTAND?

4. Reasoning How can you use what you know about dividing fractions and mixed numbers to estimate a quotient?

_____

_____

_____

_____

5. Error Analysis Explain the error and find the correct answer to the problem below.

$$4\frac{3}{10} \div 2\frac{1}{5}$$

$$4 \div 2 = 2 \text{ and } \frac{3}{10} \div \frac{1}{3} = \frac{3}{2}$$

$$2 + \frac{3}{2} = 3\frac{1}{2}$$

_____

_____

_____

_____

Problem Solving

CCSS: 6.NS.A.1: Interpret and compute quotients of fractions, and solve word problems involving division of fractions by fractions, e.g., by using visual fraction models and equations to represent the problem.

Launch

© MP2, MP3, MP4

A city plans a $\frac{1}{8}$-square-mile rectangular dog park. City workers bring $1\frac{1}{2}$ miles of fencing to build a fence around the park. After putting up one side of the fence, one worker says to the next, "I think we will need more fencing."

Do you agree? Explain.

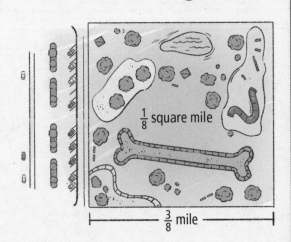

Reflect Would you rather divide by a fraction or multiply by a fraction? Can you always do what you want? Explain.

_____

_____

_____

_____

Got It?

PART 1 Got It (1 of 2)

A construction supervisor orders a 5-pound box of nails for a job. There are 16 ounces in 1 pound. If each nail weighs $\frac{1}{10}$ ounce, how many nails are in the box?

PART 1 Got It (2 of 2)

Why might a supervisor want to know how many nails are in a 5-pound box?

Discuss with a classmate
Compare your solutions to this problem.
What does a supervisor do?
What kinds of decisions does a supervisor make?
How would these decisions involve materials like how many nails are in a box?

Got It?

PART 2 Got It

What is the solution of $\frac{3}{4}n = 12$?

PART 3 Got It (1 of 2)

At a point $\frac{3}{5}$ of the way along a canoe route, there is a portage around a dam. If the dam is $14\frac{2}{3}$ miles from the start of the route, which equation could you use to find the total distance, x, of the canoe route?

I. $14\frac{2}{3}x = \frac{3}{5}$ II. $\frac{3}{5}x = 14\frac{2}{3}$ III. $x + 14\frac{2}{3} = \frac{3}{5}$

PART 3 Got It (2 of 2)

Is the solution of $b + \frac{5}{6} = 25$ *greater than* or *less than* 25? How do you know without solving?

Close and Check

> **Focus Question**
>
> What kinds of real-world problems can be solved by dividing fractions?
>
> _____
>
> _____
>
> _____

Do you know HOW?

1. A box of canned goods weighs 18 pounds. If each can weighs $14\frac{2}{5}$ ounces, how many cans are in the box?

 cans

2. What is the solution of $\frac{7}{9}d = \frac{2}{3}$?

3. The student council is creating a banner for a football game. The students will decorate $\frac{3}{8}$ of the banner, using $8\frac{1}{7}$ square feet. The remaining space will display the school name and mascot. How many total square feet is the banner?

4. The teachers make a $4\frac{5}{6}$ square foot banner, using $\frac{5}{6}$ of the total banner area. How many total square feet is the banner?

Do you UNDERSTAND?

5. Writing A riverboat travels 37 miles upstream, which is $\frac{4}{7}$ of the total trip. Show two different methods to find the total distance of the trip in miles.

_____

_____

_____

_____

6. Error Analysis Your uncle's motorcycle holds $9\frac{2}{5}$ gallons of gas and gets $53\frac{1}{3}$ miles per gallon. He says he can go $477\frac{2}{15}$ miles on a full tank. Explain his error and find how many miles he can travel on a tank of gas.

$$9\frac{2}{5} \cdot 53\frac{1}{3} = 9 \cdot 53 + \frac{2}{5} \cdot \frac{1}{3} =$$
$$477 + \frac{2}{15} = 477\frac{2}{15}$$

_____

_____

_____

_____

New Vocabulary: reciprocals
Review Vocabulary: denominator, divisor, fraction, improper fraction, mixed number, numerator, quotient

Vocabulary Review

Identify two challenging vocabulary terms from this topic. Write one vocabulary term in the center oval, and fill in the surrounding boxes with details that will help you better understand the term.

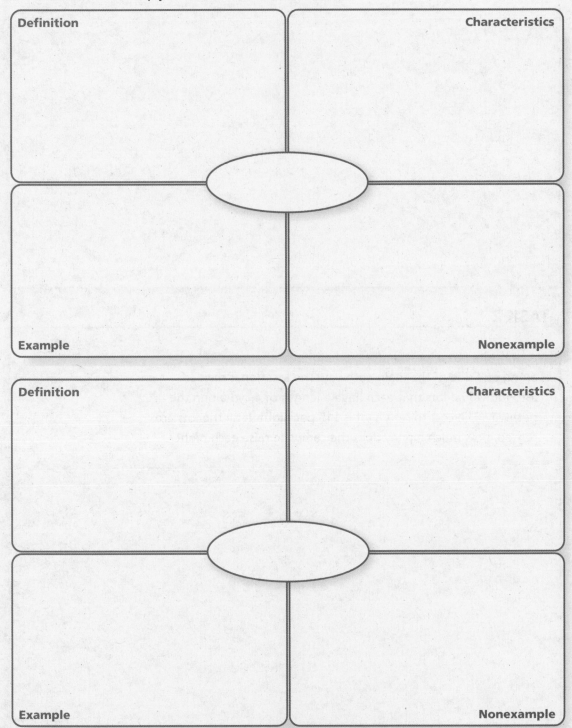

Definition	Characteristics
Example	Nonexample

Definition	Characteristics
Example	Nonexample

Pull It All Together

TASK 1

A rock concert hosting several bands is scheduled to last for 5 hours, including a $\frac{1}{2}$-hour intermission. Each band will have $\frac{3}{4}$ hour to play. How many bands can play in the concert?

TASK 2

A campsite has a location for pitching tents that runs $87\frac{1}{2}$ yd along one side of the main pathway. The location is divided into individual lots that each have a length of $4\frac{1}{6}$ yd along the pathway. The cost to rent a lot is $15 per night. If all the lots are rented, how much money does the campsite raise each night?

Adding and Subtracting Decimals

Digital Resources

CCSS: 6.NS.B.3: Fluently add, subtract, multiply, and divide multi-digit decimals using the standard algorithm for each operation.

Launch

© MP2, MP6

Your friend hands $20 to a circus store clerk and says, "I know exactly how much change you owe me for these, clown." The clerk replies, "Don't you want the deluxe noses, too? They blink."

Will the deluxe, decimal-priced, blinking noses change how your friend figures out her change? If so, how? And what will the change be?

All Prices Include Tax!

$7 $9 $0.75 $0.75

Reflect Why do you use decimals with money?

_____

_____

_____

Got It?

In the Example, you found that the suspended portion of the Golden Gate Bridge is 1.966 km long. The non-suspended approaches add another 0.771 km to the total length of the bridge. What is the total length of the Golden Gate Bridge?

How does writing a zero as a placeholder for decimal change the value of the decimal?

Got It?

PART 2 Got It

Quality control engineers use tools called micrometers that can measure part sizes to thousandths of an inch. The table shows measurements an engineer made. How much thicker than Tube A is Tube C?

Tube Thickness

Tube A	Tube B	Tube C	Tube D
0.247 in.	0.251 in.	0.25 in.	0.252 in.

PART 3 Got It

Find $19.501 - 9.45$.

Close and Check

Focus Question

How can you add and subtract decimals as easily as you do whole numbers?

_____

_____

_____

_____

Do you know **HOW?**

1. Find $26.054 + 5.7 + 0.92$.

2. A shuttle bus travels 3.045 miles to the first bus stop. Then, the bus travels another 0.34 mile to the next stop. Finally, the bus travels 2.9 miles to the last stop. Find the total distance the bus travels.

3. Find $73.7 - 8.61$.

4. Paper comes in a variety of thicknesses. A single sheet of card stock is 0.014 mm thick. Newsprint is only 0.0025 mm thick. What is the difference between the thickness of one sheet of cardstock and one sheet of newsprint?

Do you **UNDERSTAND?**

5. Writing What is the first step when adding and subtracting decimals? Explain why it is important.

_____

_____

_____

_____

6. Error Analysis Your friend says she ignores the decimal point when adding and subtracting decimals. After she finds the solution, she goes back and puts a decimal in the solution. Does this strategy work? Explain.

_____

_____

_____

_____

Multiplying Decimals

Digital Resources

CCSS: 6.NS.B.3: Fluently add, subtract, multiply, and divide multi-digit decimals using the standard algorithm for each operation.

Launch

Five bags of lemons and five boxes of cups arrive for your lemonade stand. Calculate the bill for each item. Explain the method you chose for calculating each bill.

Ⓒ MP2, MP4

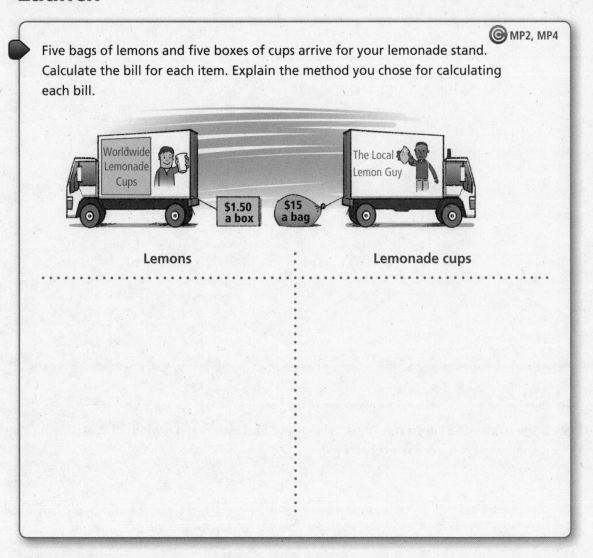

Lemons	Lemonade cups

Reflect Did you change your method of calculating each bill because one bill included a decimal-priced item and the other did not? Explain.

_____

_____

_____

_____

Got It?

PART 1 Got It

Find 0.066×0.05.

PART 2 Got It

If the screen of a big-screen TV has a length of 52.3 inches and a width of 29.4 inches, what is the area of the screen?

Discuss with a classmate

How did you know what formula to use to find the area of the screen?
Explain how you calculated the area of the screen using a diagram with all the important parts labeled.

Got It?

PART 3 Got It

Suppose you also decide to buy 1 pear for your lunch. The pear you choose weighs 0.45 pound. How much does the pear cost? Round your answer to the nearest penny.

Pears
$1.49/lb

Close and Check

Focus Question

How can you multiply decimals as easily as you multiply whole numbers?

Do you know HOW?

1. Find 0.041×0.07.

2. A glass shop cuts a piece of replacement glass for a door. Find the area of the piece of glass.

27.5 in.

18.25 in.

3. The price of gas is figured to the thousandth of a penny. The current price is $3.049 per gallon. A customer puts 7.45 gallons in her car. How much does she pay for the gas?

Do you UNDERSTAND?

4. Reasoning Does the customer in Exercise 3 pay the exact price of the gas? Explain.

5. Error Analysis Your friend says that when multiplying decimals, you must place zeros at the end of the number so both factors have the same number of decimal places. Do you agree? Explain.

Dividing Multi-Digit Numbers

Digital Resources

CCSS: 6.NS.B.2: Fluently divide multi-digit numbers using the standard algorithm.

Launch

MP2, MP7

Well, life gave your two friends lemons, 56 lemons in fact. They need 4 lemons for every pitcher of lemonade.

Find the number of pitchers of lemonade they can make. You can use any method but the standard long division method.

Reflect Are there any benefits to doing a division problem using a method other than the standard long division method? Explain.

_____

_____

_____

_____

Got It?

PART 1 Got It

Find 9,738 ÷ 18.

PART 2 Got It

Find 8,585 ÷ 17.

Got It?

PART 3 Got It (1 of 2)

Washington, D.C., has a land area of about 159 km^2 and its 2010 population was 601,723 people. Find 601,723 ÷ 159 to calculate about how many people per square kilometer lived in Washington, D.C., in 2010.

PART 3 Got It (2 of 2)

Why can you use standard long division to divide easily with greater numbers?

Close and Check

Focus Question

MP6, MP7

How can you use place value to divide any two whole numbers?

_____

_____

_____

_____

Do you know **HOW?**

1. Find $8,593 \div 12$.

2. Find $4,697 \div 23$.

3. A large apartment complex contains 55,000 square feet of living space. There are 132 individual apartments. What is the average number of square feet per apartment?

4. Windsor Castle is the largest inhabited castle in the world. It has 484,000 square feet of living space. There are 150 people in permanent residence in the castle. What is the average number of square feet per permanent resident?

Do you **UNDERSTAND?**

5. Reasoning Explain why it is important to be able to apply the arithmetic method of long division rather than drawing models to find quotients.

_____

_____

_____

_____

6. Error Analysis Identify the error in the division problem. What is the correct quotient?

$$
\begin{array}{r}
1150 \text{ R}17 \\
26\overline{)3007} \\
-26 \\
\hline
40 \\
-26 \\
\hline
147 \\
-130 \\
\hline
17
\end{array}
$$

_____

_____

_____

Dividing Decimals

Digital Resources

CCSS: 6.NS.B.3: Fluently add, subtract, multiply, and divide multi-digit decimals using the standard algorithm for each operation.

Launch

Divide 50.4 by 3 without using the standard long division method.

Show your method. Tell what you like and don't like about your method.

© MP1, MP7

Reflect Do you like your method or the long division method better for dividing? Explain.

_____

_____

_____

_____

_____

Got It?

PART 1 Got It

Find 9.012 ÷ 3.

PART 2 Got It (1 of 2)

Find 1.2 ÷ 0.005.

Got It?

When you multiply a decimal divisor by a power of 10 to change it to a whole number, why do you need to multiply the dividend by the same power of 10?

PART 3 Got It

A shelf used to store DVDs is 60.96 cm long. If each DVD is 1.5 cm wide, what is the maximum number of DVDs that can be stored on the shelf?

Close and Check

Focus Question

How can you divide decimals as easily as you divide whole numbers?

_____

_____

_____

_____

Do you know HOW?

1. Find 24.15 ÷ 6.

2. Find 8.183 ÷ 83.5.

3. There is 197.625 square feet of floor space in the back of a moving van. The van is 7.75 feet wide. Find the length of the space in the back of the van.

4. A grocer orders boxes of macaroni and cheese for the store. The shelf is 8.43 feet wide. Each box is 0.125 foot wide. Find the number of boxes that will fit in each row on the shelf.

Do you UNDERSTAND?

5. Reasoning Is it always possible to find an exact quotient when dividing with decimals? Explain.

_____

_____

_____

_____

6. Error Analysis A classmate says you can change decimal division to whole number division by moving the decimals to the end of both numbers before dividing. Do you agree with this problem-solving strategy? Explain.

_____

_____

_____

_____

_____

_____

Decimals and Fractions

CCSS: 6.NS.C.7: Understand ordering and absolute value of rational numbers.

Launch

MP3, MP6

Use at least one decimal and at least one fraction to represent the quantity shown in four new and different ways. Tell whether one of these representations is more useful than the others and why.

> **four hundredths**

Reflect Which offers you more possibilities to represent the same quantity in different ways – fractions or decimals? Explain.

_____

_____

_____

_____

_____

Got It?

PART 1 Got It

Virginia has a land and water area that is about 0.011 of the total area of the United States. What fraction of the total area of the United States does Virginia make up?

PART 2 Got It (1 of 2)

Use division to write $\frac{3}{5}$ as a decimal.

PART 2 Got It (2 of 2)

How can you write $\frac{3}{5}$ as a decimal without using division?

Got It?

PART 3 Got It (1 of 2)

The average depth of Lake Michigan, the second-largest Great Lake, is about $\frac{4}{7}$ of the average depth of Lake Superior. Write $\frac{4}{7}$ as a decimal rounded to the nearest hundredth.

PART 3 Got It (2 of 2)

When writing a fraction as a decimal, why does it make sense to round the decimal when you see that the decimal is beginning to repeat?

Close and Check

Focus Question

When might you want to communicate a fraction as a decimal? When might you want to communicate a decimal as a fraction?

_____

_____

_____

_____

Do you know HOW?

1. The area of land in the United States is about 0.052 of the total area of land on Earth. What fraction of total land on Earth does the United States make up?

2. A math class surveys the students in the school. The survey shows that $\frac{5}{8}$ of the students ride the bus to school on a regular basis. Write the fraction as a decimal.

3. The U.S. currency exchange rate determines the value of foreign dollars. If 1 U.S. dollar equals 12 foreign dollars, the value of the foreign currency is $\frac{1}{12}$ the value of U.S. currency. Write the fraction as a decimal to the nearest hundredth.

Do you UNDERSTAND?

4. Writing Think of one real-world example when fractions are primarily used and one example when decimals are primarily used. Explain why each form is used in that situation.

_____

_____

_____

_____

_____

5. Reasoning One student uses multiplication to find the decimal equivalent of $\frac{17}{20}$. Another student uses division. Which student is correct? Explain.

_____

_____

_____

_____

Comparing and Ordering Decimals and Fractions

Digital Resources

CCSS: 6.NS.C.7: Understand ordering and absolute value of rational numbers.

Launch

(C) MP5, MP6

Complete the number line by adding and labeling at least two more tick marks at regular intervals. Then, place and label points on the number line at the following locations: 2.1, $2\frac{1}{3}$, 2.75, $2\frac{5}{8}$.

Explain the decisions you made.

2

Reflect What did you consider most important about how you made your number line?

_____

_____

_____

_____

_____

Got It?

PART 1 Got It

Compare 2.99 and 2.9900.

PART 2 Got It (1 of 2)

Compare 0.67 and $\frac{6}{7}$.

Got It?

PART 2 Got It (2 of 2)

When comparing a decimal and a fraction, do you prefer to change the decimal to a fraction or change the fraction to a decimal? Why?

PART 3 Got It

$\frac{1}{3}$, ?, 0.36, $\frac{3}{8}$

Which of the numbers below could replace the question mark above so that the numbers are ordered from *least* to *greatest*?

I. 0.3   II. 0.32   III. $\frac{7}{20}$

Discuss with a classmate

Number lines are useful models for ordering and comparing numbers.
Use a number line to justify why the answer you selected allows the numbers to be ordered from least to greatest.
Use a number line to explain why the other answer choices are incorrect.

Close and Check

Focus Question

Which are usually easier to compare and order, fractions or decimals? Why?

Do you know HOW?

1. Write the numbers in order from least to greatest.

Least

75.93 ▢

75.9 ▢

75.902 ▢

75.951 ▢

Greatest

2. Compare the fraction and decimal by using $>$, $<$, or $=$ to make the statement true.

0.29 ▢ $\frac{2}{9}$

3. Circle the number in the box that could replace the question mark so that the numbers are ordered from least to greatest.

$\frac{3}{4}$	0.32	$\frac{2}{3}$	0.43

$0.14, \frac{1}{4}, ?, \frac{2}{5}$

Do you UNDERSTAND?

4. **Writing** Describe a real-world situation in which you compare fractions and a situation in which you compare decimals.

5. **Error Analysis** You have finished $\frac{8}{9}$ of your science project. Your friend has finished 0.9 of her project. You say your project is more complete than your friend's project. She disagrees. Who is correct? Explain.

Problem Solving

CCSS: 6.NS.C.7: Understand ordering and absolute value of rational numbers. **6.EE.B.7:** . Solve real-world and mathematical problems by writing and solving equations of the form $x + p = q$ and $px = q$ for cases in which p, q and x are all nonnegative rational numbers.

Launch

© MP1, MP4

An avid runner runs 1.75 miles per day each weekday. On Saturday and Sunday, he runs twice as far as he does each weekday.

How many miles does he run each week? Show how you know.

Reflect Would the problem have been easier, harder, or about the same if the runner ran whole number distances? Explain.

_____

_____

_____

_____

_____

Got It?

PART 1 Got It

The Lafayette Dollar has a mass of 26.73 grams. This is 18.63 grams more than the mass of the Washington Dollar. Which equations could you use to find the mass m of the Washington Dollar?

$$\textbf{I. } m + 18.63 = 26.73 \qquad\qquad \textbf{II. } m + 18\tfrac{63}{100} = 26\tfrac{73}{100}$$

PART 2 Got It

The carpenter paid $817.96 for 4 solar attic fans. The price of each fan is the same. Which equation could you write and solve to find the price p of 1 fan?

$$\textbf{I. } 817.96p = 4 \qquad\qquad \textbf{II. } 4p = 817.96$$

Discuss with a classmate

Use a graphic organizer, such as Know-Need-Plan, to organize the information given in the problem.

Check for the following:
Why did you choose the organizer?
How does the organizer help you solve the problem?
How does the organizer help you explain your solution?

PART 3 Got It

Which is equivalent to $6.75\overline{)2.25}$?

$$\textbf{I. } 675\overline{)225} \qquad\qquad \textbf{II. } \tfrac{1}{3}$$

Close and Check

Focus Question

© MP3, MP4

What kinds of problems can you solve using equations with decimals?

_____

_____

_____

_____

Do you know HOW?

1. A store sells team sweatshirts for $32.95. This is $7.36 more than the competitor's price on the same sweatshirt. Find the cost of the competitor's sweatshirt.

   [   ]

2. Five friends earn a total of $127.20 doing odd jobs on the weekend. Each friend gets an equal share s of the earnings. Write a multiplication equation to represent the situation.

   [   ]

3. Circle the expressions that are equivalent to $62.4\overline{)12.48}$.

   $124.8 \div 624$ $\dfrac{2}{100}$

   $624\overline{)1248}$ $\dfrac{1}{5}$

4. A quilt pattern calls for $\dfrac{7}{8}$ yard of blue fabric and 0.75 yard of yellow fabric. How many total yards of blue and yellow fabric are needed to make 3 quilts?

   [   ] yards

Do you UNDERSTAND?

5. **Compare and Contrast** The friends in Exercise 2 decide to invest $\dfrac{1}{6}$ of the earnings in their small business. Explain how to set up the equation to show how much money is left to be shared equally among the 5 friends.

   _____

   _____

   _____

   _____

   _____

6. **Reasoning** A woman walks 0.6 of a 2-mile track. Another woman walks $\dfrac{4}{5}$ of the same track. Which woman walks farther? Explain.

   _____

   _____

   _____

   _____

   _____

This page intentionally left blank.

New Vocabulary: compatible numbers
Review Vocabulary: decimal, rounding, whole number

Vocabulary Review

Identify two challenging vocabulary terms from this topic. Write one vocabulary term in the center oval, and fill in the surrounding boxes with details that will help you better understand the term.

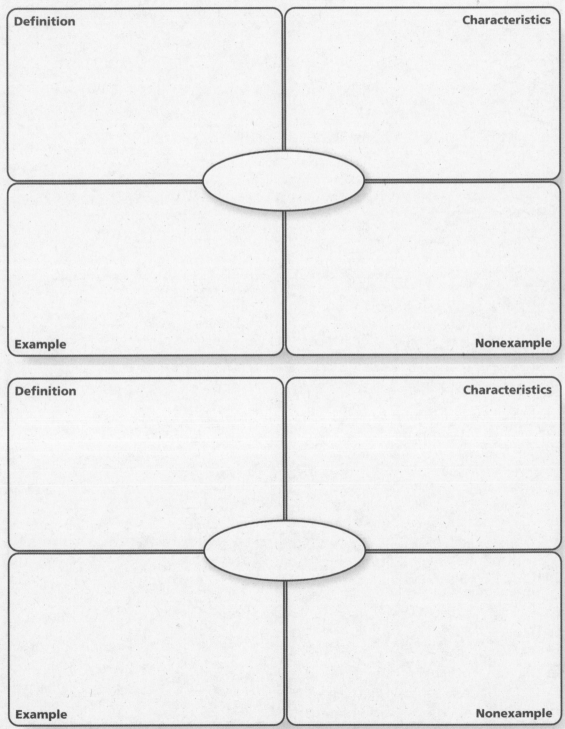

| Definition | Characteristics |
| Example | Nonexample |

| Definition | Characteristics |
| Example | Nonexample |

Pull It All Together

TASK 1

You are planning a party. The food for each guest costs $3.50, and you want each guest to have a party hat costing $2.20. You have a total budget of $95.00 for the party. How many guests can you invite?

Integers and the Number Line

CCSS: 6.NS.C.5: ... use positive and negative numbers to represent quantities in real-world contexts ... .
6.NS.C.6a: Recognize opposite signs of numbers as indicating locations on opposite sides of 0 on the number line ... . Also, 6.NS.C.6c.

Launch

Ⓒ MP4, MP7, MP8

To prepare for an overnight camping trip, you begin checking the temperature to see what clothes to bring.

If the trend continues, what might the temperature be at 8 P.M.?

Describe or show a possible temperature.

Time	Temperature
4 P.M.	6°F
5 P.M.	5°F
6 P.M.	2°F
7 P.M.	0°F
8 P.M.	??

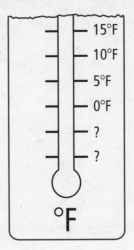

Reflect Why do you need numbers less than zero?

_____

_____

_____

_____

_____

Got It?

PART 1 Got It (1 of 2)

What is the opposite of 9?

PART 1 Got It (2 of 2)

What is the opposite of the opposite of 4? How do you know?

PART 2 Got It (1 of 2)

Electrons and protons are particles in an atom with equal but opposite charges. Electrons have a negative charge and protons have a positive charge. What is the charge of an atom with 2 more electrons than protons?

Got It?

PART 2 Got It (2 of 2)

What does it mean if an atom has a charge of 0?

PART 3 Got It

The lowest point in the United States is in Death Valley. Its elevation is 282 ft below sea level. Express this elevation as an integer.

Close and Check

Focus Question

What are integers? Why do we need integers? What do integers allow you to do that whole numbers do not?

_____

_____

_____

_____

Do you know HOW?

1. Complete the number line.

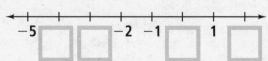

2. What is the opposite of −17?

3. What integer represents 6 strokes below par in golf?

4. A man enters a parking garage at street level (0). He parks on a level that is 4 floors below the street. What integer can represent where the man parked?

Do you UNDERSTAND?

5. Vocabulary How do you know that 8 and −8 are opposites?

_____

_____

6. Reasoning What integer can represent the position of the bait below the water line? Explain.

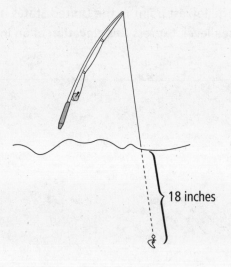

18 inches

_____

_____

_____

_____

Comparing and Ordering Integers

CCSS: 6.NS.C.7a: Interpret statements of inequality as statements about the relative position of two numbers on a number line diagram... . **6.NS.C.7b:** Write, interpret, and explain statements of order for rational numbers in real-world contexts ... . Also, **6.NS.C.7.**

Launch

© MP2, MP6

The world's top four video game players square off in a new game called Zombie Pretzel Attack 2! Rank the final scores of the players. Explain how you decided.

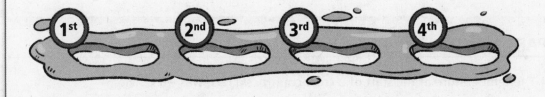

Reflect How do you score a negative number like −100 in a game?

_____

_____

_____

_____

Got It?

PART 1 Got It

What symbol correctly completes the statement? Justify your answer using a number line.

$$-5 \boxed{} -3$$

PART 2 Got It

The temperature at the start of a cross-country ski race was $-8°C$. The temperature at the end of the race was $-2°C$. Write an inequality comparing the temperatures. When was it colder?

Got It?

PART 3 Got It

Scores in a golf tournament are reported by the number of strokes each player is above or below par. The scores for five players are −5, 5, −10, 3, and −8. Order the scores from the lowest score to the highest score.

Scores:
−5
5
−10
3
−8

Close and Check

▶ Focus Question

What does it mean for one negative number to be greater than another negative number? How can you use that information?

_____

_____

_____

_____

▶ Do you know **HOW?**

In Exercises 1 and 2, write the symbol < or > that correctly completes each statement.

1. −12 ☐ −10

2. −12 ☐ −15

3. Each day, the stock market records the changes in stock values for investors.

Stocks	Net Change
Computer	10
Health Care	−3
Financial	5
Airlines	−20
Energy	−8

Order the integers from least to greatest.

▶ Do you **UNDERSTAND?**

4. Reasoning Is −5 to the left or right of −8 on a number line? How does this help you know which integer is greater?

_____

_____

_____

_____

_____

5. Writing In golf, the player with the lowest score wins. Player A scores a −1. Player B scores a −5. Explain how you know that Player B wins.

_____

_____

_____

Absolute Value

Digital Resources

CCSS: **6.NS.C.7b:** Write ... statements of order for rational numbers ... . **6.NS.C.7c:** Understand the absolute value of a rational number as its distance from 0 on the number line ... . **6.NS.C.7d:** Distinguish comparisons of absolute value from statement about order ... . Also, **6.NS.C.7.**

Launch

Two discus throwers try out for the track team. Thrower 1 throws the discus forward, but Thrower 2 slips and throws the discus the wrong way.

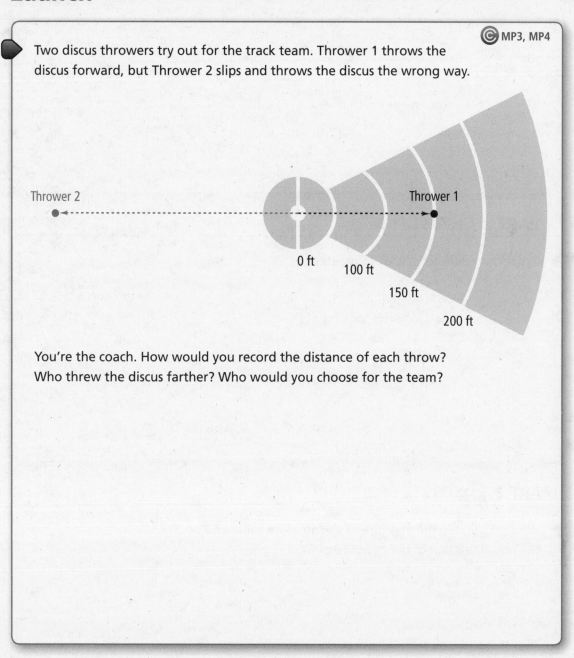

You're the coach. How would you record the distance of each throw? Who threw the discus farther? Who would you choose for the team?

Reflect What is the shortest distance a discus can travel?

_____

_____

_____

Got It?

PART 1 Got It

Find $|-6|$.

PART 2 Got It (1 of 2)

Order the values from least to greatest:

$|-5|$, -5, $|2|$, -2, -3

PART 2 Got It (2 of 2)

Which is greater, the opposite of the absolute value of 3 or the absolute value of the opposite of 3?

Got It?

You are diving off a boat into the ocean. You record your position relative to sea level on each dive.

Dive	Position Relative to Sea Level (ft)
First	−12.5
Second	−14
Third	−10
Fourth	−8

On which dive did you dive the deepest?

For each statement, give an example that shows the statement is false.

I. The absolute value of a number is less than the given number.

II. The absolute value of a number always equals the number.

III. The absolute value of a number is always the opposite of the number.

Close and Check

Focus Question

© MP6, MP8

How can you express the distance of any number from 0? When might you need to know the distance from 0?

_____

_____

_____

_____

Do you know HOW?

In Exercises 1 and 2, find each absolute value.

1. $|2|$

2. $|-13|$

3. Order the values from least to greatest.

$$-9, 7, |-3|, 0, |1|$$

4. Which number has a greater absolute value, -3 or -7?

5. The Dead Sea Depression near Israel has an elevation of 422 meters below sea level. Death Valley, CA has an elevation of 86 meters below sea level. Write an integer that represents the place with the lower elevation.

Do you UNDERSTAND?

6. Reasoning If two different integers have the same absolute value, what do you know about the integers? Explain.

_____

_____

_____

_____

7. Error Analysis Suppose a number line represents your street. Each mile of your street is represented by an integer. Your house is located at 0. Your friend lives no more than 2 miles from you. He says his house is located at -3. Is your friend correct? Explain.

_____

_____

_____

Integers and the Coordinate Plane

CCSS: 6.NS.C.6b: Understand signs of numbers in ordered pairs as indicating locations in quadrants of the coordinate plane; recognize that when two ordered pairs differ only by signs, the locations of the points are related by reflections across one or both axes. Also, **6.NS.C.6c** and **6.NS.C.8.**

Launch

Ⓒ MP6, MP7

Write the missing coordinates (?, ?) for points A, B, and C. Explain how you know you are right.

Reflect How does the numbering of coordinates relate to your earlier work on integers on the number line?

_____

_____

_____

_____

_____

Got It?

PART 1 Got It

Which point is located at (3, −2)?

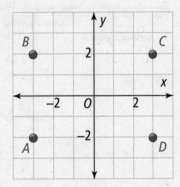

Got It?

PART 2 Got It

In which quadrant is the point (−4, 4) located?

PART 3 Got It

What is the reflection of (3, 4) across the *y*-axis?

Close and Check

Focus Question

© MP2, MP8

How is a number line related to the coordinate plane? How are integers used within the coordinate plane?

_____

_____

_____

_____

Do you know HOW?

Use the coordinate plane for Exercises 1-4.

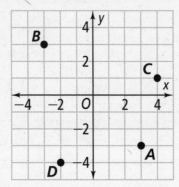

1. Plot points $X(2, 3)$, $Y(-4, 2)$, and $Z(-3, -1)$ on the coordinate plane.

2. What are the coordinates of point D?

3. In what quadrant does point D lie?

4. What is the reflection of $(3, -3)$ across the x-axis?

Do you UNDERSTAND?

5. **Compare and Contrast** Explain how the coordinates of a point and its reflection across the x-axis are the same and how they are different.

_____

_____

_____

6. **Error Analysis** Your classmate identifies the coordinates of point $P(1, -3)$. Explain the error.

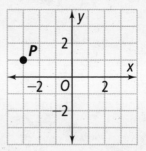

_____

_____

_____

_____

Distance

Digital Resources

CCSS: 6.NS.C.8: ... Include use of coordinates and absolute value to find distances between points with the same first ... or ... second coordinate. **6.G.A.3:** ... use coordinates to find the length of a side joining points with the same first ... or ... second coordinate ... .

Launch

© MP1, MP2

A park worker gets a call from her boss who says, "Build a rectangular sandbox with your 20 feet of board. Put a corner at (0, 0), (0, 5), (4, 0), and... ." The phone goes dead.

Show how the worker can plot the sandbox on the grid without calling her boss back. Tell why she has more than enough board.

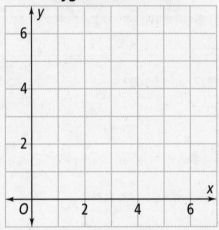

Playground Grid Plan

Reflect Why would a grid be useful when planning to build a sandbox at a playground?

_____

_____

_____

_____

_____

Got It?

PART 1 Got It

What is the distance between the points (4, 2) and (4, −2)?

PART 2 Got It

What is the distance between the points (−3, 2) and (2, 2)?

PART 3 Got It

A right triangle has its vertices at (−3, 4), (−3, 7), and (5, 4). What is the area of the triangle? Use the formula $A = \frac{1}{2}bh$, where b is the base of the triangle and h is the height.

Close and Check

> ## Focus Question
> © MP4, MP7
>
> How are integers used to express distance? What does a negative number mean when you are talking about distance?
>
> _____
>
> _____
>
> _____
>
> _____

Do you know HOW?

1. What is the distance between the points (10, −8) and (10, 8)?

> [ ]

2. What is the distance between the points (10, 3) and (−2, 3)?

> [ ]

3. You draw a square diagram of your science project on a coordinate grid. The corners of the diagram are located at (5, −4), (−2, −4), (−2, 3), and (5, 3). How many units long is each side of the diagram?

> [ ]

4. The distance between two points is 10. The coordinates of one point are (3, −4). Fill in the y-coordinate of the second point, which is in Quadrant I.

> (3, [ ])

Do you UNDERSTAND?

5. Writing Find the perimeter and area of the square diagram in Exercise 3. Explain how you found your answer.

_____

_____

_____

_____

6. Error Analysis There are two points on a coordinate grid at (7, 12) and (7, −5). A classmate says the distance between the two points is 7. Tell whether your classmate is correct. Explain your reasoning.

_____

_____

_____

_____

_____

_____

This page intentionally left blank.

Problem Solving

CCSS: 6.NS.C.6b: ... recognize that when two ordered pairs differ only by signs, the locations of the points are related by reflections across ... axes. 6.NS.C.7c: ... interpret absolute value as magnitude for a positive or negative quantity in a real-world situation ... . Also, 6.G.A.4.

Launch

© MP1, MP6

Draw your own go-cart racecourse that starts and finishes at the clubhouse, forms a rectangle, passes by another given point on one turn, and is 24 blocks long. Each grid line represents 1 block.

Label the coordinates on each turn. Explain why your racecourse works.

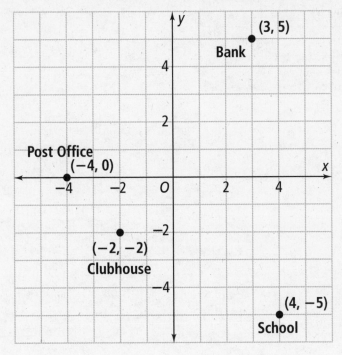

Reflect Can the drivers ever go a negative distance? Explain.

_____

_____

Got It?

PART 1 Got It

The table shows the lowest elevations for four states.
Which elevation is closest to sea level?

Elevation Relative to Sea Level

State	Elevation (ft)
Arizona	70
California	−282
Louisiana	−8
Oklahoma	289

Got It?

PART 2 Got It

Reflect the point (−2, 3) across the *x*-axis, then across the *y*-axis, and then across the *x*-axis again. In which quadrant is the final image located?

Close and Check

Focus Question

MP1, MP4

In this topic, you have learned different ways to use integers. How do integers help you to solve problems?

_____

_____

_____

_____

Do you know HOW?

Use the story for Exercises 1-3.
The mail carrier walks 6 blocks on her route before noticing she has dropped a package. She walks back 4 blocks and finds it on the ground. She continues her route, walking 10 blocks. She decides she needs a bottle of water, so she goes back 2 blocks to a corner store. After finishing her water, she walks another 15 blocks to complete her route.

1. Describe the mail carrier's route in integers.

   ☐ ☐ ☐ ☐ ☐

2. How many blocks did the mail carrier walk?

   ☐

3. How many actual blocks is the mail carrier's route?

   ☐

Do you UNDERSTAND?

4. **Reasoning** The map of your town is on a coordinate grid. Each square is a town block. The town center is at the origin. If your house is located at $(-10, 0)$, explain how -10 and $|-10|$ can both represent where you live.

   _____

   _____

   _____

   _____

   _____

5. **Writing** Point $(-3, 5)$ is reflected across the x-axis, and then the image is reflected across the y-axis. The same point $(-3, 5)$ is reflected across the y-axis, and the image is reflected across the x-axis. What do you know about the final images? Is this true for any point?

   _____

   _____

   _____

Topic Review

New Vocabulary: absolute value, coordinate plane, image, integers, line of reflection, opposites, ordered pair, quadrant, reflection, transformation

Review Vocabulary: distance, negative numbers, positive numbers

Vocabulary Review

Identify two challenging vocabulary terms from this topic. Write one vocabulary term in the center oval, and fill in the surrounding boxes with details that will help you better understand the term.

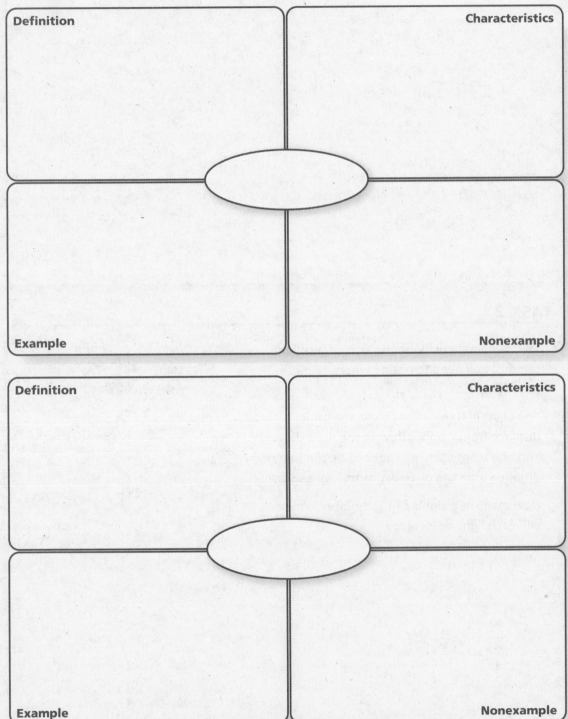

Definition

Characteristics

Example

Nonexample

Definition

Characteristics

Example

Nonexample

Pull It All Together

TASK 1

Consider an iceberg in the North Atlantic Ocean. The position of the top of the iceberg relative to sea level is 27 ft. The position of the bottom of the same iceberg relative to sea level is −193 ft. What is total height of the iceberg?

TASK 2

The coordinate plane shows part of a college campus. You need to decide where to place new lights.

You want each new light to be the same distance from Campus Row as the light shown. You also want each new light to be the same distance from the driveway as the light shown.

How many new lights can you place? Where will each light be located?

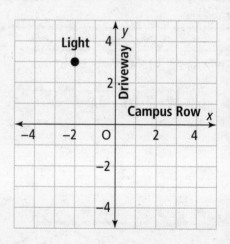

Rational Numbers and the Number Line

CCSS: 6.NS.C.5: … Use positive and negative numbers to represent quantities in real-world contexts … .
6.NS.C.6a: Recognize opposite signs of numbers as indicating locations on opposite sides of 0 on the number line … . Also, 6.NS.C.6c.

Launch

MP1, MP6

The skateboard club's exacting executive manager creates a new scoring system for the boarders' moves. The boarders say the system is suspect because "none of our scores land on a number."

Do you agree with the boarders? What could their scores be? Explain.

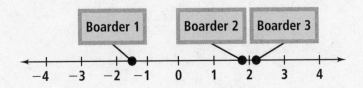

Reflect How many scores do you think are between 0 and 1? Explain.

_____

_____

_____

_____

_____

Got It?

PART 1 Got It (1 of 2)

Find the opposite of the rational number represented by the point *N*.

PART 1 Got It (2 of 2)

What is the opposite of the opposite of $-\frac{1}{3}$? How do you know?

Got It?

PART 2 Got It

In a checking account, a *debit* represents a decrease in the account balance and a *credit* represents an increase. Which rational number or numbers represent debits?

I. −4.40   II. −11.21   III. 4.40   IV. 11.21

PART 3 Got It

In Australia, the highest point on land is the peak of Mt. Kosciuszko, at an elevation of 7,130 feet above sea level. Which of the following express this elevation as a rational number?

I. 7,310 ft   II. $2,436\frac{2}{3}$ yd   III. $\frac{7,310}{3}$ yd

Close and Check

Focus Question

What are rational numbers? How can you use rational numbers?

_____

_____

_____

_____

Do you know HOW?

1. What rational number is the opposite of point *R*?

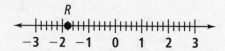

2. Altitude is measured in relation to sea level, which is 0. Circle the rational number(s) that represents a position below sea level.

   A. −2,480 ft

   B. 503 ft

   C. 1,403$\frac{2}{3}$ ft

   D. −729$\frac{1}{2}$ ft

3. In golf, scores are recorded in relation to par, which is 0. Write each score as a rational number.

Golfer	A	B	C
Score (par)	3 under	4 over	1 under
Rational Number			

Do you UNDERSTAND?

4. **Vocabulary** Explain the difference between rational numbers and integers.

   _____

   _____

   _____

   _____

   _____

   _____

5. **Error Analysis** A friend says −3.7 is not a rational number because it isn't written in the form $-\frac{a}{b}$. Do you agree? Explain.

   _____

   _____

   _____

   _____

   _____

   _____

Comparing Rational Numbers

CCSS: 6.NS.C.6c: Find and position ... rational numbers on a ... number line diagram ....
6.NS.C.7a: Interpret statements of inequality as statements about the relative position of two numbers on a number line diagram ... . Also, **6.NS.C.7b, 6.NS.C.7c.**

Launch

Ⓒ MP4, MP6

On the second day of skateboard practice, Boarder 1 asks the exacting executive manager for a verbal description of her score and how it compares to the other boarders' scores. Boarder 1 doesn't want her exact score if it's not a whole number.

Describe Boarder 1's score and how it compares to the other boarders' scores without saying Boarder 1's score.

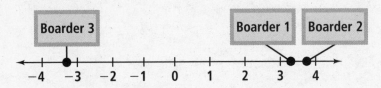

Description of Boarder 1's score:

How Boarder 1 compares to Boarder 2:

How Boarder 1 compares to Boarder 3:

Reflect How could you let Boarder 1 know her exact score for sure without giving her the score? Explain.

_____

_____

_____

_____

_____

Got It?

PART 1 Got It

You can use the number line. What symbol correctly compares the pair of rational numbers below?

$-\dfrac{1}{2}$ ☐ -0.5

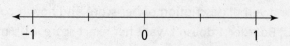

PART 2 Got It

What symbol correctly compares the absolute values below?

$\left|-\dfrac{2}{3}\right|$ ☐ $\left|-\dfrac{1}{2}\right|$

Got It?

PART 3 Got It

Compare the absolute value of a bottlenose dolphin's regular dive for food to the absolute value of the deepest trained dive ever recorded for a bottlenose dolphin. Then explain the meaning of the absolute values you compared.

Elevation of Bottlenose Dolphin Dives

	Elevation
Regular dive	−0.045 km
Deepest trained dive	−0.547 km

Close and Check

MP2, MP6

Focus Question

What does it mean for one rational number to be greater than another rational number? How can you compare absolute values of rational numbers?

Do you know HOW?

Use the number line for Exercises 1 and 2.

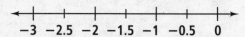

−3 −2.5 −2 −1.5 −1 −0.5 0

1. Write the symbol <, >, or = to compare the pair of rational numbers.

   $-2\frac{3}{4}$ ☐ -2.7

2. Write the symbol <, >, or = to compare the absolute values of the pair of rational numbers.

   $\left|-2\frac{3}{4}\right|$ ☐ $\left|-2.7\right|$

3. After reaching the summit, a climbing expedition descends the mountain in two groups. Circle the group that is farthest from the summit.

Group	A	B
Position relative to summit	−675 ft	−831 ft

Do you UNDERSTAND?

4. **Reasoning** You want to find which is greater, the total amount of savings account deposits or the total amount of withdrawals. Would you use the rational numbers or their absolute values? Explain.

5. **Error Analysis** A classmate says the value and the absolute value of a number are the same. Do you agree? Explain.

Comparing and Ordering Rational Numbers

CCSS: 6.NS.C.6c: Find and position … rational numbers on a … number line diagram… . **6.NS.C.7a:** Interpret statements of inequality as statements about the relative position of two numbers on a number line diagram … . Also, **6.NS.C.7b, 6.NS.C.7c, 6.NS.C.7d.**

Launch

© MP4, MP6

The skateboard manager posts her final boarder ratings. After much complaint, she deducts a half point and then posts each boarder's completely final rating.

Draw a line from the Boarders' scores to order the Completely Final Ratings. Tell if you would have solved the problem differently if the ratings were integers instead of rational numbers.

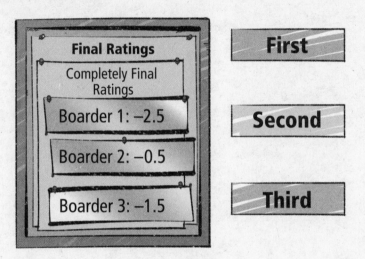

Final Ratings

Completely Final Ratings

Boarder 1: −2.5

Boarder 2: −0.5

Boarder 3: −1.5

First

Second

Third

Reflect What's the most important thing about ordering any kind of numbers—whole numbers, integers, or rational numbers?

_____

_____

_____

_____

Got It?

PART 1 Got It

Order 6.8, -3, $-\dfrac{15}{7}$, and -0.22 from greatest to least.

Got It?

PART 2 Got It

Now use the table to order those animals swimming at depths less than 1 km, from greatest depth to least depth. Explain your reasoning.

Ocean Animal Elevations

Animal	Elevation (km)
Deep sea anglerfish	$-\frac{2}{3}$
Fanfin anglerfish	$-2\frac{1}{4}$
Gulper eel	-1.19
Pacific blackdragon	$-\frac{3}{10}$

PART 3 Got It

Which expression says that an account balance of ($18.18) is less than an account balance of $18.18?

I. $-18.18 < 18.18$

II. $|-18.18| < |18.18|$

III. $|-18.18| = |18.18|$

Close and Check

Focus Question

How can you interpret the ordering of rational numbers in real-world situations?

_____

_____

_____

_____

Do you know HOW?

1. Write the numbers in order from least to greatest.

$$\frac{14}{5},\ -2.46,\ -\frac{10}{4},\ 2.5$$

, , , ____

2. Order the archeological excavation sites from the least depth to the greatest depth.

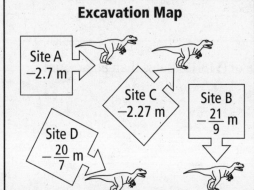

Excavation Map

Site A −2.7 m

Site C −2.27 m

Site B −$\frac{21}{9}$ m

Site D −$\frac{20}{7}$ m

Site ____ Site ____ Site ____ Site ____

Do you UNDERSTAND?

3. **Reasoning** How might using absolute value be helpful when ordering negative rational numbers?

_____

_____

_____

_____

4. **Error Analysis** A classmate ordered these numbers from greatest to least. What error did she make? Explain.

$$4.4,\ 4.2,\ -4.42,\ -4.24$$

_____

_____

_____

_____

_____

_____

Ordered Pairs in the Coordinate Plane

CCSS: 6.NS.C.6b: Understand signs of numbers in ordered pairs as indicating locations in quadrants of the coordinate plane; recognize that when two ordered pairs differ only by signs, the locations of the points are related by reflections across one or both axes. Also, 6.NS.C.6c.

Launch

MP2, MP6

Write the missing coordinates (?, ?) for points *A* and *B*. Explain how you know you are right.

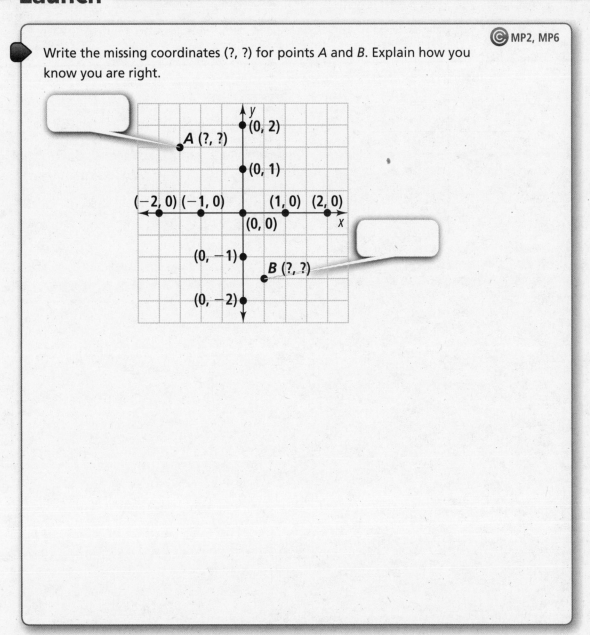

Reflect How does the numbering of coordinates relate to your earlier work on rational numbers on the number line?

_____

_____

_____

Got It?

What ordered pair names Point *V*?

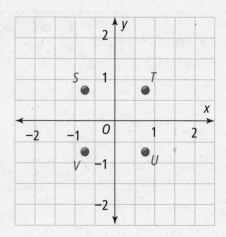

Got It?

PART 2 Got It

Which point is located at $\left(2.4, -\frac{7}{10}\right)$?

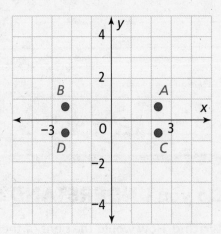

Discuss with a classmate

Circle four words in the problem that are important for understanding the problem.

Take turns reading one of the circled words, and explain what the word means.

PART 3 Got It

What is the reflection of $(-2.5, 2.75)$ across the x-axis?

Close and Check

▶ **Focus Question**

How is a number line related to the coordinate plane? How are rational numbers used within the coordinate plane?

_____

_____

_____

_____

▶ Do you know **HOW?**

1. Write the coordinates for each point.

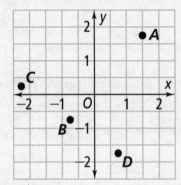

A: [ ]   B: [ ]

C: [ ]   D: [ ]

2. Plot and label the points on the coordinate grid.

$W(-2.25, -1.75)$ $X(1\frac{1}{4}, \frac{3}{4})$

$Y(-1.25, 2.25)$ $Z(1\frac{3}{4}, -2\frac{1}{4})$

3. Write the coordinates of point W reflected across the y-axis.

W: [ ]

4. Write the coordinates of point Z reflected across the x-axis.

Z: [ ]

▶ Do you **UNDERSTAND?**

5. Writing How would the signs of the coordinates of point X in Exercise 2 change if the point were moved to Quadrant III? Explain.

_____

_____

_____

6. Reasoning Point G is located at $(-1.23, 2.23)$. Compare the coordinates of point G and point Y. Is point G closer or farther away from the origin than point Y? Explain.

_____

_____

_____

_____

_____

Polygons in the Coordinate Plane

CCSS: 6.G.A.3: Draw polygons in the coordinate plane given coordinates for the vertices; use coordinates to find the length of a side joining points with the same first coordinate or the same second coordinate. Apply these techniques in the context of solving ... problems.

Launch

© MP4, MP7

A park worker has to use all 22 feet of board to make a square sandbox. She tries but all she can come up with is the plan as shown.

Tell what she got wrong and right. Then show a plan that does work. Include coordinates for your plan.

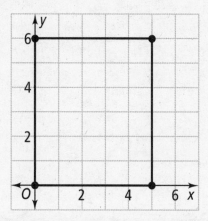

Reflect Do you think objects in the real world use whole number measurements, rational number measurements, or both? Explain.

_____

_____

_____

_____

_____

Got It?

PART 1 Got It

Which ordered pair (or pairs) name the coordinates of a vertex of pentagon *ABCDE*?

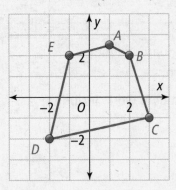

I.   (2, 2)

II. (−2, −2)

III. $\left(1, 2\frac{1}{2}\right)$

PART 2 Got It

Find the length of segment *BC*.

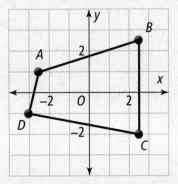

Got It?

PART 3 Got It

Each unit is 1 inch. Use the ordered pairs to find the length of the front of home plate, segment *AE*, in inches.

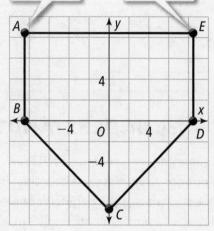

Close and Check

Focus Question

What makes a figure a polygon? Why might you want to draw a polygon in the coordinate plane?

_____

_____

_____

_____

Do you know HOW?

1. Draw polygon *QRST* with vertices at $Q(-1\frac{3}{4}, 1\frac{1}{4})$, $R(1.25, 1.25)$, $S(1\frac{3}{4}, -2)$, $T(-1.75, -1.5)$.

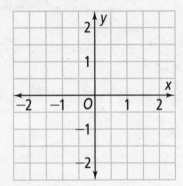

2. Find the length of segment *QR*.

3. Assume each unit of the grid represents 3.5 cm. Find the length of segment *QT*.

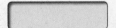

Do you UNDERSTAND?

4. Reasoning Two students each draw a polygon using the same coordinates. One student says the perimeter of his figure is 12 units. The other student says the perimeter of her figure is 36 m. Can both students be correct? Explain.

_____

_____

_____

_____

_____

5. Error Analysis A classmate writes an equation to find the distance between two points $X(-4.24, 3.39)$ and $Y(5.19, 3.39)$. Explain his error. Find the actual distance between the points.

$$-4.24 + 5.19 = 0.95$$

_____

_____

_____

Problem Solving

Digital Resources

CCSS: 6.NS.C.6b: Understand signs of numbers in ordered pairs as indicating locations in quadrants of the coordinate plane; recognize that when two ordered pairs differ only by signs, the locations of the points are related by reflections across one or both axes. Also, **6.NS.C.6c, 6.NS.C.7b,** and **6.G.A.3.**

Launch

© MP5, MP7

A famous artist starts planning four kite-shaped reflecting pools in a park. She wants each pool to be a reflection of the pool across from it on the *x* and *y* walking paths.

Draw and label the three other pools to finish the plan.

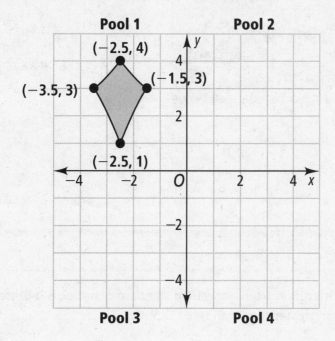

Reflect What pattern do you see between the coordinates of the pools that are reflections of each other?

_____

_____

_____

_____

_____

Got It?

PART 1 Got It (1 of 2)

If the length of a portable music player must be less than 0.05 cm from standard, which of the tested players below meet the requirement?

Difference from Standard

Player	Difference (cm)
Player 8	−0.05 cm
Player 9	+0.03 cm
Player 10	−0.03 cm
Player 11	+0.05 cm

PART 1 Got It (2 of 2)

When measuring differences from a specified standard quantity, is it better to be less than standard or greater than standard? Explain.

Got It?

A student started to draw a 3 × 2 rectangle but was interrupted after he graphed only the two vertices shown in the diagram. What are the coordinates of the two missing vertices?

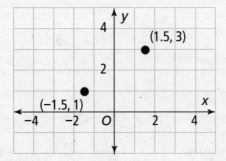

Close and Check

Focus Question

MP1, MP4

In this topic you have learned different ways to use rational numbers. How do rational numbers help you to solve problems?

Do you know HOW?

1. The diameter of a nail head must be less than 0.15 mm from the standard. Circle the nails that meet the requirement.

Difference from Standard	
Nail A	−0.14 mm
Nail B	+0.16 mm
Nail C	−0.15 mm
Nail D	+0.13 mm

2. A student started to draw trapezoid $ABCD$ with vertices $A(-1\frac{1}{4}, 1\frac{3}{4})$ and $B(-2\frac{1}{4}, -2\frac{1}{4})$. Vertex C is a reflection of point B across the y-axis. Vertex D is a reflection of point A across the y-axis. What are the coordinates of point C and point D?

C:

D:

Do you UNDERSTAND?

3. **Reasoning** How much greater is the length of segment BC than segment AD in Exercise 2? Explain how you found you answer.

---

4. **Writing** Card games are often scored using integers. Is it possible to have more negative scores than your opponent and still win the game? Explain.

Topic Review

New Vocabulary: polygon, rational numbers, vertex of a polygon
Review Vocabulary: absolute value, opposites, ordered pair, segment

Vocabulary Review

◗ Identify two challenging vocabulary terms from this topic. Write one
vocabulary term in the center oval, and fill in the surrounding boxes with
details that will help you better understand the term.

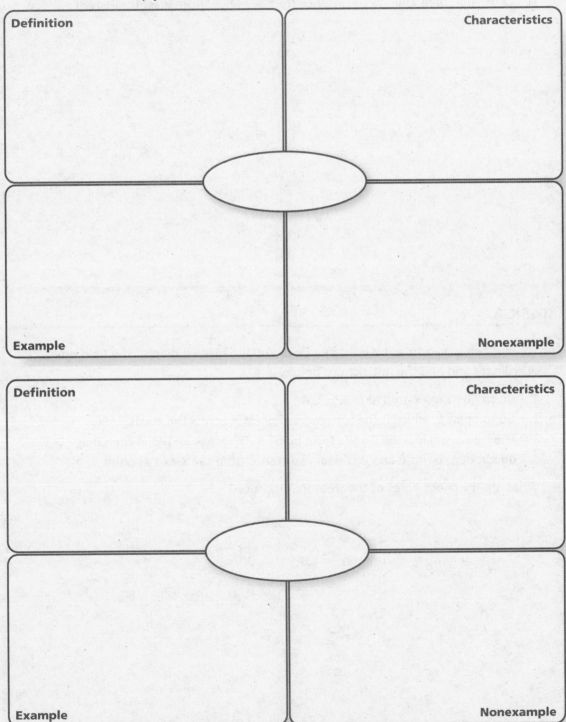

Pull It All Together

TASK 1

An albatross flies at an elevation of 16.5 meters. At the same time, an octopus is feeding at an elevation of −32.5 meters, and an orca is swimming at an elevation of −13.2 meters.

a. Order the three animals by elevation, from lowest to highest.

b. Order the three animals by distance from sea level, from least to greatest.

TASK 2

You are going on a treasure hunt in a field. You are given a map of the field on a coordinate grid and the instructions below.

1. Go to point *A*, located at (−2.5, 3.5).

2. Go to point *B*, which is the reflection of point *A* across the *x*-axis.

3. The treasure is located 8 units from point *B*. The treasure lies in the same quadrant as point *B* and is the same distance from the *x*-axis as point *B*.

What are the coordinates of the treasure's location?

Ratios

CCSS: 6.RP.A.1: Understand the concept of ratio and use ratio language to describe a relationship between two quantities.

Launch

© MP2, MP6

A gift shop sells boxes of fruit online, including this box of apples and pears. Use numbers to compare the fruit in three different ways.

Comparison 1	Comparison 2	Comparison 3

Reflect Choose one of your comparisons. Describe a situation where you could use it.

_____

_____

_____

_____

_____

Got It?

PART 1 Got It

Write the ratio of the number of fish to the number of plants.

PART 2 Got It

You have read 20 books from a series of 23 books. Write the ratio of the number of books you have *not* read to the number of books you have read.

Got It?

PART 3 Got It (1 of 2)

In a class, 15 students are wearing sneakers, 10 students are wearing boots, and 5 students are wearing sandals. Write the ratio of the number of students wearing sneakers to the total number of students.

PART 3 Got It (2 of 2)

Determine whether the following statement is *always, sometimes,* or *never* true. Explain your reasoning.

Suppose you have a basket of fruit. Let $a : b$ equal the ratio of the number of apples to the number of bananas. Then the ratio of the number of apples to the total number of pieces of fruit in the basket is $a : a + b$.

Close and Check

Focus Question

© MP1, MP3

In this lesson you learned some ways to compare quantities.
What are some ways to compare quantities? How can you use them?

_____

_____

_____

_____

Do you know HOW?

1. A sixth-grade band has 4 guitarists, 2 drummers, and 3 singers. Write a ratio for each comparison.

number of singers to number of guitarists ☐ to ☐

number of guitarists to number of band members ☐ to ☐

number of drummers to number of singers ☐ to ☐

2. For each ratio, tell what items are being compared.

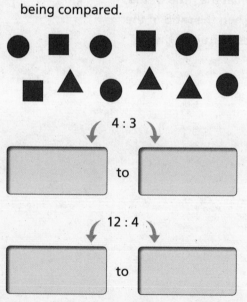

4 : 3

☐ to ☐

12 : 4

☐ to ☐

Do you UNDERSTAND?

3. Vocabulary What is a ratio?

_____

_____

4. Reasoning A class has 15 boys and 12 girls. Write at least three different ratios using this information.

_____

_____

_____

5. Error Analysis Your friend says the ratio of the number of Hs to the number of Gs is 4 : 3. Is this correct? If not, tell what mistake he makes.

H   H   G   H
  G   G   G

_____

_____

_____

Exploring Equivalent Ratios

Digital Resources

CCSS: 6.RP.A.3: Use ratio and rate reasoning to solve real-world and mathematical problems, e.g., by reasoning about tables of equivalent ratios, tape diagrams, double number line diagrams, or equations.

Launch

© MP1, MP7

A website sells song downloads for $2 each and movie downloads for $5 each. Your friend buys the same number of movies as songs. If he spends $20 on movies, how much does he spend on songs?

Use the multiplication table to show the solution.

x	1	2	3	4	5
1					
2					
3					
4					
5					

My friend buys [　] songs and [　] movies.

My friend spends [　] on songs and [　] on movies.

Reflect Do you need to complete the whole multiplication table to solve the problem? Explain.

_____

_____

_____

_____

Got It?

PART 1 Got It

Use the multiplication table to find ratios equivalent to
24 : 28. Find one ratio with lower terms and one ratio with greater terms.

×	5	6	7	8
1	5	6	7	8
2	10	12	14	16
3	15	18	21	24
4	20	24	28	32
5	25	30	35	40
6	30	36	42	48
7	35	42	49	56
8	40	48	56	64

PART 2 Got It

Complete the equivalent ratio.

[   ] : 28 = 18 : 36

Got It?

PART 3 Got It

In the same class of 32 students, 1 of every 4 students wears glasses. How many of the students wear glasses?

Close and Check

Focus Question

MP1, MP4

In this lesson, you learned about equivalent ratios. Can you use one ratio to write another ratio? Why might you want to do this?

_____

_____

_____

_____

Do you know HOW?

1. Fill in three ratios equivalent to 2 : 3 on the multiplication table.

x	1	2	3	4
1				
2				
3				
4				

2. Make a domino with 12 dots and an equivalent ratio of dots on the left to dots on the right as the first domino. Use the multiplication table above to help.

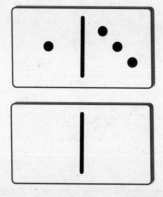

Do you UNDERSTAND?

3. **Reasoning** An animal shelter can hold only 60 cats and dogs. The current ratio of cats to dogs is 5 : 7. Can the shelter plan to take in more dogs and cats? Tell whether you know.

_____

_____

_____

_____

_____

4. **Writing** Describe a situation where you could use the ratio of cats to dogs to make a plan or decision at the shelter.

_____

_____

_____

_____

_____

_____

CCSS: 6.RP.A.3: Use ratio and rate reasoning to solve real-world and mathematical problems, e.g., by reasoning about tables of equivalent ratios, tape diagrams, double number line diagrams, or equations.

Launch

 MP3, MP5

The table shows votes for a new school team name. One friend says two grades voted the same. A second friend says the total vote for team name was the same.

Use ratios to show how both friends could be correct. Which team name should the school choose? Explain.

Votes for New Team Name

Grade	Wolves	Flyers
6th	20	10
7th	5	30
8th	30	15

The first friend is correct because:

The second friend is correct because:

The school should choose:

Reflect How can ratios use different numbers but be the same?

Got It?

PART 1 Got It

Use number lines to find ratios equivalent to 8 : 10. Find one ratio with lesser terms and one ratio with greater terms.

Discuss with a classmate

What does it mean to write a ratio with lesser terms?

Compare the ratios with lesser terms that you wrote. Were they the same? If not, how were they different?

Compare the ratios with greater terms that you wrote. Were they the same? If not, how were they different?

PART 2 Got It

Write a ratio equivalent to 3 : 4.

Got It?

PART 3 Got It

Write two different ratios equivalent to 4 : 10.

Close and Check

Focus Question

What does it mean for two ratios to be equivalent? Why might you want to use an equivalent ratio?

_____

_____

_____

_____

Do you know HOW?

1. Complete the equivalent ratios on the double number line.

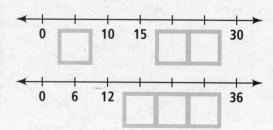

2. Each marble bag has a ratio of red to blue marbles of 3 to 4. You have 12 blue marbles. Complete the table to show how many marbles you have in your bag.

Number of Marbles

Red	Blue	Total
3	4	

I have ⬚ marbles in my bag.

Do you UNDERSTAND?

3. Writing Tell how the ratios 6 : 2 and 3 : 1 describe a similar situation among the shapes.

_____

_____

_____

4. Reasoning The ratio of consonants to vowels for two words are shown below. Explain how you can tell that the words are not the same.

Word One	Word Two
3 : 1	9 : 4

_____

_____

_____

_____

Ratios as Fractions

CCSS: 6.RP.A.1: Understand the concept of ratio and use ratio language to describe a relationship between two quantities. **6.RP.A.3:** Use ratio and rate reasoning to solve real-world and mathematical problems ... .

Launch

Ⓒ MP6, MP7

Due to high demand, a gift shop wants more fruit boxes with a 1 : 3 ratio of the number of apples to the total number of fruit.

Use letters to complete each plan. Write the fraction $\dfrac{\text{number of apples}}{\text{total number of fruit}}$. Cross out any plan that does not have the correct ratio.

b = banana   a = apple   p = pear   o = orange

Box Plan 1

____ apples
____ fruit

Box Plan 2

____ apples
____ fruit

Box Plan 3

____ apples
____ fruit

Reflect How do the ratio and the fractions in the problem both describe the apples in the boxes?

_____

_____

_____

_____

_____

Got It?

A school baseball team has 5 pitchers, 2 catchers, and 12 other fielders. Write the ratio of the number of pitchers to the total number of players in three ways.

Suppose you have a fruit box in which the ratio of the number of pears to the number of apples is $\frac{2}{3}$. Explain what this ratio tells you about the relationship between the types of fruit in the box.

Got It?

PART 2 Got It

Write two different ratios equivalent to $\frac{6}{8}$.

PART 3 Got It (1 of 2)

Write the ratio 12 to 40 in simplest form.

PART 3 Got It (2 of 2)

How can you determine whether a ratio is in simplest form?

Close and Check

▶ Focus Question

©MP2, MP3

Why might you want to write a ratio as a fraction?

_____

_____

_____

▶ Do you know **HOW?**

1. You propose a new mix of fruit for a fruit box. Write the ratio of apples to fruit (apples, pears, oranges, and mangoes) in three ways.

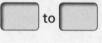 to

2. The ratio of rock songs to all songs on a playlist is $\frac{36}{60}$. Write this ratio in simplest form.

3. Circle the ratios that are equivalent to $\frac{36}{60}$.

$\frac{6}{10}$ $\frac{9}{15}$ $\frac{15}{20}$

$\frac{24}{36}$ $\frac{48}{80}$

▶ Do you **UNDERSTAND?**

4. **Writing** Your class visits the zoo. Your friend says that the ratio of elephants to giraffes is $\frac{3}{8}$. You describe the relationship of elephants to giraffes as $\frac{9}{24}$. Can both you and your friend be correct? Explain.

_____

_____

_____

_____

5. **Compare and Contrast** How would the problem above have been the same or different if the ratios would have been written as 3 : 8 and 9 : 24? Explain.

_____

_____

_____

_____

_____

_____

_____

Ratios as Decimals

CCSS: 6.RP.A.1: Understand the concept of ratio and use ratio language to describe a relationship between two quantities. **6.RP.A.3:** Use ratio and rate reasoning to solve real-world and mathematical problems ... .

Launch

© MP4, MP7

Two students take turns recording daily rain totals. When the teacher sees their work, she exclaims, "Give me the daily results and total rainfall in one way!"

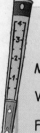

Student 1 Rain Totals

Monday: $\frac{1}{2}$ inch

Wednesday: $\frac{2}{10}$ inch

Friday: no rain

Student 2 Rain Totals

Tuesday: 0.3 inch

Thursday: 0.6 inch

Show how you would revise the results for the teacher.

Explain your work.

Reflect Does it matter whether you choose decimals or fractions? Are there situations where using one is better than using the other?

_____

_____

_____

_____

Got It?

PART 1 Got It

Write the ratio 3 : 8 as a fraction and a decimal.

PART 2 Got It

The ratio of the number of sixth graders to the total number of students at a school is 0.45. Write the ratio 0.45 as a fraction in simplest form.

Got It?

PART 3 Got It (1 of 2)

Another player's batting average is .290. The player has 200 at bats. How many hits does the player have?

PART 3 Got It (2 of 2)

Which player has the best batting average? Explain how you found your answer.

Player Batting Averages

Player	Number of Hits	Number of At Bats	Batting Average
Player 1	33	120	
Player 2	39	150	
Player 3	22	80	

Discuss with a classmate

Read each other's explanation for the problem.
Is the explanation clear?
Are there any words or phrases that you do not understand? If so, ask your teacher to explain them to you.

Close and Check

Focus Question

Why might you want to write a ratio as a decimal?

_____

_____

_____

_____

Do you know HOW?

1. According to a recent study, the ratio of households in the United States that have high-speed Internet access is 0.64. Cross out the fractions that cannot be used to describe this ratio.

$\frac{64}{100}$ $\frac{1}{64}$ $\frac{16}{25}$ $\frac{6}{4}$

2. Each row of the table shows a star basketball player's ratio of free throws made to free throws attempted. Complete the table. Circle the game with the best ratio.

Free Throw Ratios			
Game 1	7 : 8	$\frac{}{8}$	
Game 2	: 4	$\frac{3}{}$	0.75
Game 3	4 :	$\frac{4}{5}$	

3. In Game 4, the star player makes 0.6 of her free throws attempted. She attempts 5 free throws. How many did she make?

☐ free throws

Do you UNDERSTAND?

4. Writing Describe why writing each ratio of free throws made as a decimal makes it easier to compare the ratios.

_____

_____

_____

_____

_____

5. Error Analysis A study shows that approximately 0.08 of the population are left handed. Your friend says, "8 out of 10 people are left handed." What mistake does your friend make?

_____

_____

_____

_____

Problem Solving

CCSS: 6.RP.A.1: Understand the concept of ratio and use ratio language to describe a relationship between two quantities. **6.RP.A.3:** Use ratio and rate reasoning to solve real-world and mathematical problems ... .

Launch

MP1, MP4

One hundred students vote for a drama, comedy, or action movie for a party. Drama gets one fifth of the votes. Action gets three times as many votes as comedy.

Write the vote totals.

All Votes: ☐   Drama: ☐   Action: ☐   Comedy: ☐

Tell which of these ratios correctly describe the results of the voting.

comedy votes
to action votes

1 to 3

all votes to
comedy votes

5 : 1

action votes to
drama votes

$\frac{3}{1}$

action votes
to all votes

0.6

Reflect Which ratio is the best for showing which movie type won the vote? Explain.

_____

_____

_____

Got It?

PART 1 Got It

A gym teacher has 20 soccer balls and 12 footballs. The teacher wants to put four times as many soccer balls as footballs in one bin. The teacher wants to put twice as many footballs as soccer balls in another bin. How many soccer balls and footballs should the teacher put in the first bin?

PART 2 Got It (1 of 2)

A biscuit recipe uses 2 cups flour, 1 tablespoon baking powder, $\frac{1}{2}$ teaspoon salt, $\frac{1}{4}$ cup butter, and $\frac{2}{3}$ cup milk. How much milk should you use to make 4 batches of biscuits?

Got It?

Suppose you have a pancake recipe that makes enough pancakes for 12 people. How would you change the recipe to make pancakes for 6 people?

PART 3 Got It

The famous chef's gumbo recipe uses a total of 21 pounds of celery and onions. The ratio of pounds of celery to pounds of onions is 2 : 5. How many pounds of celery and how many pounds of onions are in the soup?

Close and Check

Focus Question

MP2, MP6

In this topic you have learned different ways to work with ratios. How can you use what you learned to make plans and decisions?

Do you know HOW?

1. Your friend makes dough for a model volcano that turns out too dry. She changes the ratio of water to dry ingredients to 1 : 4. Then she doubles each ingredient to make more dough. Write the new ingredient amounts.

Volcano Dough Recipe

Item	Old Amounts	New Amounts
flour (cups)	3	
salt (cups)	1	
water (cups)	$\frac{1}{2}$	
cooking oil	2	

2. You can make green paint by mixing blue paint to yellow paint in a $\frac{3}{5}$ ratio. How many gallons of blue and yellow paint do you need to make 40 gallons of green paint?

Blue paint: ☐ gallons

Yellow paint: ☐ gallons

Do you UNDERSTAND?

3. **Error Analysis** For each class of 30 students, the ratio of boys to girls or girls to boys can be no more than 3 to 2. The principal plans Class A and B. What error does the principal make?

Class A
19 Boys
11 Girls

Class B
13 Boys
17 Girls

4. **Reasoning** Tell how to fix the error by moving the fewest students between Class A and B. Each class must have 30 students.

New Vocabulary: equivalent ratios, ratio, terms of a ratio
Review Vocabulary: decimal, greatest common factor, simplest form

Vocabulary Review

Identify two challenging vocabulary terms from this topic. Write one vocabulary term in the center oval, and fill in the surrounding boxes with details that will help you better understand the term.

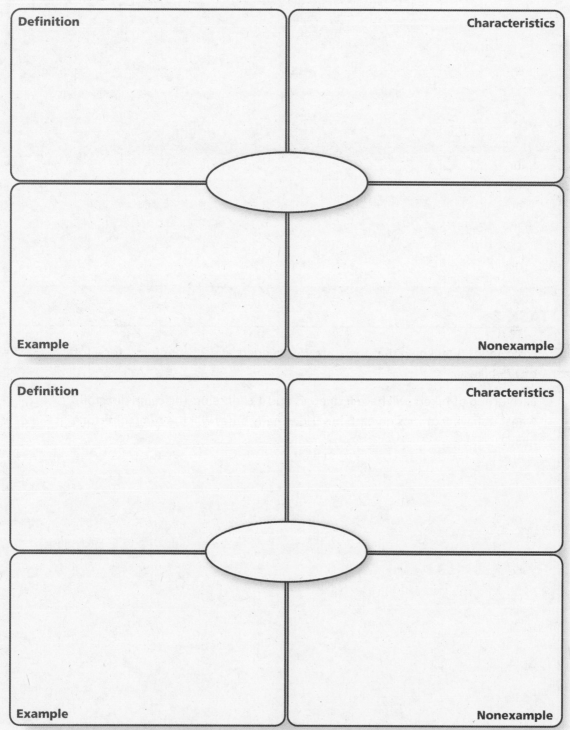

Definition

Characteristics

Example

Nonexample

Definition

Characteristics

Example

Nonexample

Pull It All Together

TASK 1

A camp director is planning a hike for 150 campers. There will be a counselor hiking with each group of 6 campers. The camp director needs to have 2 jugs of water for every 5 people going on the hike. How many jugs of water does the camp director need?

TASK 2

From Task 1, you know that there are 150 campers and 25 counselors for a total of 175 hikers.

Each group of hikers will have 6 campers and 1 counselor. The camp director wants to have 5 groups on each bus. How many buses will the camp director need?

Unit Rates

CCSS: 6.RP.A.2: Understand the concept of a unit rate $\frac{a}{b}$ associated with a ratio $a : b$ with $b \neq 0$, and use rate language in the context of a ratio relationship ... . **6.RP.A.3:** Use ratio and rate reasoning to solve real-world and mathematical problems ... .

Launch

© MP2, MP7

The label shows nutritional benefits for an entire 12-fluid-ounce sports drink. The beverage company wants to produce a 16-fluid-ounce bottle of the same drink.

How many calories and grams (g) of carbohydrates should the company put on the label?

Reflect How many calories does 1 fluid ounce of sports drink have? How would knowing this be useful?

_____

_____

_____

_____

Got It?

PART 1 Got It

A basketball player scores 60 points in 4 games. What is the basketball player's unit rate for points per game?

PART 2 Got It

A blade of grass grew 5 inches in 50 days. How much did the grass grow per day?

Got It?

PART 3 Got It

Your dishwasher uses 11 gallons of water to wash 2 loads of dishes. How many gallons of water will your dishwasher use to wash 7 loads of dishes?

Close and Check

Focus Question

MP2, MP3

What makes a ratio a rate? When could rates be useful?

_____

_____

_____

_____

Do you know **HOW?**

1. Write each as a rate and as a unit rate.

32 flowers to 8 vases

rate

unit rate

22 gallons to 5 buckets

rate

unit rate

4 boats to 20 days

rate

unit rate

2. The boat company makes 4 boats in 20 days. At that rate, how many boats could they make in 25 days?

[ ] boats

Do you **UNDERSTAND?**

3. Vocabulary How is a unit rate different from other rates?

_____

_____

_____

_____

_____

4. Error Analysis Your aunt works at a pet store that is about to receive a shipment of birds. She counts how many cages are available to know how many birds to place in each. She tells her boss the unit rate is 1 cage per 4 birds. Explain her mistake.

_____

_____

_____

_____

Digital Resources

CCSS: 6.RP.A.3b: Solve unit rate problems including those involving unit pricing and constant speed. *For example, if it took 7 hours to mow 4 lawns, then at that rate, how many lawns could be mowed in 35 hours? At what rate were lawns being mowed?*

Launch

© MP3, MP4

Your cousin shops for movies online. He sees three different offers.
Which offer should your cousin choose? Explain your reasoning.

Offer 1	Offer 2	Offer 3

Reflect Should you always choose the lowest unit rate? Why might your cousin not choose the lowest unit rate?

_____

_____

_____

_____

_____

Got It?

PART 1 Got It

A sports store sells 5 baseballs for $12.50. What is the price per baseball?

PART 2 Got It

A pack of 6 bottles of a sports drink sells for $4.50. What is the unit price of one bottle of the sports drink?

PART 3 Got It

Four of your friends buy album downloads online. Ilana buys 1 album for $8.95, Kyle buys 2 albums for $17, Joe buys 3 albums for $30, and Aimee buys 4 albums for $44. Which friend gets the best buy?

Close and Check

Focus Question

How can you compare the prices of different amounts of the same item? Why might you want to do this?

_____

_____

_____

_____

Do you know HOW?

1. If 5 gallons of gas costs $17.50, what is the unit price of the gas?

[ ]

2. A grocery store advertises weekly specials for fruit. Write the unit price for each type of fruit.

Weekly Specials

Fruit	Total Price	Unit Price
7 oranges	$3.01	
5 kiwis	$1.85	
9 plums	$2.88	
3 pears	$1.68	

3. A movie theater offers different ticket packages. Order them by the unit price for a ticket from greatest (1) to least (3).

Junior 4-pack! $25   Senior 2-pack! $12   Adult 5-pack! $32

[ ]   [ ]   [ ]

Do you UNDERSTAND?

4. Reasoning 10 binders cost $1. 10 notebooks cost $1. Can you tell which is the better buy? Explain.

_____

_____

_____

_____

5. Error Analysis Your friend says that the unit price of Pack A is lower because Pack A costs less than Pack B. Explain your friend's error.

Pack A
10 pencils
for $1

Pack B
50 pencils
for $4

_____

_____

_____

_____

This page intentionally left blank.

Constant Speed

CCSS: 6.RP.A.3b: Solve unit rate problems including those involving unit pricing and constant speed. *For example, if it took 7 hours to mow 4 lawns, then at that rate, how many lawns could be mowed in 35 hours? At what rate were lawns being mowed?*

Launch

© MP2, MP6

Three riders try out for one spot on a bike team with different coaches for different distances with different times.

What factors should the coaches consider when picking a rider? Which rider should they pick? Justify your choice.

Rider	Distance (miles)	Time (minutes)
Rider 1	5	20
Rider 2	6	30
Rider 3	8	40

Factors to Consider:

. . . .

The Rider to Pick:

Reflect What could the coaches have done to make the try-outs better?

_____

_____

_____

_____

Got It?

PART 1 Got It

Lisa bikes at a constant speed of 8 miles per hour. If she bikes for 30 minutes, how far does she travel?

PART 2 Got It

A bus travels 70 miles in 2 hours. What is the speed of the bus in miles per hour? Use the equation $d = rt$.

Got It?

PART 3 Got It (1 of 2)

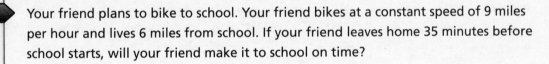

On an even busier road, your friend's mother drives 12 miles in 36 minutes. At this speed, how long does it take your friend's mother to drive 2 miles?

PART 3 Got It (2 of 2)

Your friend plans to bike to school. Your friend bikes at a constant speed of 9 miles per hour and lives 6 miles from school. If your friend leaves home 35 minutes before school starts, will your friend make it to school on time?

Close and Check

Focus Question   © MP3, MP7

What is the relationship between distance and time? How can you use this relationship?

Do you know HOW?

1. Millions of monarch butterflies migrate from Canada to Mexico each year. They travel at an average rate of 12 miles per hour. How far will the butterflies travel in 7 hours?

2. Some monarch butterflies complete the 1,800-mile journey in about 60 hours of flight time. What is their average speed?

3. If a bicyclist travels 3 miles in 15 minutes, how far will he travel in 25 minutes maintaining a constant speed?

4. You have completed 4 miles of a 10-mile race in 32 minutes. At this pace, how long will it take you to complete the entire race?

Do you UNDERSTAND?

5. Writing Two hikers start from the opposite ends of the same 18-mile trail. You know Hiker A's average speed r and Hiker B's finishing time t. Explain how you can determine which hiker completes the trail first.

6. Reasoning Your friend runs a 500-yard race with a goal to complete it in less than 3 minutes. If her average speed is 200 yards per minute, will she achieve her goal? Explain.

Measurements and Ratios

CCSS: 6.RP.A.3d: Use ratio reasoning to convert measurement units; manipulate and transform units appropriately when multiplying or dividing quantities.

Launch

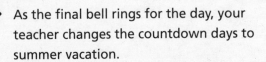

© MP3, MP4

As the final bell rings for the day, your teacher changes the countdown days to summer vacation.

At the same time, your friend writes three ways other than days to count down the time in his notebook.

Show what he might have written.

Way 1	Way 2	Way 3

Reflect Which way would you use to keep track of time left until summer vacation? Explain.

_____

_____

_____

Got It?

PART 1 Got It

A summer camp has a milk dispenser that holds 1,536 fluid ounces. How many cups of milk are in the dispenser?

PART 2 Got It (1 of 2)

One of the rails on the roller coaster needs to be replaced. The old rail is 250 centimeters long. The new piece is 8 feet long. Will the new piece fit? Use the conversion factor 1 inch = 2.54 centimeters.

Got It?

How many inches are in one centimeter? Explain.

PART 3 Got It

You have 2 gallons of a bubble solution. About how many liters of bubble solution do you have? Use 1 quart ≈ 0.95 liter.

Close and Check

Focus Question

MP4, MP8

You can express measurements of time, length, weight, and capacity in many different units. Why would you want to convert measurements? How can rates help you find a common measurement?

_____

_____

_____

_____

Do you know HOW?

1. The average dairy cow produces 1,500 gallons of milk per year. The milk-bottling factory puts milk into quart bottles. About how many quarts of milk can it bottle each year from the average dairy cow?

   [_____] quarts

2. There are 1,760 yards in one mile. There are 2.54 centimeters in one inch. How many centimeters are there in one mile?

   [_____] centimeters

3. About how many meters tall is the tree? One inch is approximately 0.025 meter.

   13.2 ft

   [_____] meters

Do you UNDERSTAND?

4. **Error Analysis** Your aunt runs 3 miles in 30 minutes. Your uncle runs 4 kilometers in 30 minutes. He claims he ran farther. Explain why he is incorrect.

   _____

   _____

   _____

   _____

   _____

5. **Writing** Your best friend needs 150 centimeters of ribbon for his school project. At the store, he sees that ribbon is sold in spools of 60 inches. Explain how he can decide whether one spool is enough.

   _____

   _____

   _____

   _____

Choosing the Appropriate Rate

Digital Resources

CCSS: **6.RP.A.3:** Use ratio and rate reasoning to solve real-world and mathematical problems ... .
6.RP.A.3b: Solve unit rate problems including those involving unit pricing and constant speed ... .

Launch

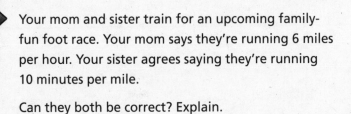

Your mom and sister train for an upcoming family-fun foot race. Your mom says they're running 6 miles per hour. Your sister agrees saying they're running 10 minutes per mile.

Can they both be correct? Explain.

Ⓒ MP2, MP4

Reflect Are miles per hour and minutes per mile the only two rates that can describe how fast your mom and sister are running? Explain.

_____

_____

_____

_____

_____

Got It?

PART 1 Got It

In some states, you can return bottles for recycling and receive 5¢ per bottle.
What is the rate in bottles per dollar?

PART 2 Got It

Which song download site offers the best deal?
Site A: 3 songs for $4
Site B: $3 for 4 songs
Site C: 5 songs for $5
Site D: 90¢ per song

Got It?

PART 3 Got It

A bushel of apples weighs about 40 pounds.

a. How many pounds of apples are there in 5 bushels?

b. How many bushels of apples should a cafeteria order if it needs about 75 pounds of apples?

Close and Check

Focus Question

If you know two measurements, you can write two different rates. How do you know which rate is best to use in a situation?

_____

_____

_____

_____

Do you know HOW?

1. The presidential jet, Air Force One, can fly 10.5 miles per minute. How many miles per hour can Air Force One travel?

   [ ]

2. How many hours would it take Air Force One to travel 2,268.6 miles from Washington, DC to San Diego, California?

   [ ]

3. A local plant nursery offers the following weekend deals. Circle the deal that offers the lowest price per plant.

Weekend Deals	
Deal 1	6 plants for $10
Deal 2	$7 for 4 plants
Deal 3	Buy 2 plants for $4, get one free
Deal 4	$1.50 per plant

Do you UNDERSTAND?

4. **Compare and Contrast** Your friend jumps rope at a rate of 25 jumps every minute. You know she jumped 85 times. If you want to know how many minutes she jumped rope, would you use the rate 25 jumps per minute or 1 minute per 25 jumps? Explain.

   _____

   _____

   _____

   _____

5. **Reasoning** You and a friend have to walk 0.85 mile to a play that begins in 20 minutes. You walk at a rate of 3.5 miles per hour. Is this the most useful way to write the rate to see if you will make it on time? Explain.

   _____

   _____

   _____

   _____

   _____

Problem Solving

CCSS: 6.RP.A.3: Use ratio and rate reasoning to solve real-world and mathematical problems, e.g., by reasoning about tables of equivalent ratios, tape diagrams, double number line diagrams, or equations.

Launch

© MP2, MP3

A restaurant chain develops three possible slogans based on the number of people it serves. The chain has 10,000 restaurants and serves about 24 million people every day.

Is each slogan accurate using a 30-day month?

720 million people served every month

1 million people served every hour

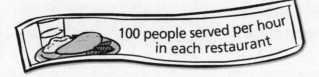

100 people served per hour in each restaurant

Which slogan would you choose if you ran the company?

Reflect Why did you choose the slogan you chose?

_____

_____

Got It?

PART 1 Got It

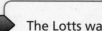

Last June, you baby-sat a total of 120 hours. You estimate that you spend 840 minutes each week talking to your friends online. Did you spend more time baby-sitting or talking to your friends online?

PART 2 Got It

The Lotts want to decrease their water usage. Mrs. Lott switches from taking baths to taking a 6-minute shower each day. Mr. Lott shortens his shower to 4 minutes each day. They still flush the toilet a total of 6 times a day. How much water do the Lotts now use per week?

Water Source	Water Use Rate
Shower	2.2 gallons per minute
Toilet	1.5 gallons per flush

Discuss with a classmate

Did your answers match? Explain the steps you took to arrive at your answer, especially how you used the information in the table as well as words and phrases in the problem to arrive at your answer.

Close and Check

Focus Question

MP2, MP6

In this topic, you have learned different ways to use rates. How do you use rates to make predictions and decisions?

_____

_____

_____

_____

Do you know HOW?

1. Your friend works 15 hours at the corner market and volunteers 780 minutes a week at the boys and girls club. Does your friend spend more time working or volunteering?

   [   ]

2. The additional fees a cell phone company charges are shown below. How much extra can the customer expect to pay in a four-week period?

Additional Service	Fee per use	Additional Cost (per week)
3 additional minutes per day	$0.45	
2 ring tones each week	$1.99	
13 text messages each day	$0.05	
	Total	

Four-week Total = [   ]

Do you UNDERSTAND?

3. **Reasoning** Describe a situation in which comparing unit rates is a useful problem-solving strategy and tell how you would apply the strategy.

   _____

   _____

   _____

   _____

   _____

4. **Writing** A member of the track team runs one mile in 7 minutes and 54 seconds. Use unit rates to find how fast he runs 4 miles at the same pace. Explain each step.

   _____

   _____

   _____

   _____

   _____

This page intentionally left blank.

New Vocabulary: conversion factor, rate, unit rate, unit price
Review Vocabulary: constant speed, ratio, reciprocals

Vocabulary Review

Identify two challenging vocabulary terms from this topic. Write one vocabulary term in the center oval, and fill in the surrounding boxes with details that will help you better understand the term.

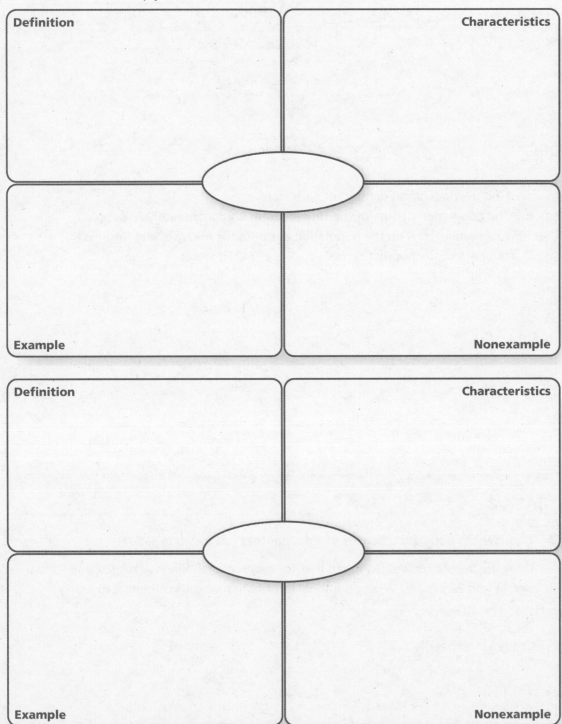

Definition

Characteristics

Example

Nonexample

Definition

Characteristics

Example

Nonexample

Pull It All Together

TASK 1

Population density is the number of persons per unit of land area. It is frequently measured in persons per square mile.

Consider these two US states.

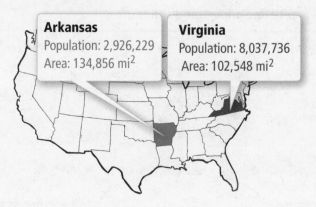

Arkansas
Population: 2,926,229
Area: 134,856 mi²

Virginia
Population: 8,037,736
Area: 102,548 mi²

a. Find the population density for each state.

b. The population density of the United States is approximately 76 people/ square mile. How do the population densities for Arkansas and Virginia compare to the population density of the United States?

TASK 2

Consider the population density of Arkansas that you found in Task 1.

Does the population density mean that for every square mile in Arkansas, you would find 22 people? What additional information would you collect to justify your reasoning?

Plotting Ratios and Rates

Digital Resources

CCSS: 6.RP.A.3a: Make tables of equivalent ratios relating quantities with whole number measurements … and plot the pairs of values on the coordinate plane … . **6.EE.C.9:** … Analyze the relationship between … variables using graphs and tables … .

Launch

© MP2, MP4

An electronics company plans a 16-gigabyte model player that will hold the same ratio of songs to gigabytes of memory as their other players.

How many songs will the 16-gigabyte player hold? Tell how you know.

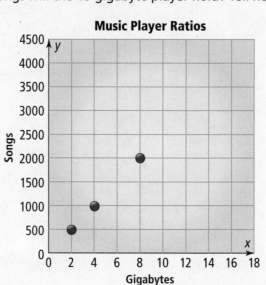

Music Player Ratios

Reflect Did having the ratios plotted on a graph help you solve the problem? Explain.

_____

_____

_____

_____

Got It?

PART 1 Got It

A local access television station charges $150 for every 10 seconds of commercials bought. Complete the table and graph the ratios.

Commercial Pricing

Commercial Length (seconds)	Cost ($)
	300
30	
40	
	900

PART 2 Got It (1 of 2)

You buy oats for your oatmeal bars in bulk. Use the graph to find the unit price of oats.

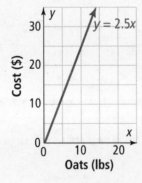

Got It?

Based on the graph, could the unit rate also be 0.25 of a cup of flour per cup of oats?

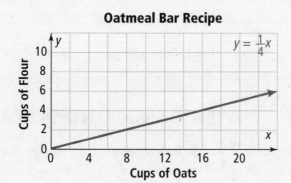

Oatmeal Bar Recipe

$y = \frac{1}{4}x$

Cups of Flour

Cups of Oats

PART 3 Got It

During one bullet train trip, the equation $y = \frac{5}{2}x$ describes the number of miles y the bullet train traveled in x minutes. Write a statement that describes the speed of the bullet train.

Discuss with a classmate

What words are used to describe the speed at which a vehicle travels? What are some examples of signs that you see near school, in your neighborhood, or on local roads, to indicate the speed a car should be traveling?

Close and Check

Focus Question

How can you use a graph that represents equivalent ratios?

_____

_____

_____

Do you know HOW?

1. A recipe calls for 3 cups of sugar for every stick of butter used. Complete the table below.

Sticks of Butter	Cups of Sugar
1	
3	
	15
6	

2. Make a graph of the information from the table above. Plot and label each point.

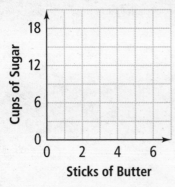

Do you UNDERSTAND?

3. **Reasoning** Could you use the graph in Exercise 2 to find how much sugar is needed for 4 sticks of butter? Explain.

_____

_____

_____

4. **Compare and Contrast** Two friends analyze this equation. One friend says the volume of water increases $\frac{3}{4}$ ft^3 every minute. The other says the volume of water increases 3 ft^3 every 4 minutes. Which friend is correct? Explain.

$$y = \frac{3}{4}x$$

x = minutes
y = volume of water in cubic feet

_____

_____

_____

_____

Recognizing Proportionality

CCSS: 6.RP.A.2: … Use rate language in the context of a ratio relationship … . **6.RP.A.3:** Use ratio and rate reasoning to solve real-world and mathematical problems … . **6.RP.A.3a:** … Plot the pairs of values on the coordinate plane … .

Launch

©MP2, MP6

You invent two robots to paint cars. Each robot works at a constant rate, but Robot 2 works faster than Robot 1.

Draw a line from the cards to the correct robot.

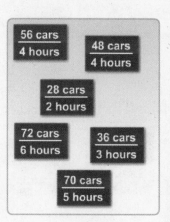

56 cars / 4 hours

48 cars / 4 hours

28 cars / 2 hours

72 cars / 6 hours

36 cars / 3 hours

70 cars / 5 hours

Tell how you know you're right.

Reflect Could you predict how many cars Robot 2 would paint in only 1 hour? How?

_____

_____

_____

_____

_____

Got It?

PART 1 Got It

Which pair(s) of ratios have a proportional relationship?

I. $\frac{4}{3}$ and $\frac{16}{12}$ II. $\frac{2}{3}$ and $\frac{4}{9}$ III. $\frac{2}{3}$ and $\frac{4}{6}$

PART 2 Got It

Which table(s) shows a proportional relationship between x and y?

I.

x	3	4	6	12
y	9	12	18	36

II.

x	5	10	20	25
y	2	4	8	10

Got It?

Does the equation $y = 2x$ represent a proportional relationship? Explain.

Close and Check

Focus Question

A proportional relationship can be represented by equivalent ratios. How can you recognize proportional relationships in tables and graphs? Why is it important to be able to recognize proportional relationships in multiple ways?

_____

_____

_____

_____

Do you know **HOW**?

1. Circle the ratios that are proportional to $\frac{3}{4}$.

$\frac{6}{8}$ $\qquad$ $\frac{12}{16}$ $\qquad$ $\frac{13}{14}$

$\frac{36}{48}$ $\qquad$ $\frac{4}{3}$ $\qquad$ $\frac{15}{25}$

2. Circle each representation that shows a proportional relationship.

x	4	8	10	20	25
y	16	32	40	80	100

$\frac{8}{10}$ and $\frac{12}{16}$

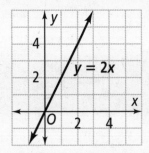

Do you **UNDERSTAND**?

3. Reasoning Explain why this graph does not represent a proportional relationship.

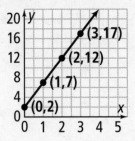

_____

_____

_____

_____

4. Error Analysis Explain the mistake in the following table of a proportional relationship.

x	12	32	45	80
y	3	8	11	20

_____

_____

Introducing Percents

CCSS: 6.RP.A.3c: Find a percent of a quantity as a rate per 100 (e.g., 30% of a quantity means $\frac{30}{100}$ times the quantity); solve problems involving finding the whole, given a part and the percent.

Launch

© MP4, MP7

Describe two part-to-whole situations that could relate to each ratio. Use words to describe one situation. Use a picture to describe the other situation.

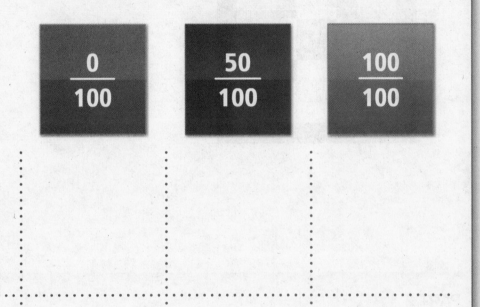

	$\frac{0}{100}$	$\frac{50}{100}$	$\frac{100}{100}$
Words			
Picture			

Reflect Would the task have been different if the ratios were $\frac{0}{92}$, $\frac{46}{92}$, and $\frac{92}{92}$? Explain.

_____

_____

_____

_____

Got It?

> What percent of the crossword puzzle is black?

> Write $\frac{3}{100}$ as a percent.

Got It?

At your last soccer game, 15 out of every 20 spectators wore sunglasses. What percent of the spectators wore sunglasses?

At the same soccer game where 15 out of every 20 spectators were wearing sunglasses, 18 out of every 25 spectators were wearing hats. Were hats or sunglasses more popular?

Close and Check

Focus Question

What is a common language for comparing ratios? What is the value of having a common language for comparing ratios?

_____

_____

_____

_____

Do you know HOW?

1. Look at the checkerboard below. What percent of the squares are white?

[____] %

2. Complete the table.

Ratio	Fraction	Percent
7 : 10	$\frac{}{100}$	70%
4 : 5	$\frac{}{100}$	[ ] %
8 : [ ]	$\frac{32}{100}$	[ ] %
[ ] : 50	$\frac{}{100}$	6%
9 : [ ]	$\frac{}{100}$	45%

Do you UNDERSTAND?

3. Writing How does using percents help when comparing the ratios 7 out of 20 and 11 out of 25?

_____

_____

_____

_____

4. Error Analysis At a football game, 21 out of 25 people wore a red shirt. Your friend states that 4% of the people did not wear a red shirt. Explain the mistake your friend made. What percent of people did not wear a red shirt?

_____

_____

_____

_____

Using Percents

CCSS: 6.RP.A.3c: Find a percent of a quantity as a rate per 100 (e.g., 30% of a quantity means $\frac{30}{100}$ times the quantity); solve problems involving finding the whole, given a part and the percent.

Launch

The teacher tells your friend she got 90% correct on a 20-question math quiz. Your friend says to you, "I think I got questions 5 and 17 wrong."

Is this possible? Tell how you know.

MP3, MP4

Math Quiz

Identify the equivalent expressions.

Grade 90%

1. $4 \times 3 = 2 \times 6$ True

2. $5 \times 2 = 10 \times 1$ True

3. $3 \times 8 = 6 \times 5$ False

Reflect Would you rather have a teacher write your score on your paper as a percent or as a fraction? Does it matter? Explain.

_____

_____

_____

_____

Got It?

PART 1 Got It

What is 15% of 300?

PART 2 Got It

In one community, 84% of the animal shelters microchip cats and dogs before adoption. If 21 shelters in the community microchip cats and dogs, how many animal shelters are in that community?

PART 3 Got It (1 of 2)

During one year, 60% of the hurricanes that struck the U.S. were Category 1 hurricanes. If nine Category 1 hurricanes struck the U.S. that year, what was the total number of hurricanes that struck the U.S. during that year?

Got It?

During a different year, 60% of the hurricanes that struck the U.S. were Category 1 hurricanes. That year there were only 10 hurricanes and 6 were Category 1 hurricanes. How is that possible?

PART 4 Got It

What number is 44% of 25?

Close and Check

Focus Question

Percents are another language you can use for comparisons. What does 100% represent? How are the terms of a ratio represented in a percent?

_____

_____

_____

_____

Do you know HOW?

1. Complete each statement.

☐ is 95% of 20.

☐ is 60% of 10.

☐ is 30% of 50.

☐ is 40% of 25.

2. If 14 students choose red as their favorite color, how many students were surveyed?

Favorite Color

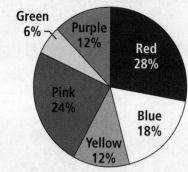

 students

Do you UNDERSTAND?

3. Reasoning Can you determine the number of people who choose football as their favorite sport? Explain your reasoning.

Favorite Sport

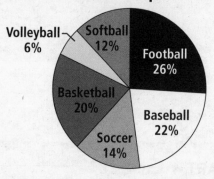

_____

_____

_____

4. Error Analysis Your friend said that 200 students were surveyed for the circle graph above and used it to conclude that 26 students chose football. What mistake did she make?

_____

_____

Problem Solving

Digital Resources

CCSS: 6.RP.A.3: Use ratio and rate reasoning to solve real world and mathematical problems, e.g., by reasoning about tables of equivalent ratios ... . **6.RP.A.3c:** Find a percent of a quantity as a rate per 100 ... .

Launch

© MP1, MP6

The championship game is on the line. Which Wolves' basketball player should take the last shot? Explain.

Wolves Season Shooting Results

Player	Makes	Attempts
10	11	25
4	22	50
8	16	40
40	12	30
31	24	60

Reflect Player #31 made the most shots. Should this player then take the last shot? Explain.

_____

_____

_____

Got It?

PART 1 Got It

Over the past 6 months, an online newspaper published 360 articles about the local sports teams. Write the ratio of the number of basketball articles to the number of football articles.

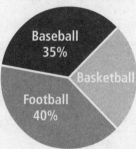

Sports Articles

Baseball 35%
Basketball
Football 40%

PART 2 Got It (1 of 2)

The U.S. Mint makes nickel coins out of an alloy that is made of nickel and copper. The alloy contains 3 grams of copper for every gram of nickel. How many grams of copper are needed to make 96 grams of the alloy?

Discuss with a classmate

Highlight the word *alloy* in the problem statement.
What do you understand *alloy* to mean, based on the information in the problem?
Write a basic definition for *alloy*.
Compare your definition with other classmates.
Discuss your definition with your teacher.

Got It?

Your friend says that because the ratio of nickel to copper is $\frac{1}{3}$, the alloy is about 33% nickel. Is your friend correct? Explain.

Close and Check

Focus Question

In this topic you have learned about percents and proportional relationships. How can you use percents and proportional relationships to solve problems?

_____

_____

_____

_____

Do you know HOW?

1. You have 30 coins in your bank.

a. Complete the table.

Coin	Number	Percent
Quarter	6	
Dime		30%
Nickel		10%
Penny	12	

2. Using the table above, tell the ratio of nickels to dimes in simplest form.

3. At a local sporting event, the ratio of green shirts to yellow shirts was 3 : 5. If 160 people attended the sporting event, how many people were wearing green shirts?

[   ] people

Do you UNDERSTAND?

4. Reasoning The ratio of cars to trucks in the parking lot is 5 to 3. Can you use just this information to determine the total number of vehicles in the parking lot?

_____

_____

_____

_____

5. Error Analysis The ratio of red marbles to green marbles in a bag is 3 : 4. Describe the mistake in the statement.

"If there are 120 red marbles, there must be 121 green marbles."

_____

_____

_____

_____

_____

New Vocabulary: circle graph, percent
Review Vocabulary: equivalent ratios, proportional relationship, ratio

Vocabulary Review

Identify two challenging vocabulary terms from this topic. Write one vocabulary term in the center oval, and fill in the surrounding boxes with details that will help you better understand the term.

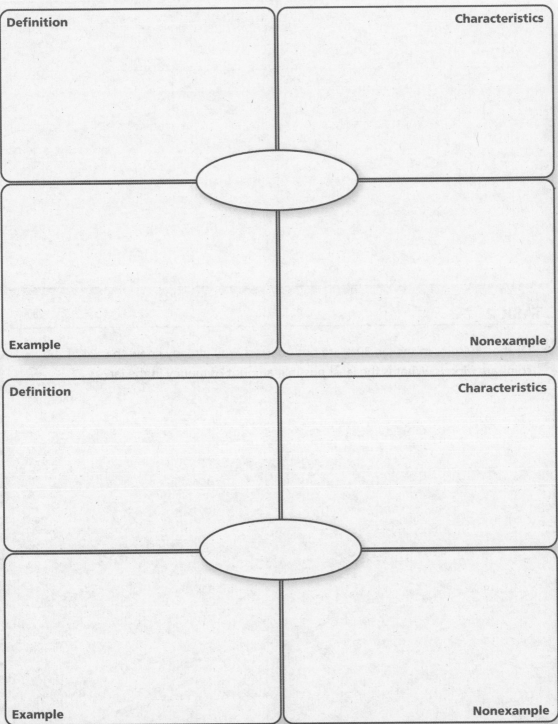

Definition

Characteristics

Example

Nonexample

Definition

Characteristics

Example

Nonexample

Pull It All Together

TASK 1

You have a jar that contains 150 coins. You know 16% of the coins are nickels. What is the value of the nickels in the jar?

TASK 2

Of the 150 coins in the jar, 30% are not quarters. You already know that 24 of the coins are nickels. What is the least possible amount of money in the jar?

Rectangles and Squares

Digital Resources

CCSS: 6.G.A.1: Find the area of right triangles, other triangles, special quadrilaterals, and polygons by composing into rectangles or decomposing into triangles and other shapes; apply these techniques in the context of solving real-world and mathematical problems.

Launch

MP5, MP7

Your friend uses small squares to make a rectangle and a square. Shape 1 uses 9 small squares, and Shape 2 uses 8 small squares.

Tell which shape is a rectangle and which is a square.

Shape 1 is a [   ]. Shape 2 is a [   ].

Then make and label each shape on the grid.

Reflect Can you make more than one possible rectangle? Can you make more than one possible square? Explain.

_____

_____

_____

_____

_____

Got It?

PART 1 Got It (1 of 2)

What is the area of the basketball court?

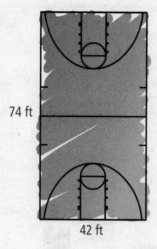

74 ft

42 ft

PART 1 Got It (2 of 2)

To find the area of a rectangle, does it matter which side you use as the base and which side you use as the height? Explain.

Discuss with a classmate

Compare the explanations you wrote for this problem.

What key terms did you include in your explanation?

Add a diagram to your explanation. Be sure to label all important parts.

Got It?

What is the area of the square clock?

13 in.

13 in.

A rectangular tabletop has an area of 28 ft^2. The tabletop is $3\frac{1}{2}$ ft wide. How long is the tabletop?

Given only the area of a square, can you find the dimensions of the square? Explain.

Close and Check

Focus Question

You find the area of a rectangle by multiplying its base and height. What happens to the area of a rectangle when you change its dimensions?

_____

_____

_____

_____

Do you know HOW?

1. What is the length of each side of the square?

$$A = 121 \text{ in.}^2$$

$s = $ [_____]

2. What is the width of the rectangle?

$$A = 31 \text{ ft}^2$$

$$\ell = 7\frac{3}{4} \text{ ft}$$

$w = $ [_____]

3. A square table has a side length of 1.52 m. What is the area of the table to the nearest hundredth meter?

Do you UNDERSTAND?

4. Compare and Contrast Explain how finding the area of a square and the area of a rectangle are alike and different.

_____

_____

_____

_____

_____

5. Reasoning Three friends each drew a rectangle with an area of 18 in.² The rectangles each looked different no matter how the friends turned them. Explain how this is possible.

_____

_____

_____

_____

_____

_____

Right Triangles

CCSS: 6.G.A.1: Find the area of right triangles, other triangles, special quadrilaterals, and polygons by composing into rectangles or decomposing into triangles and other shapes; apply these techniques in the context of solving real-world and mathematical problems.

Launch

MP6, MP8

The principal of a middle school wants students to help restore a nearby lot. The school asks each grade to submit a plan for part of the lot. The sixth grade plans a nature zone split evenly as shown between a garden and a mini-forest.

What is the area of each part of the nature zone? Explain.

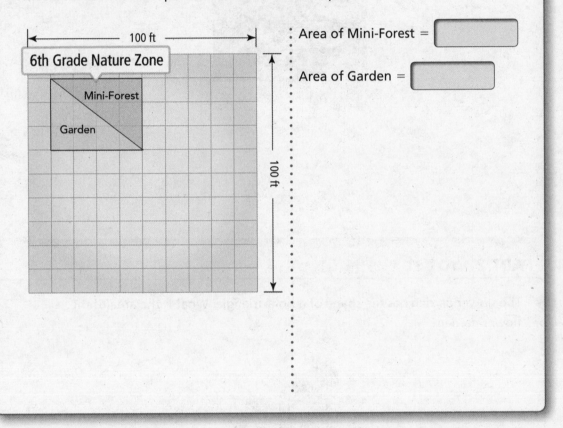

Area of Mini-Forest =

Area of Garden =

Reflect How does knowing the area of a rectangle help you find the area of the two triangle-shaped spaces in the rectangle?

_____

_____

_____

_____

_____

Got It?

PART 1 Got It

A quilt pattern has rectangular pieces of fabric divided into right triangles as shown. What is the area of one of the triangular pieces?

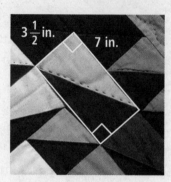

PART 2 Got It

The flower garden has the shape of a right triangle. What is the area of the flower garden?

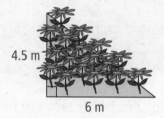

Got It?

PART 3 Got It

What is the area of the right triangle?

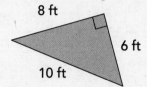

8 ft

6 ft

10 ft

Close and Check

Do you know **HOW?**

1. Triangle Park takes up $\frac{1}{2}$ of a small, square city block. What is the area of Triangle Park?

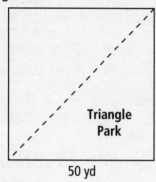

Triangle
Park

50 yd

2. A school banner is sewn in the shape of a right triangle. What is the area of the banner?

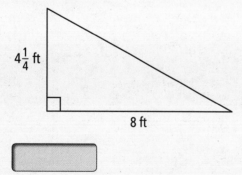

$4\frac{1}{4}$ ft

8 ft

Do you **UNDERSTAND?**

3. Writing Describe two different ways you could solve Exercise 2.

4. Error Analysis A storeowner advertises a triangular deck kit. The owner lists the area of the deck. What error do you think the owner made?

NEW!
Triangular
Deck Kit!
Area = 12 m²

4 m   5 m

3 m

Parallelograms

CCSS: 6.G.A.1: Find the area of right triangles, other triangles, special quadrilaterals, and polygons by composing into rectangles or decomposing into triangles and other shapes; apply these techniques in the context of solving real-world and mathematical problems.

Launch

© MP2, MP6

The seventh grade adds their plan for restoring the lot. They plan an art center shaped like a parallelogram for displaying student work.

What is the area of the art center? Explain.

100 ft

6th Grade Nature Zone

Mini-Forest

Garden

100 ft

7th Grade Art Center

Area of Art Center: _____

Reflect Can you find the area of the art center in more than one way? Explain.

_____

_____

_____

_____

_____

Got It?

PART 1 Got It

Find the area of the parallelogram by decomposing the parallelogram into a rectangle.

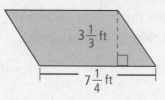

$3\frac{1}{3}$ ft

$7\frac{1}{4}$ ft

PART 2 Got It

What is the area of the parallelogram?

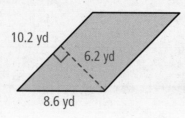

10.2 yd

6.2 yd

8.6 yd

Close and Check

Focus Question

How can you show that the area formulas for parallelograms and rectangles are the same?

_____

_____

_____

_____

Do you know HOW?

1. Draw lines to decompose the parallelogram into pieces that can be rearranged into a rectangle. Then find its area.

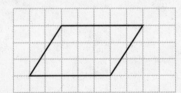

2. What is the area of the parallelogram?

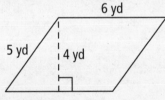

6 yd

5 yd   4 yd

3. A historical marker is in the shape of a parallelogram. The height is 5.7 m. The area of the marker is 22.8 m². What is the length of the base of the marker?

Do you UNDERSTAND?

4. Reasoning Two teams make posters to show how to find the area of a parallelogram. Which team has the correct start? Explain.

Team A	Team B
We made two triangles and a rectangle to find the area!	We cut off the triangle on one side and taped it to the other to make a rectangle!

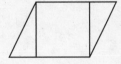 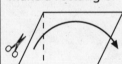

_____

_____

_____

_____

_____

This page intentionally left blank.

Digital Resources

CCSS: 6.G.A.1: Find the area of right triangles, other triangles, special quadrilaterals, and polygons by composing into rectangles or decomposing into triangles and other shapes; apply these techniques in the context of solving real-world and mathematical problems.

Launch

MP6, MP8

The seventh grade changes their plan for the art center on the lot. They decide to split the art center into two triangle-shaped spaces as shown.

What is the area of the space devoted to paintings? Explain.

Area for paintings =

100 ft

6th Grade Nature Zone

Mini-Forest

Garden

100 ft

Paintings

Sculptures

7th Grade Art Center

Reflect Suppose the seventh grade had split the art center by drawing a diagonal from the bottom left to the top right instead of what is shown. Would the area devoted to paintings be the same or different?

_____

_____

_____

_____

Got It?

PART 1 Got It

Compose the acute triangle into a parallelogram to find the area of the triangle.

12 m

8 m

11 m

PART 2 Got It

What is the area of the obtuse triangle?

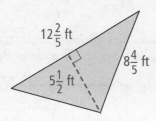

$12\frac{2}{5}$ ft

$8\frac{4}{5}$ ft

$5\frac{1}{2}$ ft

Discuss with a classmate

Write the definition of obtuse triangle.

Then, make a graphic organizer summarizing the names used to classify triangles by their sides and by their angles.

Finally, identify all the triangles in the figure and classify them by their sides and angles.

Got It?

What is the area of the triangle?

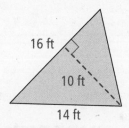

16 ft

10 ft

14 ft

Suppose you know the perimeter and height of an equilateral triangle. Explain how you would find the area of the triangle.

Close and Check

Focus Question

You can divide any parallelogram into two matching triangles. How is this useful?

_____

_____

_____

Do you know HOW?

1. What is the area of the acute triangle? Use the triangle to compose a parallelogram to find the area.

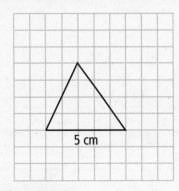

5 cm

2. Three houses share a yard in the shape of an obtuse triangle. What is the area of the triangular yard?

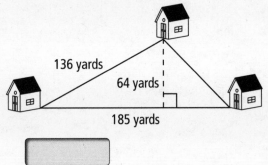

136 yards

64 yards

185 yards

Do you UNDERSTAND?

3. Reasoning The perimeter of the parallelogram is 44 cm. Do you have enough information to find the area of one of the triangles? Explain.

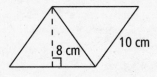

8 cm   10 cm

_____

_____

_____

_____

4. Vocabulary The height of a triangle can be inside a triangle, outside a triangle, or on the side of a triangle. Draw and label an example of each.

Polygons

CCSS: 6.G.A.1: Find the area of right triangles, other triangles, special quadrilaterals, and polygons by composing into rectangles or decomposing into triangles and other shapes; apply these techniques in the context of solving real-world and mathematical problems.

Launch

MP2, MP6

The eighth grade adds their plan for restoring the lot. They plan a music center for student concerts in the shape of a pentagon.

What is the area of the planned music center? Explain.

Area for Music Center = _____

100 ft

6th Grade Nature Zone

Mini-Forest

Garden

100 ft

Paintings

Sculptures

8th Grade Music Center

7th Grade Art Center

Reflect Can you find the area of the music center in more than one way? Explain.

_____

_____

_____

_____

Got It?

PART 1 Got It (1 of 2)

What is the area of the trapezoid?

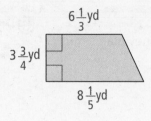

$6\frac{1}{3}$ yd

$3\frac{3}{4}$ yd

$8\frac{1}{5}$ yd

PART 1 Got It (2 of 2)

The figure shown below is a trapezoid that has been composed into a parallelogram. The bases of the trapezoid have lengths b_1 and b_2. The height of the trapezoid is h. Use this information to find a formula for the area of a trapezoid. Explain how you got your formula.

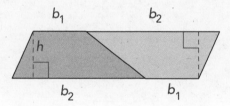

b_1 b_2

h

b_2 b_1

Got It?

PART 2 Got It

Decompose the regular hexagon into six matching triangles to find the area of the hexagon.

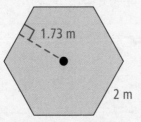

PART 3 Got It

Decompose the regular octagon into eight matching triangles to find the area of the octagon. Round your answer to the nearest whole number.

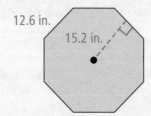

Close and Check

Focus Question

When you find the area of a polygon, how do you know whether to compose or decompose? Does it matter?

_____

_____

_____

_____

Do you know HOW?

1. What is the area of the trapezoid?

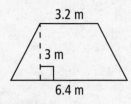

3.2 m

3 m

6.4 m

2. A theater company uses a hexagonal stage that can be rotated to change scenes. What is the area of the entire stage?

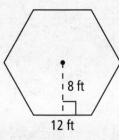

8 ft

12 ft

Do you UNDERSTAND?

3. Reasoning Can you find the area of the stage in Exercise 2 by decomposing it into trapezoids? Explain.

_____

_____

_____

4. Writing Suppose that a part of the stage in Exercise 2 is removed to make room for the orchestra. Explain how you can find the area of the remaining stage.

_____

_____

_____

_____

_____

Problem Solving

CCSS: 6.G.A.1: Find the area of right triangles, other triangles, special quadrilaterals, and polygons by composing into rectangles or decomposing into triangles and other shapes; apply these techniques in the context of solving real-world and mathematical problems.

Launch

© MP1, MP5

Combine some or all of the polygons to make a rectangle with an area of 20 square units.

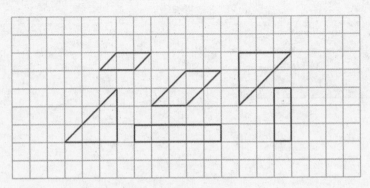

Draw your rectangle. Explain your work.

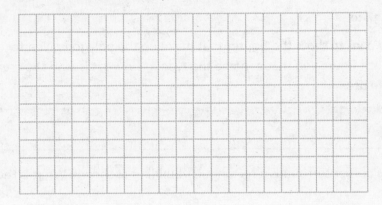

Reflect Describe a situation where you might rearrange polygons into a rectangle.

_____

_____

_____

_____

Got It?

What is the area of the polygon?

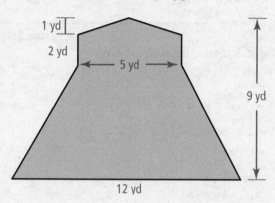

Discuss with a classmate

Use color pencils or pens to show the figures that make up the polygon given for this problem. For each figure you shade, name the type of figure it is, and the area formula you need to use.

A 3-foot-wide grass border surrounds a rectangular building as shown. What is the area of the grass?

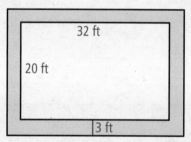

Got It?

A regular hexagon has a side length of 10 cm. The area of the shaded region is 130 cm^2. What is the value of x? Round to the nearest tenth.

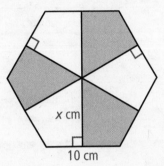

x cm

10 cm

Close and Check

Focus Question   © MP2, MP7

How can you find the area of any polygon? What does this allow you to do that you couldn't do before?

_____

_____

_____

_____

Do you know **HOW?**

1. What is the area of the polygon?

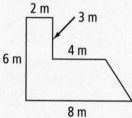

2 m   3 m
6 m   4 m
8 m

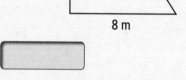

2. A picture is placed in a wooden frame. The dimensions of the picture and frame are equivalent ratios. Find the area of the frame.

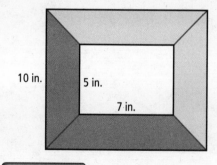

10 in.   5 in.
7 in.

Do you **UNDERSTAND?**

3. Writing A homeowner wants to buy the exact amount of sod needed for her lawn. Describe what she needs to do.

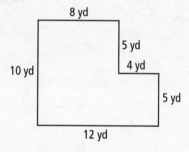

8 yd
5 yd
10 yd   4 yd
5 yd
12 yd

_____

_____

4. Error Analysis Explain her mistake in calculating the amount of sod needed.

$$A_1 = 10 \cdot 12 = 120 \text{ yd}^2$$
$$A_2 = 5 \cdot 4 = 20 \text{ yd}^2$$
$$A = 120 \text{ yd}^2 + 20 \text{ yd}^2 = \mathbf{140 \text{ yd}^2}$$

_____

_____

_____

13-R / **Topic Review**

New Vocabulary: area, compose a shape, decompose a shape, polygon, regular polygon
Review Vocabulary: acute triangle, diagonal, obtuse triangle, parallelogram, rectangle, right triangle, square

Vocabulary Review

Identify two challenging vocabulary terms from this topic. Write one vocabulary term in the center oval, and fill in the surrounding boxes with details that will help you better understand the term.

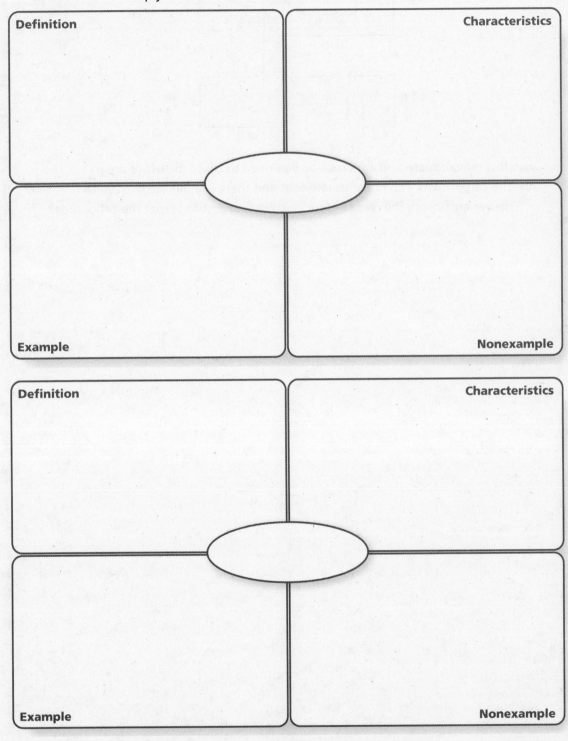

Definition

Characteristics

Example

Nonexample

Definition

Characteristics

Example

Nonexample

Pull It All Together

TASK 1

Suppose you are a carpet salesperson who just sold carpet for the office area shown in the figure. All angles in the figure are right angles.

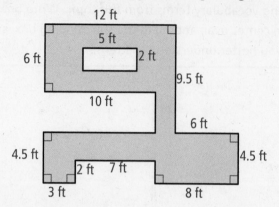

a. How many square feet of carpet do you need to cover the office area?

b. The carpet costs $12.99 per square foot and there is a flat fee of $200 to deliver and install the carpet. How much does it cost to carpet the office area?

Analyzing Three-Dimensional Figures

Digital Resources

CCSS: 6.G.A.4: Represent three-dimensional figures using nets made up of rectangles and triangles, and use the nets to find the surface area of these figures. Apply these techniques in the context of solving real-world and mathematical problems.

Launch

© MP2, MP3

You play a "guess my word" card game with a friend. Your friend must name the figure on your card. You pick this card.

cube

Write at least five things you could say to get your friend to guess your word. You cannot use the word "cube" in your descriptions.

Reflect Why is it useful to be able to describe solid figures?

_____

_____

_____

_____

_____

Got It?

PART 1 Got It

How many faces, edges, and vertices does the three-dimensional figure have?

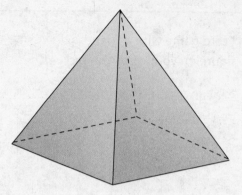

PART 2 Got It (1 of 2)

Name the figure shown.

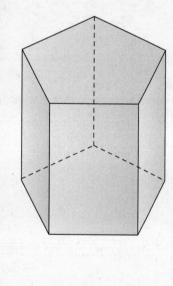

Got It?

How is the number of lateral faces of a prism related to the shape of a base of the prism?

Name the three-dimensional figure shown.

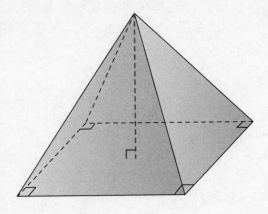

How is a pentagonal pyramid similar to a pentagonal prism? How is it different?

Close and Check

Focus Question

© MP3, MP7

What does it mean for a figure to be 3-D?

_____

_____

_____

_____

Do you know HOW?

1. Look at the following 3-D figures. Complete the table.

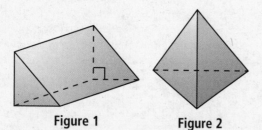

Figure 1   Figure 2

	Figure 1	Figure 2
Name		
Number of Faces		
Number of Edges		
Number of Vertices		
Shapes of Faces		

Do you UNDERSTAND?

2. Compare and Contrast How are a cube and a square pyramid alike? How are they different?

_____

_____

_____

_____

_____

_____

3. Reasoning How many lateral faces does a pentagonal prism have? Explain.

_____

_____

_____

_____

Digital Resources

CCSS: 6.G.A.4: Represent three-dimensional figures using nets made up of rectangles and triangles, and use the nets to find the surface area of these figures. Apply these techniques in the context of solving real-world and mathematical problems.

Launch

MP4, MP6

A toy store displays robotic dogs in cube-shaped boxes without fronts so kids can easily see what kind of dog is inside. A worker needs one more box. The boxes in the back room are all unfolded.

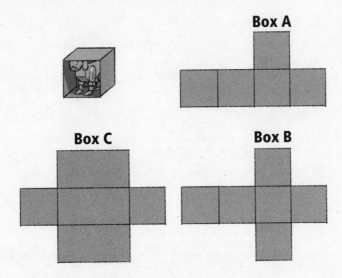

Box A

Box C

Box B

Can the worker choose a box without building it? Explain.

Reflect How are the unfolded boxes useful?

_____

_____

_____

_____

Got It?

PART 1 Got It

Match the cube with its net.

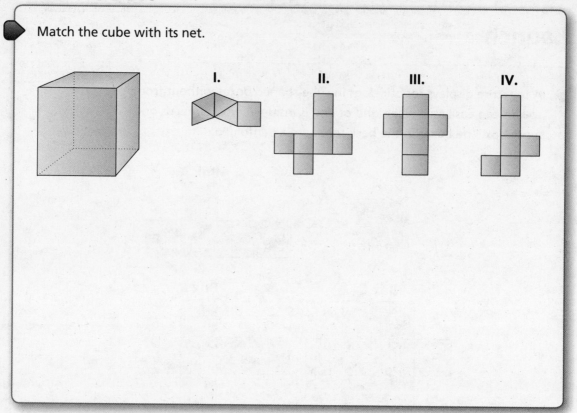

PART 2 Got It

Identify the three-dimensional figure that the given net forms.

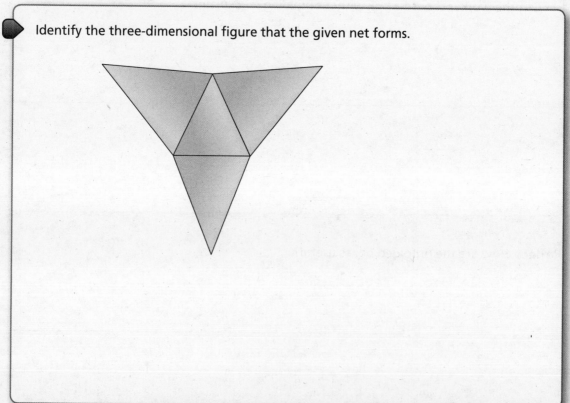

Got It?

PART 3 Got It

Draw a net for the square pyramid.

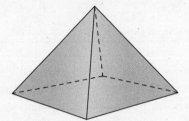

Close and Check

Focus Question

MP5, MP6

How can you tell which 3-D figure a 2-D model will form?

_____

_____

_____

_____

Do you know HOW?

1. Name the three-dimensional figure the given net forms.

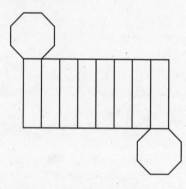

[_____]

2. Draw a net that forms a pentagonal pyramid.

Do you UNDERSTAND?

3. **Writing** Explain how you found your answer for Exercise 1.

_____

_____

_____

_____

_____

4. **Reasoning** A student wants to build a square pyramid using 2 squares and 3 triangles. Is this possible? Explain.

_____

_____

_____

_____

_____

_____

Surface Areas of Prisms

Digital Resources

CCSS: 6.G.A.4: Represent three-dimensional figures using nets made up of rectangles and triangles, and use the nets to find the surface area of these figures. Apply these techniques in the context of solving real-world and mathematical problems.

Launch

© MP2, MP8

A box factory stamps out nets to make the cube-shaped robotic dog boxes. The manager shows the workers a sample net for the box.

The worker says, "Ok, I know how much cardboard I need for each box."

10 in.

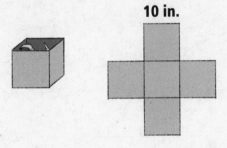

Explain how the worker knows.

Reflect How does a net help you find how much cardboard was needed? Would the problem have been easier or harder if you just saw the folded box? Explain.

_____

_____

_____

_____

Got It?

PART 1 Got It

 Use a net to find the surface area of a cube with edge length $2\frac{3}{4}$ in.

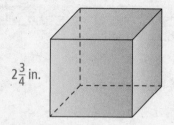

$2\frac{3}{4}$ in.

PART 2 Got It

 Find the surface area of the rectangular prism.

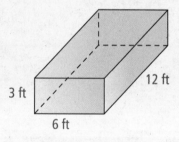

12 ft

3 ft

6 ft

Got It?

PART 3 Got It

 Find the surface area of the triangular prism.

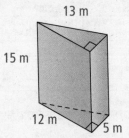

Close and Check

Focus Question

How do you describe the surface area of a prism? How does the prism's net help you do that?

_____

_____

_____

Do you know **HOW?**

1. Find the surface area of the figure below.

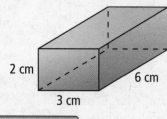

2. How many square inches of paper is needed to create the triangular prism shown below?

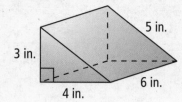

Do you **UNDERSTAND?**

3. **Writing** Explain how to find the surface area of a 3-D figure.

_____

_____

_____

_____

4. **Error Analysis** A student calculated the surface area of the figure below. What mistake did the student make? Find the correct surface area.

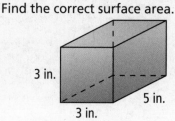

$$6 \cdot (3)(3) = 6 \cdot 9 = 54 \text{ in.}^2$$

_____

_____

_____

_____

Surface Areas of Pyramids

CCSS: 6.G.A.4: Represent three-dimensional figures using nets made up of rectangles and triangles, and use the nets to find the surface area of these figures. Apply these techniques in the context of solving real-world and mathematical problems.

Launch

© MP1, MP6

The toy company plans to sell their new robotic puppies in pyramid-shaped boxes instead of a cube-shaped box without a front.

A worker says, "I can tell which box will need more cardboard by just looking." Explain how the worker knows. Justify your response by finding the surface area of each box.

Robotic Dog Box

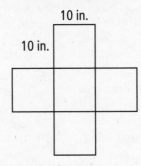

10 in.

10 in.

Robotic Puppy Box

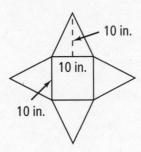

10 in.

10 in.

10 in.

Surface area of robotic dog box:

Surface area of robotic puppy box:

How the worker knows:

Reflect How does this problem relate to your past work on composing and decomposing shapes?

_____

_____

_____

Got It?

PART 1 Got It

Use a net to find the surface area of the square pyramid.

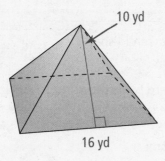

10 yd

16 yd

PART 2 Got It

Find the surface area of the rectangular pyramid to the nearest square foot.

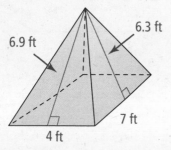

6.9 ft

6.3 ft

4 ft

7 ft

Got It?

Find the surface area of the regular triangular pyramid to the nearest square meter.

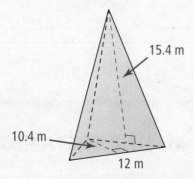

15.4 m

10.4 m

12 m

Close and Check

Focus Question

How do you describe the surface of a pyramid? How does the pyramid's net help you do that?

_____

_____

_____

Do you know HOW?

1. What is the surface area of the figure below?

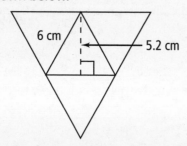

12.65 ft
12 ft
10 ft
6 ft

[   ]

2. A triangular pyramid is made using 4 equilateral triangles. The net is shown below.

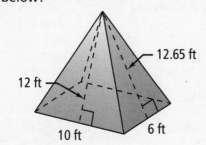

6 cm
5.2 cm

What is the surface area of this figure?

[   ]

Do you UNDERSTAND?

3. **Writing** Explain how you found your answer to Exercise 2.

_____

_____

_____

4. **Error Analysis** What error was made in calculating the surface area of the square pyramid? Calculate the correct surface area.

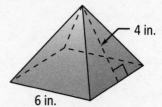

4 in.
6 in.

$$4[\tfrac{1}{2}(6)(4)] = 4(12) = 48 \text{ in.}^2$$

_____

_____

_____

_____

Volumes of Right Rectangular Prisms

CCSS: 6.G.A.2: Find the volume of a right rectangular prism ... by packing it with unit cubes ... show that the volume is the same as would be found by multiplying the edge lengths of the prism. Apply ... $V = lwh$ and $V = Bh$ to find volumes of right rectangular prisms ... .

Launch

© MP1, MP2

City park workers plan to dig a rectangular hole for a small fishpond.

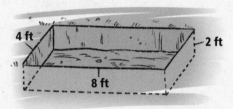

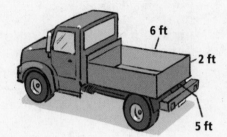

Will they be able to haul away the dirt in one truckload? Justify your reasoning.

Reflect Suppose the dimensions of the hole were 4 ft long, 2 ft wide, and 8 ft deep. Would the hole hold the same amount of dirt? Explain.

_____

_____

_____

_____

Got It?

PART 1 Got It

What is the volume of the rectangular prism?

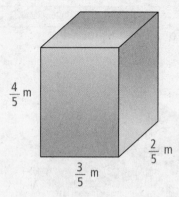

$\frac{4}{5}$ m

$\frac{2}{5}$ m

$\frac{3}{5}$ m

PART 2 Got It

Use two different methods to find the volume of the rectangular prism.

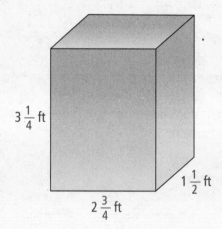

$3\frac{1}{4}$ ft

$1\frac{1}{2}$ ft

$2\frac{3}{4}$ ft

Got It?

Use a formula to find the volume of the rectangular prism.

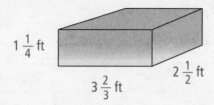

$1\frac{1}{4}$ ft

$3\frac{2}{3}$ ft

$2\frac{1}{2}$ ft

Close and Check

MP2, MP7

Focus Question

You use nets to find the surface area of a box. How do you figure out how much fits in a box?

_____

_____

_____

_____

Do you know HOW?

1. How many $\frac{1}{2}$ in. by $\frac{1}{2}$ in. by $\frac{1}{2}$ in. cubes does it take to fill the box below?

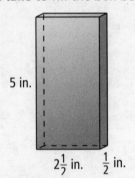

5 in.

$2\frac{1}{2}$ in. $\frac{1}{2}$ in.

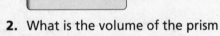

2. What is the volume of the prism below?

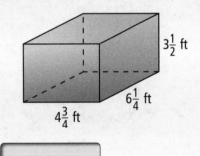

$3\frac{1}{2}$ ft

$6\frac{1}{4}$ ft

$4\frac{3}{4}$ ft

Do you UNDERSTAND?

3. Reasoning Will 500 ft^3 of gravel fit inside a container that measures $7\frac{1}{4}$ ft by $15\frac{3}{4}$ ft by $4\frac{3}{4}$ ft? Explain.

_____

_____

_____

_____

4. Writing How many $\frac{1}{3}$ cm by $\frac{1}{3}$ cm by $\frac{1}{3}$ cm cubes will fit in a 1 cm by 1 cm by 1 cm box? Explain how you know.

_____

_____

_____

_____

_____

_____

Problem Solving

CCSS: 6.G.A.2: Find the volume of a right rectangular prism … solving real-world and mathematical problems. **6.G.A.4:** Represent three-dimensional figures using nets … And use the nets to find the surface area … solving real-world and mathematical problems.

Launch

© MP1, MP4

The toy company offers a robotic dog condo made of wood with openings for a square window and a square entrance.

Draw a net for the dog condo.

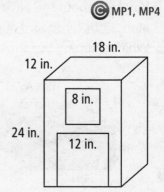

Then find the surface area of the condo.

Reflect Could you draw more than one correct net for the dog condo? Explain.

_____

_____

_____

_____

Got It?

PART 1 Got It

The two shipping boxes have the shape of rectangular prisms. The item you want to mail fits in either box.

You care about the environment so you want to buy the box that uses the least amount of cardboard and needs the least number of packing peanuts to fill it. Which shipping box should you buy? Explain.

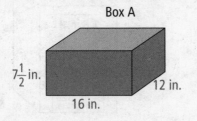

Box A

$7\frac{1}{2}$ in.   12 in.   16 in.

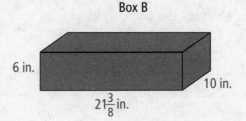

Box B

6 in.   10 in. $21\frac{3}{8}$ in.

PART 2 Got It

You plan to build a birdhouse with one square doorway as shown. How many square centimeters of wood do you need to make the birdhouse?

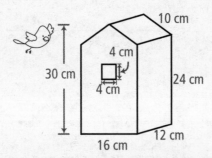

10 cm

4 cm

30 cm   24 cm

4 cm

16 cm   12 cm

Discuss with a classmate

How did you organize your work to find the answer to this problem? Compare your work and use diagrams or organizers to make your solution and explanation more clear.

Close and Check

Focus Question

What can surface area and volume help you describe? What can knowing the surface area and volume of 3-D figures allow you to do?

_____

_____

_____

_____

Do you know HOW?

1. Find the surface area and volume of each figure. Then circle the figure that has the greatest surface area and the least volume.

Figure 1

1 in.

4 in.

4 in.

4 in.

Figure 2

4 in.

2 in.

2 in.

Figure 3

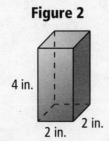

1.5 in.

6 in.

2 in.

	Surface area	Volume
Figure 1		
Figure 2		
Figure 3		

Do you UNDERSTAND?

2. **Reasoning** Using an 8-inch by 10-inch sheet of paper, is it possible to build a rectangular prism with a length of 5 in., a width of 4 in., and a volume of 60 in.^{3}? Explain.

_____

_____

_____

_____

3. **Writing** Is it possible for two solids to have the same volume, but different surface areas? Tell when this would be helpful to know.

_____

_____

_____

_____

This page intentionally left blank.

New Vocabulary: net, prism, pyramid, surface area of a three-dimensional figure, three-dimensional figure, volume of a prism

Review Vocabulary: center, cube, cubic unit, regular polygon

Vocabulary Review

Identify two challenging vocabulary terms from this topic. Write one vocabulary term in the center oval, and fill in the surrounding boxes with details that will help you better understand the term.

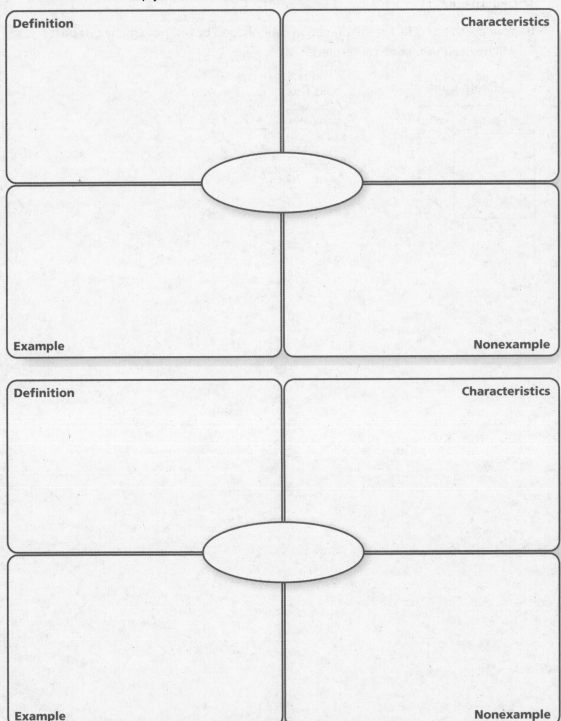

Definition	Characteristics

Example	Nonexample

Definition	Characteristics

Example	Nonexample

Pull It All Together

TASK 1

Your basketball coach is making centerpieces for the team banquet. Each centerpiece is a photo cube with an open top.

a. Your coach wants to cover the photos on each cube with a plastic wrap. To the nearest square foot, how much plastic wrap will the coach need for one centerpiece?

b. Your coach has gifts for the players in cube-shaped boxes. How many gift boxes will he need to fill one centerpiece?

Photo Cube

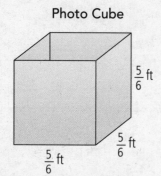

Gift Box

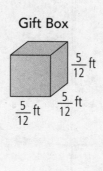

Statistical Questions

CCSS: 6.SP.A.1: Recognize a statistical question as one that anticipates variability in the data related to the question and accounts for it in the answers. **6.SP.B.5b:** ... Describing the nature of the attribute under investigation ... .

Launch

© MP3, MP8

Sort these questions into two categories. Then describe your categories.

> How long does it take students to get to school?

> What is your favorite color?

> Did the cafeteria serve pizza today?

> How many books do students read each month?

> What fruits do students like to eat?

Category 1 Questions ⋮ **Category 2 Questions**

Description ⋮ **Description**

Reflect Will some of the questions provide more useful information than others? Explain.

_____

_____

_____

_____

Got It?

PART 1 Got It

Why is *"How many hours do students play video games in one day?"* a statistical question?

Discuss with a classmate

How did your knowledge about video games help you answer this question?
How did you apply this knowledge in your answer?

PART 2 Got It (1 of 2)

Which questions are statistical questions?

I. How much time did students spend on the computer yesterday?
II. What kind of calculator do I have?
III. How many emails will I get each day for the next week?

Got It?

Suppose you asked students how long they spent on the computer yesterday. Suppose all of the students gave the same answer. Does this mean that "How much time did students spend on the computer yesterday?" is not a statistical question? Explain.

PART 3 Got It

Water boils at different temperatures based on its distance above sea level. In a laboratory, 1,000 feet above sea level, a scientist recorded the temperature of water in twelve pots just as they each started to boil. If you were the scientist, what would you conclude to be the specific boiling point of water at 1,000 feet? Justify your answer.

Temperature of the water in each pot:

210.2°F	210.1°F	210.3°F
209.9°F	210.0°F	210.1°F
210.4°F	209.8°F	209.9°F
210.0°F	209.7°F	210.0°F

Close and Check

▶ Focus Question

How can a question have more than one answer? How do you decide which answer to use?

_____

_____

_____

_____

▶ Do you know HOW?

1. Fill in the chart with Y or N to identify whether the question is statistical.

Question	Statistical Question? Y or N
How long do students spend on homework each night?	
How tall are you?	
How many students in your class rode the bus to school today?	
What is your favorite season?	

2. Read the statements about statistical questions. Put an X in the box next to statements that are correct.
   A statistical question...

   ☐ has more than one answer.

   ☐ will always have the same answer.

   ☐ is used to collect data about an aspect of the world.

▶ Do you UNDERSTAND?

3. **Vocabulary** Is _"What is the high temperature each day this month?"_ a statistical question? Explain.

   _____

   _____

   _____

4. **Reasoning** The data set shown answers the question _"How many eggs does a Blue Jay lay at one time (clutch size)?"_

4	4	5	3
3	5	4	5
5	3	4	7
4	2	3	4

What can you conclude about the average clutch size of a Blue Jay?

   _____

   _____

   _____

Dot Plots

CCSS: 6.SP.B.4: Display numerical data in plots on a number line, including dot plots ... . **6.SP.B.5:** Summarize numerical data sets in relation to their context. **6.SP.B.5c:** ... Describing any overall pattern and any striking deviations from the overall pattern ... .

Launch

© MP2, MP6

A principal is deciding how many computers to order for a new lab. Each classroom has submitted a vote. Show the data in a better way to help the principal make a decision. Tell why your way is better.

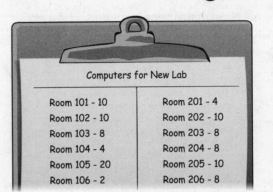

Computers for New Lab

Room 101 - 10	Room 201 - 4
Room 102 - 10	Room 202 - 10
Room 103 - 8	Room 203 - 8
Room 104 - 4	Room 204 - 8
Room 105 - 20	Room 205 - 10
Room 106 - 2	Room 206 - 8

My Way   **Why It's Better**

Reflect Is there one right way to display data? Are some ways better than others?

_____

_____

_____

_____

Got It?

PART 1 Got It

Your friends hold a basketball-shooting contest. The person who makes the most baskets in one minute wins. Use the dot plot to answer the questions.

Basketball-shooting contest

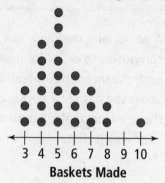

Baskets Made

a. How many people made six baskets?

b. How many baskets did the winner make?

Discuss with a classmate

Each partner should choose one of the lettered parts of the problem.
Explain how you used the dot plot to answer that part of the problem.
If your answers don't agree for a part of the problem, consult with another group to see if you can reach agreement.

PART 2 Got It

The list on the right shows the number of books each student in your class read over the summer. Make a dot plot of the data.

Books Read This Summer

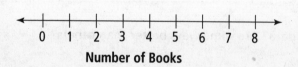

Number of Books

0, 3, 6, 2, 0, 2, 3, 5,
1, 4, 2, 4, 2, 0, 1, 1,
5, 4, 5, 8, 2, 3

Got It?

PART 3 Got It

The dot plot shows how many hours plant researchers spent in the laboratory last night. Identify the clusters, the gaps, and any data values that stray to describe the center, spread, and shape of the data distribution. What does the plot tell you about how much time researchers spent in the lab?

Time Spent in Laboratory

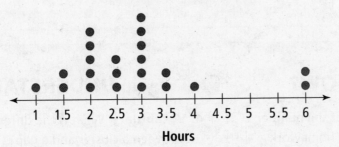

Hours

Close and Check

Focus Question

What kinds of information can a dot plot easily show you? In what types of situations might you want that information?

_____

_____

_____

_____

Do you know HOW?

1. Your class keeps track of the number of hours they spend on homework each week. Display the data in the dot plot below.

   10, 7, 5, 4, 5, 8, 10, 4, 6, 6,
   5, 7, 4, 7, 5, 4, 5, 7, 8, 8, 6

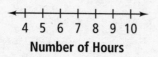

   Number of Hours

2. What is the most frequent amount of time spent on homework?

   [____] hours

3. How many students spend 6 hours on homework each week?

   [____] students

Do you UNDERSTAND?

4. **Vocabulary** What is the difference between a cluster and a gap?

   _____

   _____

   _____

   _____

5. **Error Analysis** The dot plot shows the scores on a recent math quiz. A classmate states that only 7 students took the quiz. Explain the error, and tell how many students took the quiz.

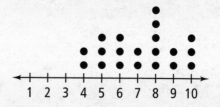

   _____

   _____

   _____

   _____

Histograms

CCSS: **6.SP.B.4:** Display numerical data in plots on a number line, including ... histograms ... .
6.SP.B.5: Summarize numerical data sets in relation to their context. **6.SP.B.5c:** ... Describing any overall pattern and any striking deviations from the overall pattern ... .

Launch

Ⓒ MP4, MP5

A park worker writes out ticket sales information for his boss.

> 18 tickets from 10 A.M. to noon
> 24 tickets from noon to 2 P.M.
> 56 tickets from 2 P.M. to 4 P.M.
> 62 tickets from 4 P.M. to 6 P.M.
> 24 tickets from 6 P.M. to 8 P.M.

What is a better way to show the sales data?

Reflect Why is your way to show the ticket sales better?

_____

_____

_____

_____

_____

Got It?

PART 1 Got It (1 of 2)

Use the histogram to determine how many of the users surveyed have fewer than 100 friends.

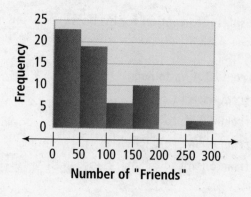

PART 1 Got It (2 of 2)

If a user has exactly 50 friends, in which interval is the user represented?

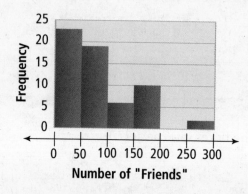

Got It?

PART 2 Got It

Twice a month for a year, a scientist measured the temperature at the top of Mt. Everest. Make a histogram of the data.

A Year at the Top of Mt. Everest

Temperature (°F)		
−35.5, −34.6	−32.8, −31.9	−26.5, −27.4
−23.8, −24.7	−13.0, −12.1	−2.2, −1.3
−0.4, 0.5	−1.3, −2.2	−6.7, −7.6
−16.6, −17.5	−22.0, −22.9	−29.2, −30.1

Got It?

PART 3 Got It

Engineers recorded the amount of energy that 300 individual households consumed in one day.

What does the histogram show about the amount of energy used?

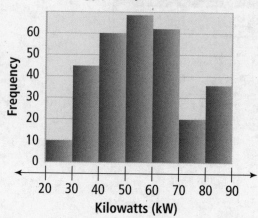

Energy Used per Household

(y-axis: Frequency, values 0, 10, 20, 30, 40, 50, 60)

(x-axis: Kilowatts (kW), values 20, 30, 40, 50, 60, 70, 80, 90)

Close and Check

Focus Question

What kinds of information can a histogram easily show you? In what types of situations might you want that information?

_____

_____

_____

_____

Do you know HOW?

1. Use the resting heart rate data in beats per minute (bpm) to complete the histogram.

Resting Heart Rate						
86	72	92	83	91	84	86
71	66	93	87	89	81	98

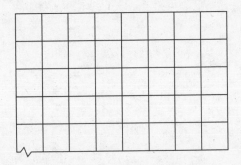

2. Use the histogram from Exercise 1 to complete the following statements.

☐ people have a resting heart rate between 80 and 85 bpm.

☐ people have resting heart rates that are under 75 bpm.

Do you UNDERSTAND?

3. **Reasoning** A weather tracker records the temperatures for a week. Would a histogram be a good way to represent this data? Explain your reasoning.

Daily Temperatures (°F)						
74	73	76	76	74	75	75

_____

_____

_____

_____

4. **Error Analysis** Your classmate says that the histogram for Exercise 1 shows that most people have a resting heart rate between 85 and 90 beats per minute. Explain why he is not correct.

_____

_____

_____

_____

This page intentionally left blank.

Box Plots

CCSS: 6.SP.B.4: Display numerical data in plots on a number line, including … box plots. **6.SP.B.5:** Summarize numerical data sets in relation to their context. **6.SP.B.5c:** … Describing any overall pattern and any striking deviations from the overall pattern … .

Launch

Ⓒ MP1, MP7

A teacher sets up a kickball game by having students choose different whole numbers from 0 to 50. The student whose number ends up in the middle of all numbers chosen gets to be the referee.

Your classmates have already chosen the numbers shown. You get to go last in choosing numbers. Can you be the referee? Explain.

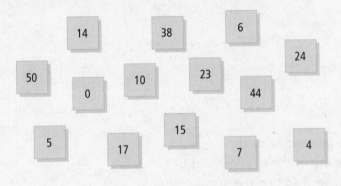

Reflect Were there any students you knew could not be the referee based on their numbers? Explain.

_____

_____

_____

_____

_____

Got It?

PART 1 Got It

What is the middle value of the following data set?

34.5   68.9   76.4   32.8   73.2   22.9   68.3

Discuss with a classmate

Define what is meant by "middle value".
What did you observe about the arrangement of the data?
Describe the steps you took to find the middle value.

PART 2 Got It

Use the box plot.

How many words do the fastest 50% of readers read per minute?

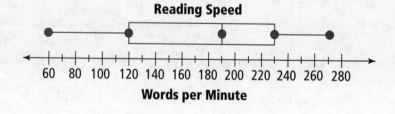

Reading Speed

Words per Minute

Got It?

An athletic trainer recorded how many miles 11 people could run in 30 minutes. Make a box plot of the results.

2.5, 4.4, 2.1, 2.3, 4.5, 1.3, 2.2, 5.0, 4.7, 2.7, 3.3

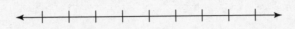

In a box plot, why doesn't the line inside the box always fall exactly halfway between the two end dots?

Close and Check

Focus Question

MP4, MP8

What kinds of information can a box plot easily show you? In what types of situations might you want that information?

_____

_____

_____

_____

Do you know HOW?

1. People at the local store were surveyed about their wait time. Find the boundary points and create a box plot. Waiting times in minutes: 5, 10, 6, 14, 3, 2, 15, 12, 11

Wait Time

0 1 2 3 4 5 6 7 8 9 10 11 12 13 14 15 16
minutes

Minimum: ☐   Middle of Data Set: ☐   Maximum: ☐

Middle of the Lower Half: ☐   Middle of the Upper Half: ☐

Do you UNDERSTAND?

2. **Reasoning** Your uncle waited for 3 minutes. Did he wait more or less than the most of the others? Explain.

_____

_____

3. **Error Analysis** The scores **86, 77, 45, 19, 53, 75, 62, 20, 42, 89, 100** are displayed in class. Your classmate says that 50% of the scores are above 75. Explain the error, and correct the statement.

_____

_____

Choosing an Appropriate Data Display

Digital Resources

CCSS: 6.SP.B.4: Display numerical data in plots on a number line, including dot plots, histograms, and box plots.

Launch

MP5, MP7

Your soccer coach posts results of ticket sales for a team fundraiser for new uniforms. You are the player who sells 94 tickets.

> **Uniform Fundraiser Tickets Sold**
>
> 44, 59, 66, 73, 74, 76
> 80, 83, 88, 91, 94

. . . .

Make a dot plot, histogram, or box plot to display the sales data.

Then tell why you chose the type of graph you made.

Reflect You chose one of three types of graphs to display the data. Which of the other two graph types did you like the least for the data and why?

_____

_____

_____

_____

Got It?

PART 1 Got It

Which data display(s) can help you answer the question:

"In the results of an opinion poll, how many people responded '80' or above on a scale from 1 to 100?"

I. Dot Plot   **II.** Box Plot   **III.** Histogram

PART 2 Got It (1 of 2)

In the talent competition, the top five scorers of the first round cannot be eliminated in the second round. Use a display to determine the top five scores. Explain why you chose the display you did.

Round 1 Results

56	42	45	67	29	60	81	50
68	58	60	61	55	49	23	39
48	48	49	64	91	52	56	51
29	73	61	49	88	50	43	47
32	87	43	53	79	55	67	82
46	90	77	61	62	51	92	46
34	68	28	37	43	85	76	72
38	52	41	79	68	70	20	58
10	35	50	80	57	62	49	36
65	40	78	36	68	79	44	41
59	84	92	54	91	38	51	54
51	96	44	87	62	47	83	63
84	32	56	67	58	56	54	40
42	57	93	24	52	94	39	75
63	81	45	49	62	40	58	48
71	59	39	19	48	88	46	

Got It?

If you scored a 74 in the first round, how did you do?

Round 1 Results

56	42	45	67	29	60	81	50
68	58	60	61	55	49	23	39
48	48	49	64	91	52	56	51
29	73	61	49	88	50	43	47
32	87	43	53	79	55	67	82
46	90	77	61	62	51	92	46
34	68	28	37	43	85	76	72
38	52	41	79	68	70	20	58
10	35	50	80	57	62	49	36
65	40	78	36	68	79	44	41
59	84	92	54	91	38	51	54
51	96	44	87	62	47	83	63
84	32	56	67	58	56	54	40
42	57	93	24	52	94	39	75
63	81	45	49	62	40	58	48
71	59	39	19	48	88	46	

PART 3 Got It

Your science class is doing an experiment to estimate the temperature at which water boils at the class's elevation. Each student puts a pot of water on the stove and measures the water temperature when it just starts to boil. Which data display should you use to find the specific temperature at which water boils at the class's elevation?

Close and Check

Focus Question ⓒ MP5, MP6

Which data displays are more useful in which situations?

_____

_____

_____

_____

Do you know HOW?

1. Circle the data display that can help you answer the question, *How many students scored exactly 80% on the test?*

dot plot   histogram   box plot

2. Write a T for true or an F for false next to each statement.

☐ A histogram is helpful to see each data value.

☐ A dot plot is helpful to see frequencies of data values.

☐ A box plot is helpful to see clusters and gaps in data values.

☐ A histogram is helpful to see large data sets in data values.

3. A graph shows the total number of inches of precipitation that falls each month. It does not show daily totals. Is the graph a dot plot, a histogram, or a box plot?

☐

Do you UNDERSTAND?

4. Reasoning A soccer coach keeps track of the goals made during the season. He wants to compare the number of goals made by each player. Should he display the data as a dot plot or histogram? Explain.

_____

_____

_____

5. Compare and Contrast How are dot plots and histograms similar? How are they different?

_____

_____

_____

_____

_____

_____

_____

Copyright © by Pearson Education, Inc., or its affiliates. All Rights Reserved.

Topic 15   384   **Lesson 15-5**

Problem Solving

CCSS: 6.SP.B.4: Display numerical data in plots on a number line, including dot plots, histograms, and box plots.

Launch

Ⓒ MP1, MP3

A marketing team asked executives how many gigabytes of storage their music players should contain. They used a box plot to describe the responses and chose the middle value, 6 gigabytes, as the preferred storage space for the player.

Gigabytes for Music Player

1, 4, 4, 8, 6, 8,
7, 4, 10, 8, 4

Music Player Plan

Gigabytes

Do you agree with the marketers' thinking? Tell why or why not.

Reflect Does it matter what graph you choose when showing data? Explain.

_____

_____

_____

_____

Got It?

PART 1 Got It

Your friend gets to stay up late if she usually spends more than 3 hours studying each day. She made a dot plot to show her study times over one month. Should your friend be able to stay up late? Why?

How Many Hours I Studied

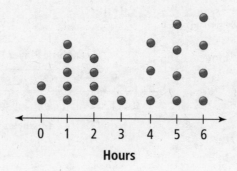

Hours

Got It?

PART 2 Got It (1 of 2)

The histogram shows the number of hours that students in a school exercised last week. If the recommended minimum level of exercise is 3 hours per week, what health advice would you give to the principal of the school?

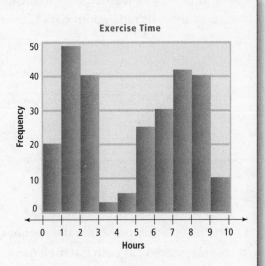

PART 2 Got It (2 of 2)

What type of students might the cluster on the right represent?

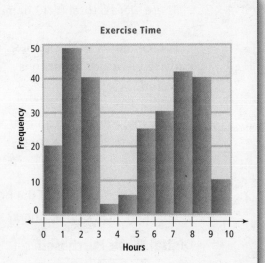

Close and Check

Focus Question

In this topic, you learned how to display different types of data. What might a display show or hide about data?

_____

_____

_____

Do you know **HOW?**

1. The dot plot below shows the number of runs scored for each baseball game. Place an X next to the statements that correctly describe the data.

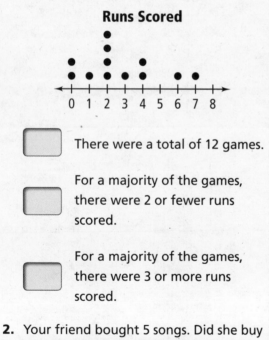

Runs Scored

There were a total of 12 games.

For a majority of the games, there were 2 or fewer runs scored.

For a majority of the games, there were 3 or more runs scored.

2. Your friend bought 5 songs. Did she buy more or less than most of the others?

Digital Music Purchased

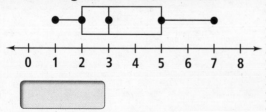

Do you **UNDERSTAND?**

3. **Reasoning** A customer service representative receives ratings from the people he helps. Scores above 6 are considered good. He makes this histogram to show his ratings. Is it misleading? Explain.

Customer Service Scores

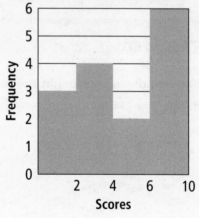

_____

_____

_____

_____

_____

New Vocabulary: box plot, data, dot plot, frequency, histogram, statistical question
Review Vocabulary: maximum, minimum

Vocabulary Review

Identify two challenging vocabulary terms from this topic. Write one vocabulary term in the center oval, and fill in the surrounding boxes with details that will help you better understand the term.

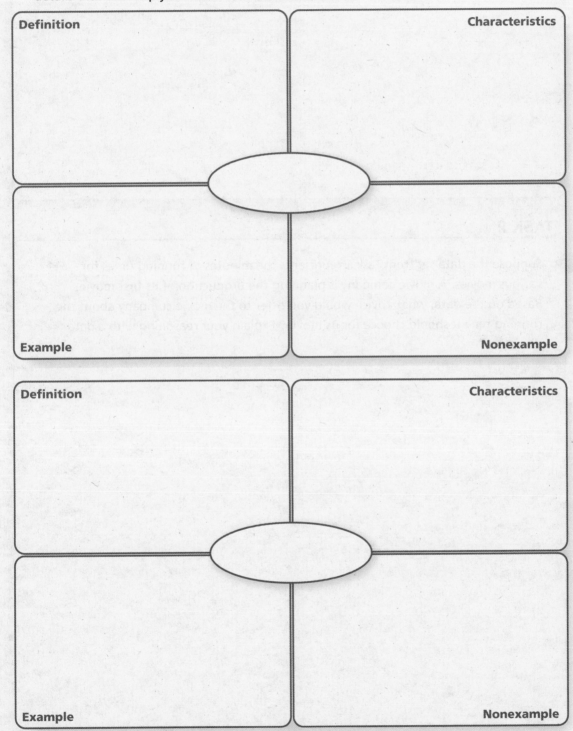

Definition

Characteristics

Example

Nonexample

Definition

Characteristics

Example

Nonexample

Pull It All Together

TASK 1

Does this data set contain any stray data values? Explain your reasoning with a data display.

95, 120, 150, 129, 94, 98, 102, 91, 111, 91, 100, 120, 127, 98, 250

TASK 2

Suppose the data set from Task 1 represents the minutes of running times for various movies. A movie company is planning the production of its first movie. Based on the data, what advice would you offer to the movie company about the running time it should choose for its movie? Explain your reasoning with a data display.

16-1

Mean and Median

CCSS: 6.SP.A.3: Recognize that a measure of center for a numerical data set summarizes all of its values with a single number ... . **6.SP.B.4:** Display numerical data in ... box plots. **6.SP.B.5:** Summarize numerical data sets in relation to their context, such as by: **6.SP.B.5c:** Giving ... median ... .

Launch

Ⓒ MP3, MP6

Before building a new version of the video game "Zombie Pretzel Attack 2!", you survey gamers on the ideal number of characters Version 3 should have.

45   8   5   12   6   4   10

Based on the data, how many characters should you have in "Zombie Pretzel Attack 3!"? Explain.

Reflect How did the result "45" affect your thinking about choosing the number of characters? Explain.

_____

_____

_____

_____

_____

Got It?

PART 1 Got It (1 of 2)

What is the median of the data set?

2, −4, 1, 7, −3, 0, −2, 6, 3, −1, −5, 4

PART 1 Got It (2 of 2)

Will the median always be a value in the original data set? Explain.

PART 2 Got It

Make a box plot of the data set.

12, 31, 25, 84, 45, 96, 54, 67, 46

Got It?

PART 3 Got It

A track coach wants to make sure that his athletes are drinking enough water throughout the day so that they are properly hydrated for their workouts. He records how many glasses of water they drank today. Is the median an appropriate measure of center for the data set below? Use a graph to justify your reasoning.

8, 3, 4, 3, 10, 4, 9

Close and Check

Focus Question

How can you represent a collection of numbers using just one number? How is using one number helpful? How is using one number *not* helpful?

Do you know HOW?

1. What is the median of the data set?

   137, −150, 55, 17, −101, 179

2. You measure the height of people in your family and record the results in inches.

   41.5, 67.2, 63.4, 64,
   46.1, 72.4, 43.7, 57.8

   Fill in the correct values to complete the box plot.

   Family Member Heights (in.)

   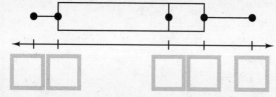

Do you UNDERSTAND?

3. **Reasoning** In Exercise 2, is the median an appropriate measure of center for the data? Explain.

4. **Error Analysis** A classmate records the gasoline prices on the way to school.

   $2.60, $2.79, $2.82, $2.67, $2.70

   He says the median of the data set is $2.82. Explain the error your classmate made and find the correct median.

Mean

CCSS: 6.SP.A.3: Recognize that a measure of center for a numerical data set summarizes all of its values with a single number... . **6.SP.B.5:** Summarize numerical data sets in relation to their context, such as by: **6.SP.B.5c:** Giving ... mean ... .

Launch

MP2, MP7

Five friends set out with their packs for a long hike. After a while, the trailing hiker yells out, "This just isn't fair!"

22 lb · 16 lb · 12 lb · 10 lb · 8 lb

What do you think the hiker means? Find a way to make the situation fair.

Reflect Could you have made it fair by having everyone carry the median amount of weight shown?

_____

_____

_____

_____

_____

Got It?

PART 1 Got It (1 of 2)

What is the mean of the data set?

> 4, 2, 90, 6, 0, 12

PART 1 Got It (2 of 2)

Will the mean always be a value in the original data set? Explain.

Discuss with a classmate

Read your explanations for this problem. How are they alike? How are they different? Is one clearer than another?

PART 2 Got It

A tour guide created a report that shows the revenue of his tourist agency for one week. As he went to post his report, he smudged a value on the table. What is the missing value?

Tourist Agency Revenue

Sun	Mon	Tues	Wed	Thurs	Fri	Sat
$6,400	$2,500	$3,200	$2,600	$4,900		$6,200

Mean daily revenue: $4,400

Got It?

PART 3 Got It (1 of 2)

A track coach wants to make sure his athletes are drinking enough water before their workouts. He records how many glasses of water they drank today: 3, 3, 4, 8, 9, and 10 glasses. Is the mean an appropriate measure of center for this data set? Use a graph to justify your reasoning.

PART 3 Got It (2 of 2)

Why is the mean affected more by stray data values than the median is?

Close and Check

Focus Question

MP3, MP6

You've learned about the median of a collection of numbers. How can you represent a collection of numbers using a different number? How do you choose which number to use?

_____

_____

_____

_____

Do you know HOW?

1. What is the mean of the data set?
   37, 50, 53, 17, 10, 49

   [   ]

2. Your teacher says the mean of your test scores is 87. You have kept a record of all your test scores except one. What is the value of your missing test score?

My Test Scores						
95		93	91	90	93	63

3. Your teacher says you may drop your lowest score if it raises the mean. What would be the new mean of your test scores?

   [   ]

Do you UNDERSTAND?

4. **Vocabulary** Your classmate describes the data below by using a measure of center, 21.5.

   25, 4, 78, 18, 7, 63

   Explain how you know which measure of center he used.

   _____

   _____

   _____

   _____

   _____

5. **Reasoning** Did your classmate use the appropriate measure of center to best describe the data? Explain.

   _____

   _____

   _____

   _____

   _____

Variability

Digital Resources

CCSS: **6.SP.A.2:** Understand that a set of data ... has a distribution which can be described by its ... spread ... . **6.SP.A.3:** Recognize that ... A measure of variation describes how its values vary with a single number. Also, **6.SP.B.5, 6.SP.B.5c.**

Launch

C MP3, MP8

While developing a new sports drink, you ask members of two groups how many sports drinks they buy each month.

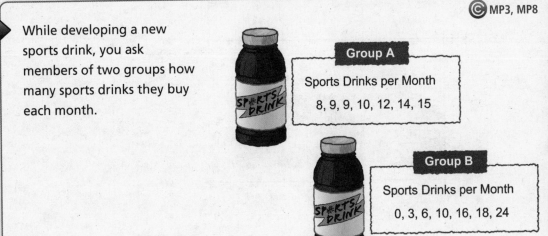

Group A

Sports Drinks per Month

8, 9, 9, 10, 12, 14, 15

Group B

Sports Drinks per Month

0, 3, 6, 10, 16, 18, 24

• •

Use the data. Give at least one way the groups are alike and one way they are different. Which group would you like to have test your new drink? Why?

Reflect Suppose you knew only the mean number of drinks purchased by each group per month. Would you choose a different group to test your drink? Explain.

_____

_____

_____

Got It?

PART 1 Got It (1 of 2)

Which data display or displays show a data set with high variability?

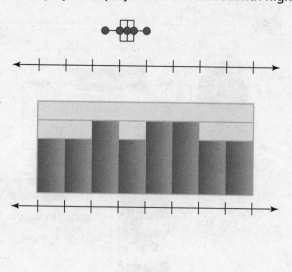

PART 1 Got It (2 of 2)

What kind of variability can you expect in the responses to this statistical equation? Explain.

How many bicycles does each student in your class own?

PART 2 Got It (1 of 2)

Find the range of the data set.

17, 39, 80, 56, 12, 8, 94

Got It?

Is the range affected by stray data values? Explain.

PART 3 Got It

In a science experiment, each team of students measures the mass of a penny on a beam balance. Which statements below are true?

Mass of a Penny (grams)

Team 1: 3.11	Team 6: 3.14	Team 11: 2.87
Team 2: 3.10	Team 7: 3.11	Team 12: 2.96
Team 3: 3.16	Team 8: 3.11	Team 13: 3.11
Team 4: 3.15	Team 9: 3.09	Team 14: 3.05
Team 5: 3.12	Team 10: 2.88	Team 15: 2.99

I.   The range of the results is 0.12 g.
II. The range of the results is 0.29 g.
III. There is high variability in the results.
IV. There is low variability in the results.

Close and Check

Focus Question

You know how to represent the middle of a collection of numbers. What else do you need to understand a data set?

_____

_____

_____

Do you know HOW?

1. Look at each graph. Label the variability as low, high, or none. Then find the range.

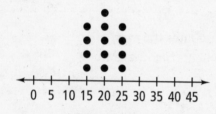

variability: [　　　　　]

range: [　　]

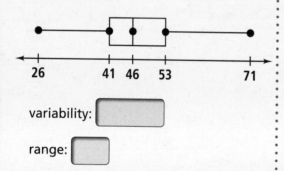

variability: [　　　　　]

range: [　　]

Do you UNDERSTAND?

2. **Writing** A veterinarian records the weight of the pets she sees in her office. Describe the data set, including measures of center and variability.

Weight of Pets (pounds)			
40.8	15.9	2.7	52.8
23	7	48.5	36
0.3	63.2	6	14.6

_____

_____

_____

_____

3. **Reasoning** If the maximum value is ignored, does the variability change? Explain.

_____

_____

_____

_____

_____

16-4 Interquartile Range

Digital Resources

CCSS: 6.SP.A.3: Recognize that ... a measure of variation describes how its values vary with a single number. **6.SP.B.5:** Summarize numerical data sets in relation to their context, such as by: **6.SP.B.5c:** Giving ... variability (interquartile range ...) ... .

Launch

 MP1, MP4

Which race was more competitive, this year's or last year's?

This Year's Car Race

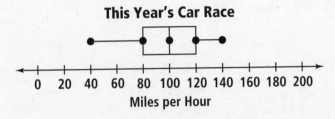

Miles per Hour

Last Year's Car Race

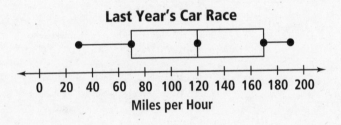

Miles per Hour

· ·

Tell how you know, and provide a possible reason for the difference in race results.

Reflect Suppose you knew only the median speed of each race. Could you tell which race was more competitive?

_____

_____

_____

Got It?

PART 1 Got It (1 of 2)

Which data set or sets have an interquartile range of 25?

I.

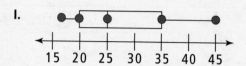

II.

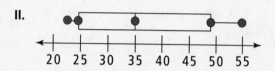

PART 1 Got It (2 of 2)

Why might the interquartile range be a more useful measure of spread than the range in certain situations?

Got It?

The data set shows the lowest pitches, measured in hertz (Hz), that various animals can hear. Find the interquartile range of the set of lowest pitches. What does the interquartile range tell about the lowest pitches various animals can hear?

Hearing Ranges of Animals

Animal	Lowest Pitch (Hz)	Animal	Lowest Pitch (Hz)
bat	2,000	horse	55
beluga whale	1,000	human	64
bullfrog	100	mouse	1,000
canary	250	opossum	500
cat	45	owl	200
chicken	125	parakeet	200
cow	23	porpoise	75
dog	67	rabbit	360
elephant	16	raccoon	100
goldfish	20	rat	200

Got It?

PART 2 Got It (2 of 2)

The interquartile range of the set of lowest pitches that various animals can hear is 245.5 Hz, and the interquartile range of the set of highest pitches that the same animals can hear is 59,750 Hz. Which set of pitches is more consistent among these animals? Explain.

PART 3 Got It (1 of 2)

The data set shows the average weights of various animals. Determine which statements are true.

I.   The first quartile is 9.
II. The third quartile is 6,020.
III. The interquartile range is 6,011.

Average Weight	
Animal	**Weights (lbs.)**
Cat	10
Dog	37
Dolphin	350
Elephant	11,500
Gorilla	330
Mouse	0.04
Rabbit	9
Tiger	540
Turtle	2
Whale	121,254

PART 3 Got It (2 of 2)

What does it mean when the interquartile range is close to zero?

Close and Check

Focus Question

How can you represent the variability of a collection of numbers with one number? Why would you want to?

_____

_____

_____

_____

Do you know HOW?

1. The drama club records the total number of tickets sold for each performance. Find the interquartile range (IQR) for the given data set.

Number of Tickets Sold

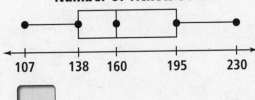

107   138   160   195   230

2. The summer reading program records the number of books that each participant reads. Use the data to complete the table.

32, 16, 43, 10, 44, 31, 48, 6
19, 27, 39, 21, 11, 25, 8, 36

Books Read over Summer Break			
Median		First Quartile	
Minimum		Third Quartile	
Maximum		Interquartile Range	

Do you UNDERSTAND?

3. **Reasoning** What does the IQR tell you about the variability of the following data set?

Monthly High Temperatures (°F)

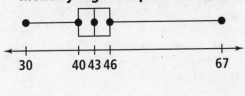

30   40 43 46   67

_____

_____

_____

_____

4. **Writing** Explain how IQR and variability are related.

_____

_____

_____

_____

_____

This page intentionally left blank.

Mean Absolute Deviation

CCSS: 6.SP.B.5: Summarize numerical data sets in relation to their context, such as by: **6.SP.B.5c:** Giving … variability (… mean absolute deviation) … Describing … any striking deviations from the overall pattern … . Also, **6.SP.A.3.**

Launch

 MP2, MP3

A coffee shop wants to serve coffee at the same temperature every time for best taste. On average, both shop workers hit the shop goal. But the shop manager thinks one worker does a better job than the other.

Coffee Temperature by Cup (°F)							
Worker A	155	160	150	145	170	175	165
Worker B	155	160	163	157	162	158	165

Tell what temperature the shop wants the coffee to be. Then explain who the manager thinks did a better job.

Reflect Can you think of another example of when you want something done just right and not too much or too little?

_____

_____

_____

_____

Got It?

PART 1 Got It

Tanner, one of the dogs that you walk, performed in a dog trick competition. The dot plot shows the scores from the entire competition. The mean is 6. Tanner's score is represented by the circled dot. What is the deviation of Tanner's score from the mean?

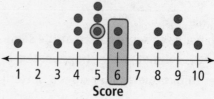

Dog Trick Competition Results

Score

PART 2 Got It (1 of 2)

The deviation of each dog's score from the mean is shown in place of its dot. Find the mean absolute deviation of the scores.

Deviations of Competition Scores

```
                    −1
              −2 −1              +3
              −2 −1  │ 0 │  +2 +3
        −5    −3 −2 −1 │ 0 │ +1 +2 +3 +4
        ◄──┬──┬──┬──┬──┬──┬──┬──┬──┬──►
           1  2  3  4  5  6  7  8  9  10
                       Score
```

PART 2 Got It (2 of 2)

Tanner's score is represented by the numeral 1. If the mean of the competition scores is 6, and the mean absolute deviation is 2, how did Tanner do?

Absolute Deviations of Competition Scores

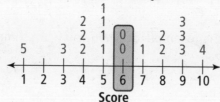

Score

Got It?

The data set shows the maximum lifespan of various animals.

The mean is 58. Which animal's lifespan has an absolute deviation from the mean of 37?

Maximum Lifespan	
Animal	**Years**
Cat	30
Dog	24
Dolphin	52
Elephant	65
Gorilla	21
Mouse	4
Rabbit	9
Tiger	26
Turtle	138
Whale	211

Median and mean are measures of center. Interquartile range and mean absolute deviation are measures of variability related to median and mean, respectively. Which measure of variability would you use for this data set? Explain.

Data set: 2, 4, 6, 7, 8, 9, 14, 15, 16, 18, 19, 60

Close and Check

Focus Question

You've learned about the interquartile range of a collction of numbers. How can you represent the variability of a collection of numbers using a different number? How do you choose which number to use?

_____

_____

_____

_____

Do you know HOW?

1. The mean of a data set is 5. The minimum of the data is 2. What is the deviation of the minimum?

   [ ]

Use the graph for Exercises 2 and 3.

Age of Skateboarders at Park

```
          14  15  16  17  18  19
```

2. The mean of the data is 16. Fill in the absolute deviation for each data point.

3. What is the mean absolute deviation (MAD) of the data?

   [ ]

Do you UNDERSTAND?

4. **Compare and Contrast** How is the deviation of a data value the same as and different from the absolute deviation of that data value?

   _____

   _____

   _____

   _____

5. **Reasoning** If the mean is a better measure of center for a given data set, does the MAD or interquartile range (IQR) better represent the variability? Explain.

   _____

   _____

   _____

   _____

   _____

Problem Solving

CCSS: 6.SP.B.5: Summarize numerical data sets in relation to their context, such as by: **6.SP.B.5d:** Relating the choice of measures of center and variability to the shape of the data distribution and the context in which the data were gathered. Also, **6.SP.A.3.**

Launch

Ⓒ MP1, MP6

You are the coach of the girls' basketball team. Two of your players each claim to be the star player on the team.

Use at least one statistical concept – median, mean, variability, or mean absolute deviation – to compare the players. Describe the qualities of each player and decide which player is the team's star.

Points Per Game

Player A	Player B
28, 8, 11, 4, 33, 2, 40	16, 19, 14, 18, 20, 17, 22

Reflect Suppose it's the eighth game of the season. Do you have the information you need to decide who should take the last shot? If not, what else would you want to know?

_____

_____

_____

_____

Got It?

PART 1 Got It

You found the mean absolute deviation of the humidity level in City A to be 9%, and the mean absolute deviation of the humidity level in City B to be 26%. If you wanted to go to college in a place with low humidity levels, which city would you choose to live in? Why?

PART 2 Got It (1 of 2)

The student council is determining the winner of a two-classroom running race. The table shows the race times of the students of Classroom A and Classroom B. The student council wants to give the prize to the faster class. Compare the mean of both classes to determine the winner.

Race Times (seconds)

Classroom A	12.7	13.0	13.3	13.4	14.0	14.1	15.2	15.4	15.4	15.5	15.8	17.2	18.3	20.0
Classroom B	13.2	13.5	13.8	13.9	13.9	14.1	14.2	14.7	15.6	15.9	16.4	17.9	18.1	18.3

PART 2 Got It (2 of 2)

The table shows measures of center for Classroom A and Classroom B. If you had to decide the winner based on a measure of center, which classroom would you choose? Explain.

Classroom A	Classroom B
median = 15.3	median = 14.45
mean ≈ 15.2	mean ≈ 15.3

Got It?

PART 3 Got It (1 of 2)

The student council is determining the winner of a two-classroom running race. The table shows the race times of the students of Classroom A and Classroom B. The student council wants to give the prize to the class that is the most consistent. Compare the interquartile ranges of the classrooms to determine the winner.

Race Times (seconds)

Classroom A	12.7	13.0	13.3	13.4	14.0	14.1	15.2	15.4	15.4	15.5	15.8	17.2	18.3	20.0
Classroom B	13.2	13.5	13.8	13.9	13.9	14.1	14.2	14.7	15.6	15.9	16.4	17.9	18.1	18.3

PART 3 Got It (2 of 2)

The table shows measures of variation of Classroom A and Classroom B. Which measure of variability would you use to choose the winner? Explain.

Classroom A	Classroom B
Range = 7.3	Range = 5.1
IQR = 2.4	IQR = 2.5

Close and Check

Focus Question

MP3, MP4

How can you use measures of center and variability to make decisions?

_____

_____

_____

_____

Do you know HOW?

1. You perform a science experiment that measures plant growth. You give only water to the control group. You give a special fertilizer to the variable group. You measure the heights of the plants in each group after 2 weeks.

Plant Heights (centimeters)

control group			variable group		
4	4.2	3.6	7.3	3.4	3.8
3.8	4.3	4.5	6.7	6.9	3.6
3.6	3.3	4.7	6.8	6.1	4.9

Use the mean of the plant heights to determine which set of plants grew taller.

[   ]

Use the mean absolute deviation (MAD) to determine which set of plants grew more consistently.

[   ]

Do you UNDERSTAND?

2. Writing The MAD of annual income is $12,000 for city A and $3,000 for city B. Explain whether this is enough information to decide where to seek employment.

_____

_____

_____

_____

_____

3. Reasoning Should Team A or Team B advance to the next competition? Justify your decision.

Long Jump Distances (meters)							
A	5.67	6.55	7.12	5.94	6.83	6.35	6.34
B	7.86	5.09	6.86	5.68	5.86	5.78	7.67

_____

_____

_____

_____

New Vocabulary: absolute deviation from the mean, deviation from the mean, interquartile range, mean absolute deviation, measure of variability, measures of center, median, range
Review Vocabulary: box plot, cluster, gap, maximum, minimum

Vocabulary Review

Identify two challenging vocabulary terms from this topic. Write one vocabulary term in the center oval, and fill in the surrounding boxes with details that will help you better understand the term.

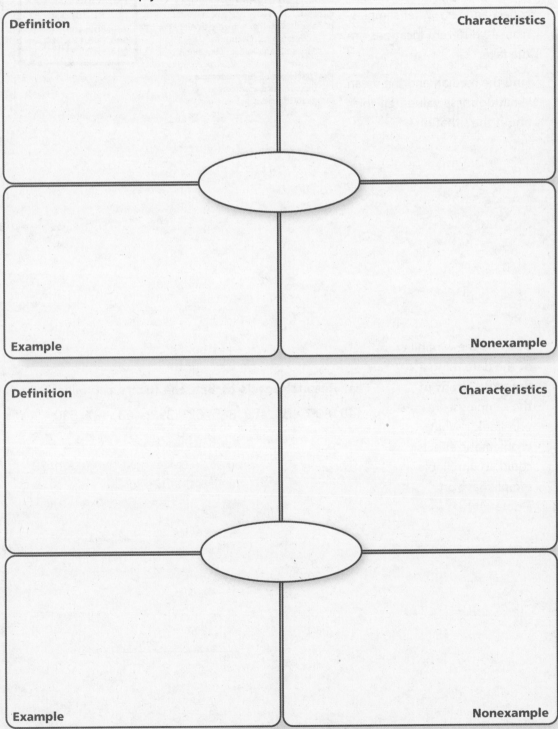

Pull It All Together

TASK 1

Suppose you are a student reporter covering unsafe levels of benzene in the town's drinking water. While doing research for your article, you collect and test water samples from 10 different locations on the lake.

Find the median and the mean. What do these values tell you about the situation?

Drinking Water Contaminated by Gasoline Leak

Recent tests have detected high levels of the toxic chemical benzene in the lake that supplies the town's drinking water. Benzene poses a serious health risk to people and animals, and it is deadly to plants and fish. The maximum contaminant level of benzene allowed in public water is 5 ppb (parts per billion). **Because benzene is a component of gasoline**, we reached a nearby factory that uses gasoline for

> Test results: Levels of Benzene (parts per billion)
> 449, 800, 405, 488, 385, 521, 392, 463, 427, 530

Describe the variability of the data using a dot plot. Do any of the samples seem unreliable? What problematic effects could an unreliable sample have on a data set?

> **Test Results: Levels of Benzene (parts per billion)**
> 449, 800, 405, 488, 385, 521, 392, 463, 427, 530

Pull It All Together

TASK 2

Three months later, a chemical company contacts you about their recent samples they collected from the lake. How does their data set differ from yours? Explain your reasoning with a dot plot.

Company Test Results: Levels of Benzene (parts per billion)

212, 211, 205, 199, 212, 217, 217, 208, 218, 199

This page intentionally left blank.

English/Spanish Glossary

············ **A** ·················

Absolute deviation from the mean Absolute deviation measures the distance that the data value is from the mean. You find the absolute deviation by taking the absolute value of the deviation of a data value. Absolute deviations are always nonnegative.

Desviación absoluta de la media La desviación absoluta mide la distancia a la que un valor se encuentra de la media. Para hallar la desviación absoluta, tomas el valor absoluto de la desviación de un valor. Las desviaciones absolutas siempre son no negativas.

Absolute value The absolute value of a number a is the distance between a and zero on a number line. The absolute value of a is written as $|a|$.

Valor absoluto El valor absoluto de un número a es la distancia entre a y cero en la recta numérica. El valor absoluto de a se escribe como $|a|$.

Accuracy The accuracy of an estimate or measurement is the degree to which it agrees with an accepted or actual value of that measurement.

Exactitud La exactitud de una estimación o medición es el grado de concordancia con un valor aceptado o real de esa medición.

Action In a probability situation, an action is a process with an uncertain result.

Acción En una situación de probabilidad, una acción es el proceso con un resultado incierto.

Acute angle An acute angle is an angle with a measure between 0° and 90°.

Ángulo agudo Un ángulo agudo es un ángulo que mide entre 0° y 90°.

Acute triangle An acute triangle is a triangle with three acute angles.

Triángulo acutángulo Un triángulo acutángulo es un triángulo que tiene tres ángulos agudos.

Addend Addends are the numbers that are added together to find a sum.

Sumando Los sumandos son los números que se suman para hallar un total.

English/Spanish Glossary

Additive inverses Two numbers that have a sum of 0.

Inversos de suma Dos números cuya suma es 0.

Adjacent angles Two angles are adjacent angles if they share a vertex and a side, but have no interior points in common.

Ángulos adyacentes Dos ángulos son adyacentes si tienen un vértice y un lado en común, pero no comparten puntos internos.

Algebraic expression An algebraic expression is a mathematical phrase that consists of variables, numbers, and operation symbols.

Expresión algebraica Una expresión algebraica es una frase matemática que consiste en variables, números y símbolos de operaciones.

Analyze To analyze is to think about and understand facts and details about a given set of information. Analyzing can involve providing a written summary supported by factual information, diagrams, charts, tables, or any combination of these.

Analizar Analizar es pensar en los datos y detalles de cierta información y comprenderlos. El análisis puede incluir la presentación de un resumen escrito sustentado por información objetiva, diagramas, tablas o una combinación de esos elementos.

Angle An angle is a figure formed by two rays with a common endpoint.

Ángulo Un ángulo es una figura formada por dos semirrectas que tienen un extremo en común.

Angle of rotation The angle of rotation is the number of degrees a figure is rotated.

Ángulo de rotación El ángulo de rotación es el número de grados que se rota una figura.

Annual salary The amount of money earned at a job in one year.

Salario annual La cantidad de dinero ganó en un trabajo en un año.

Area The area of a figure is the number of square units the figure encloses.

Área El área de una figura es el número de unidades cuadradas que ocupa.

English/Spanish Glossary

Area of a circle The formula for the area of a circle is $A = \pi r^2$, where A represents the area and r represents the radius of the circle.

Área de un círculo La fórmula del área de un círculo es $A = \pi r^2$, donde A representa el área y r representa el radio del círculo.

Area of a parallelogram The formula for the area of a parallelogram is $A = bh$, where A represents the area, b represents a base, and h is the corresponding height.

Área de un paralelogramo La fórmula del área de un paralelogramo es $A = bh$, donde A representa el área, b representa una base y h es la altura correspondiente.

Area of a rectangle The formula for the area of a rectangle is $A = bh$, where A represents the area, b represents the base, and h represents the height of the rectangle.

Área de un rectángulo La fórmula del área de un rectángulo es $A = bh$, donde A representa el área, b representa la base y h representa la altura del rectángulo.

Area of a square The formula for the area of a square is $A = s^2$, where A represents the area and s represents a side length.

Área de un cuadrado La fórmula del área de un cuadrado es $A = s^2$, donde A representa el área y l representa la longitud de un lado.

Area of a trapezoid The formula for the area of a trapezoid is $A = \frac{1}{2}h(b_1 + b_2)$, where A represents the area, b_1 and b_2 represent the bases, and h represents the height between the bases.

El área de un trapezoide La fórmula para el área de un trapezoide es $A = \frac{1}{2}h(b_1 + b_2)$, donde A representa el área, b_1 y b_2 representan las bases, y h representa la altura entre las bases.

Area of a triangle The formula for the area of a triangle is $A = \frac{1}{2}bh$, where A represents the area, b represents the length of a base, and h represents the corresponding height.

Área de un triángulo La fórmula del área de un triángulo es $A = \frac{1}{2}bh$, donde A representa el área, b representa la longitud de una base y h representa la altura correspondiente.

Asset An asset is money you have or property of value that you own.

Ventaja Una ventaja es dinero que tiene o la propiedad de valor que usted posee.

English/Spanish Glossary

Associative Property of Addition For any numbers a, b, and c:
$$(a + b) + c = a + (b + c)$$

Propiedad asociativa de la suma Para los números cualesquiera a, b y c:
$$(a + b) + c = a + (b + c)$$

Associative Property of Multiplication For any numbers a, b, and c:
$$(a \cdot b) \cdot c = a \cdot (b \cdot c)$$

Propiedad asociativa de la multiplicación Para los números cualesquiera a, b y c:
$$(a \cdot b) \cdot c = a \cdot (b \cdot c)$$

Average of two numbers The average of two numbers is the value that represents the middle of two numbers. It is found by adding the two numbers together and dividing by 2.

Promedio de dos números El promedio de dos números es el valor que está justo en el medio de esos dos números. Se halla sumando los dos números y dividiendo el resultado por 2.

B

Balance The balance in an account is the principal amount plus the interest earned.

Saldo El saldo de una cuenta es el capital más el interés ganado.

Balance of a checking Account The balance of a checking account is the amount of money in the checking account.

El equilibrio de una Cuenta Corriente Bancaria El equilibrio de una cuenta corriente bancaria es la cantidad de dinero en la cuenta corriente bancaria.

Balance of a loan The balance of a loan is the remaining unpaid principal.

El equilibrio de un préstamo El equilibrio de un préstamo es el director impagado restante.

Bar diagram A bar diagram is a way to represent part to whole relationships.

Diagrama de barras Un diagrama de barras es una forma de representar una relación de parte a entero.

Base The base is the repeated factor of a number written in exponential form.

Base La base es el factor repetido de un número escrito en forma exponencial.

English/Spanish Glossary

Base area of a cone The base area of a cone is the area of a circle. Base Area = πr^2.

Área de la base de un cono El área de la base de un cono es el área de un círculo. El área de la base = πr^2.

Base of a cone The base of a cone is a circle with radius r.

Base de un cono La base de un cono es un círculo con radio r.

Base of a cylinder A base of a cylinder is one of a pair of parallel circular faces that are the same size.

Base de un cilindro Una base de un cilindro es una de dos caras circulares paralelas que tienen el mismo tamaño.

Base of a parallelogram A base of a parallelogram is any side of the parallelogram.

Base de un paralelogramo La base de un paralelogramo es cualquiera de los lados del paralelogramo.

Base of a prism A base of a prism is one of a pair of parallel polygonal faces that are the same size and shape. A prism is named for the shape of its bases.

Base de un prisma La base de un prisma es una de las dos caras poligonales paralelas que tienen el mismo tamaño y la misma forma. El nombre de un prisma depende de la forma de sus bases.

Base of a pyramid A base of a pyramid is a polygonal face that does not connect to the vertex.

Base de una pirámide La base de una pirámide es una cara poligonal que no se conecta con el vértice.

Base of a triangle The base of a triangle is any side of the triangle.

Base de un triángulo La base de un triángulo es cualquiera de los lados del triángulo.

Benchmark A benchmark is a number you can use as a reference point for other numbers.

Referencia Una referencia es un número que usted puede utilizar como un punto de referencia para otros números.

English/Spanish Glossary

Bias A bias is a tendency toward a particular perspective that is different from the overall perspective of the population.

Sesgo Un sesgo es una tendencia hacia una perspectiva particular que es diferente de la perspectiva general de la población.

Biased sample In a biased sample, the number of subjects in the sample with the trait that you are studying is not proportional to the number of members in the population with that trait. A biased sample does not accurately represent the population.

Muestra sesgada En una muestra sesgada, el número de sujetos de la muestra que tiene la característica que se está estudiando no es proporcional al número de miembros de la población que tienen esa característica. Una muestra sesgada no representa con exactitud la población.

Bivariate categorical data Bivariate categorical data pairs categorical data collected about two variables of the same population.

Datos bivariados por categorías Los datos bivariados por categorías agrupan pares de datos obtenidos acerca de dos variables de la misma población.

Bivariate data Bivariate data is comprised of pairs of linked observations about a population.

Datos bivariados Los datos bivariados se forman a partir de pares de observaciones relacionadas sobre una población.

Box plot A box plot is a statistical graph that shows the distribution of a data set by marking five boundary points where data occur along a number line. Unlike a dot plot or a histogram, a box plot does not show frequency.

Diagrama de cajas Un diagrama de cajas es un diagrama de estadísticas que muestra la distribución de un conjunto de datos al marcar cinco puntos de frontera donde se hallan los datos sobre una recta numérica. A diferencia del diagrama de puntos o el histograma, el diagrama de cajas no muestra la frecuencia.

Budget A budget is a plan for how you will spend your money.

Presupuesto Un presupuesto es un plan para cómo gastará su dinero.

English/Spanish Glossary

C

Categorical data Categorical data consist of data that fall into categories.

Datos por categorías Los datos por categorías son datos que se pueden clasificar en categorías.

Center of a circle The center of a circle is the point inside the circle that is the same distance from all points on the circle. Name a circle by its center.

Centro de un círculo El centro de un círculo es el punto dentro del círculo que está a la misma distancia de todos los puntos del círculo. Un círculo se identifica por su centro.

Center of a regular polygon The center of a regular polygon is the point that is equidistant from its vertices.

Centro de un polígono regular El centro de un polígono regular es el punto equidistante de todos sus vértices.

Center of rotation The center of rotation is a fixed point about which a figure is rotated.

Centro de rotación El centro de rotación es el punto fijo alrededor del cual se rota una figura.

Check register A record that shows all of the transactions for a bank account, including withdrawals, deposits, and transfers. It also shows the balance of the account after each transaction.

Verifique registro Un registro que muestra todas las transacciones para una cuenta bancaria, inclusive retiradas, los depósitos, y las transferencias. También muestra el equilibrio de la cuenta después de cada transacción.

Circle A circle is the set of all points in a plane that are the same distance from a given point, called the center.

Círculo Un círculo es el conjunto de todos los puntos de un plano que están a la misma distancia de un punto dado, llamado centro.

Circle graph A circle graph is a graph that represents a whole divided into parts.

Gráfica circular Una gráfica circular es una gráfica que representa un todo dividido en partes.

English/Spanish Glossary

Circumference of a circle The circumference of a circle is the distance around the circle. The formula for the circumference of a circle is $C = \pi d$, where C represents the circumference and d represents the diameter of the circle.

Circunferencia de un círculo La circunferencia de un círculo es la distancia alrededor del círculo. La fórmula de la circunferencia de un círculo es $C = \pi d$, donde C representa la circunferencia y d representa el diámetro del círculo.

Cluster A cluster is a group of points that lie close together on a scatter plot.

Grupo Un grupo es un conjunto de puntos que están agrupados en un diagrama de dispersión.

Coefficient A coefficient is the number part of a term that contains a variable.

Coeficiente Un coeficiente es la parte numérica de un término que contiene una variable.

Common denominator A common denominator is a number that is the denominator of two or more fractions.

Común denominador Un común denominador es un número que es el denominador de dos o más fracciones.

Common multiple A common multiple is a multiple that two or more numbers share.

Múltiplo común Un múltiplo común es un múltiplo que comparten dos o más números.

Commutative Property of Addition For any numbers a and b: $a + b = b + a$

Propiedad conmutativa de la suma Para los números cualesquiera a y b: $a + b = b + a$

Commutative Property of Multiplication For any numbers a and b: $a \cdot b = b \cdot a$

Propiedad conmutativa de la multiplicación Para los números cualesquiera a y b: $a \cdot b = b \cdot a$

Comparative inference A comparative inference is an inference made by interpreting and comparing two sets of data.

Inferencia comparativa Una inferencia comparativa es una inferencia que se hace al interpretar y comparar dos conjuntos de datos.

English/Spanish Glossary

Compare To compare is to tell or show how two things are alike or different.

Comparar Comparar es describir o mostrar en qué se parecen o en qué se diferencian dos cosas.

Compatible numbers Compatible numbers are numbers that are easy to compute mentally.

Números compatibles Los números compatibles son números fáciles de calcular mentalmente.

Complementary angles Two angles are complementary angles if the sum of their measures is 90°. Complementary angles that are adjacent form a right angle.

Ángulos complementarios Dos ángulos son complementarios si la suma de sus medidas es 90°. Los ángulos complementarios que son adyacentes forman un ángulo recto.

Complex fraction A complex fraction is a fraction $\frac{A}{B}$ where A and/or B are fractions and B is not zero.

Fracción compleja Una fracción compleja es una fracción $\frac{A}{B}$ donde A y/o B son fracciones y B es distinto de cero.

Compose a shape To compose a shape, join two (or more) shapes so that there is no gap or overlap.

Componer una figura Para componer una figura, debes unir dos (o más) figuras de modo que entre ellas no queden espacios ni superposiciones.

Composite figure A composite figure is the combination of two or more figures into one object.

Figura compuesta Una figura compuesta es la combinación de dos o más figuras en un objeto.

Composite number A composite number is a whole number greater than 1 with more than two factors.

Número compuesto Un número compuesto es un número entero mayor que 1 con más de dos factores.

Compound event A compound event is an event associated with a multi-step action. A compound event is composed of events that are the outcomes of the steps of the action.

Evento compuesto Un evento compuesto es un evento que se relaciona con una acción de varios pasos. Un evento compuesto se compone de eventos que son los resultados de los pasos de una acción.

English/Spanish Glossary

Compound interest Compound interest is interest paid on both the principal and the interest earned in previous interest periods. To calculate compound interest, use the formula $B = p(1 + r)^n$, where B is the balance in the account, p is the principal, r is the annual interest rate, and n is the time in years that the account earns interest.

Interés compuesto El interés compuesto es el interés que se paga sobre el capital y el interés obtenido en períodos de interés anteriores. Para calcular el interés compuesto, usa la fórmula $B = c(1 + r)^n$ donde B es el saldo de la cuenta, c es el capital, r es la tasa de interés anual y n es el tiempo en años en que la cuenta obtiene un interés.

Cone A cone is a three-dimensional figure with one circular base and one vertex.

Cono Un cono es una figura tridimensional con una base circular y un vértice.

Congruent figures Two two-dimensional figures are congruent $\cong$ if the second can be obtained from the first by a sequence of rotations, reflections, and translations.

Figuras congruentes Dos figuras bidimensionales son congruentes $\cong$ si la segunda puede obtenerse a partir de la primera mediante una secuencia de rotaciones, reflexiones y traslaciones.

Conjecture A conjecture is a statement that you believe to be true but have not yet proved to be true.

Conjetura Una conjetura es un enunciado que crees que es verdadero, pero que todavía no has comprobado que sea verdadero.

Constant A constant is a term that only contains a number.

Constante Una constante es un término que solamente contiene un número.

Constant of proportionality In a proportional relationship, one quantity y is a constant multiple of the other quantity x. The constant multiple is called the constant of proportionality. The constant of proportionality is equal to the ratio $\frac{y}{x}$.

Constante de proporcionalidad En una relación proporcional, una cantidad y es un múltiplo constante de la otra cantidad x. El múltiplo constante se llama constante de proporcionalidad. La constante de proporcionalidad es igual a la razón $\frac{y}{x}$.

English/Spanish Glossary

Construct To construct is to make something, such as an argument, by organizing ideas. Constructing an argument can involve a written response, equations, diagrams, charts, tables, or a combination of these.

Construir Construir es hacer o crear algo, como se construye un argumento al organizar ideas. Para construir un argumento puede usarse una respuesta escrita, ecuaciones, diagramas, tablas o una combinación de esos elementos.

Convenience sampling Convenience sampling is a sampling method in which a researcher chooses members of the population that are convenient and available. Many researchers use this sampling technique because it is fast and inexpensive. It does not require the researcher to keep track of everyone in the population.

Muestra de conveniencia Una muestra de conveniencia es un método de muestreo en el que un investigador escoge miembros de la población que están convenientemente disponibles. Muchos investigadores usan esta técnica de muestreo porque es rápida y no es costosa. No requiere que el investigador lleve un registro de cada miembro de la población.

Cost of attendance The cost of attendance of one year of college is the sum of all of your expenses during the year.

El costo de asistencia El costo de asistencia de un año del colegio es la suma de todos sus gastos durante el año.

Cost of credit The cost of credit for a loan is the difference between the total cost and the principal.

El costo de crédito El costo de crédito para un préstamo es la diferencia entre el coste total y el director.

Converse of the Pythagorean Theorem If the sum of the squares of the lengths of two sides of a triangle equals the square of the length of the third side, then the triangle is a right triangle. If $a^2 + b^2 = c^2$, then the triangle is a right triangle.

Expresión recíproca del Teorema de Pitágoras Si la suma del cuadrado de la longitud de dos lados de un triángulo es igual al cuadrado de la longitud del tercer lado, entonces el triángulo es un triángulo rectángulo. $a^2 + b^2 = c^2$, entonces el triángulo es un triángulo rectángulo.

Conversion factor A conversion factor is a rate that equals 1.

Factor de conversión Un factor de conversión es una tasa que es igual a 1.

English/Spanish Glossary

Coordinate plane A coordinate plane is formed by a horizontal number line called the *x*-axis and a vertical number line called the *y*-axis.

Plano de coordenadas Un plano de coordenadas está formado por una recta numérica horizontal llamada eje de las *x* y una recta numérica vertical llamada eje de las *y*.

Corresponding angles Corresponding angles lie on the same side of a transversal and in corresponding positions.

Ángulos correspondientes Los ángulos correspondientes se ubican al mismo lado de una secante y en posiciones correspondientes.

Counterexample A counterexample is a specific example that shows that a conjecture is false.

Contraejemplo Un contraejemplo es un ejemplo específico que muestra que una conjetura es falsa.

Counting Principle If there are *m* possible outcomes of one action and *n* possible outcomes of a second action, then there are $m \cdot n$ outcomes of the first action followed by the second action.

Principio de conteo Si hay *m* resultados posibles de una acción y *n* resultados posibles de una segunda acción, entonces hay $m \cdot n$ resultados de la primera acción seguida de la segunda acción.

Coupon A coupon is part of a printed or online advertisement entitling the holder to a discount at checkout.

Cupón Un cupón forma parte de un anuncio impreso o en línea que permite al poseedor a un descuento en comprueba.

Credit card A credit card is a card issued by a lender that can be used to borrow money or make purchases on credit.

Tarjeta de crédito Una tarjeta de crédito es una tarjeta publicada por un prestamista que puede ser utilizado para pedir dinero prestado o compras de marca a cuenta.

Credit history A credit history shows how a consumer has managed credit in the past.

Acredite la historia Una historia del crédito muestra cómo un consumidor ha manejado crédito en el pasado.

English/Spanish Glossary

Credit report A report that shows personal information about a consumer and details about the consumer's credit history.

Acredite reporte Un reporte que muestra información personal sobre un consumidor y detalles acerca de la historia del crédito del consumidor.

Critique A critique is a careful judgment in which you give your opinion about the good and bad parts of something, such as how a problem was solved.

Crítica Una crítica es una evaluación cuidadosa en la que das tu opinión acerca de las partes positivas y negativas de algo, como la manera en la que se resolvió un problema.

Cross section A cross section is the intersection of a three-dimensional figure and a plane.

Corte transversal Un corte transversal es la intersección de una figura tridimensional y un plano.

Cube A cube is a rectangular prism whose faces are all squares.

Cubo Un cubo es un prisma rectangular cuyas caras son todas cuadrados.

Cube root The cube root of a number, n, is a number whose cube equals n.

Raíz cúbica La raíz cúbica de un número, n, es un número que elevado al cubo es igual a n.

Cubic unit A cubic unit is the volume of a cube that measures 1 unit on each edge.

Unidad cúbica Una unidad cúbica es el volumen de un cubo en el que cada arista mide 1 unidad.

Cylinder A cylinder is a three-dimensional figure with two parallel circular bases that are the same size.

Cilindro Un cilindro es una figura tridimensional con dos bases circulares paralelas que tienen el mismo tamaño.

D

Data Data are pieces of information collected by asking questions, measuring, or making observations about the real world.

Datos Los datos son información reunida mediante preguntas, mediciones u observaciones sobre la vida diaria.

English/Spanish Glossary

Debit card A debit card is a card issued by a bank that is linked a customer's bank account, normally a checking account. A debit card can normally be used to withdraw money from an ATM or to make a purchase.

Tarjeta de débito Una tarjeta de débito es una tarjeta publicada por un banco que es ligado la cuenta bancaria de un cliente, normalmente una cuenta corriente bancaria. Una tarjeta de débito puede ser utilizada normalmente retirar dinero de una ATM o para hacer una compra.

Decimal A decimal is a number with one or more places to the right of a decimal point.

Decimal Un decimal es un número que tiene uno o más lugares a la derecha del punto decimal.

Decimal places The digits after the decimal point are called decimal places.

Lugares decimales Los dígitos que están después del punto decimal se llaman lugares decimales.

Decompose a shape To decompose a shape, break it up to form other shapes.

Descomponer una figura Para descomponer una figura, debes separarla para formar otras figuras.

Deductive reasoning Deductive reasoning is a process of reasoning logically from given facts to a conclusion.

Razonamiento deductivo El razonamiento deductivo es un proceso de razonamiento lógico que parte de hechos dados hasta llegar a una conclusión.

Denominator The denominator is the number below the fraction bar in a fraction.

Denominador El denominador es el número que está debajo de la barra de fracción en una fracción.

Dependent events Two events are dependent events if the occurrence of the first event affects the probability of the second event.

Eventos dependientes Dos eventos son dependientes si el resultado del primer evento afecta la probabilidad del segundo evento.

Deposit A transaction that adds money to a bank account is a deposit.

Depósito Una transacción que agrega dinero a una cuenta bancaria es un depósito.

English/Spanish Glossary

Dependent variable A dependent variable is a variable whose value changes in response to another (independent) variable.

Variable dependiente Una variable dependiente es una variable cuyo valor cambia en respuesta a otra variable (independiente).

Describe To describe is to explain or tell in detail. A written description can contain facts and other information needed to communicate your answer. A diagram or a graph may also be included.

Describir Describir es explicar o indicar algo en detalle. Una descripción escrita puede incluir hechos y otra información necesaria para comunicar tu respuesta. También puede incluir un diagrama o una gráfica.

Design To design is to make using specific criteria.

Diseñar Diseñar es crear algo a partir de criterios específicos.

Determine To determine is to use the given information and any related facts to find a value or make a decision.

Determinar Determinar es usar la información dada y cualquier otro dato relacionado para hallar un valor o tomar una decisión.

Deviation from the mean Deviation indicates how far away and in which direction a data value is from the mean. Data values that are less than the mean have a negative deviation. Data values that are greater than the mean have a positive deviation.

Desviación de la media La desviación indica a qué distancia y en qué dirección un valor se aleja de la media. Los valores menores que la media tienen una desviación negativa. Los valores mayores que la media tienen una desviación positiva.

Diagonal A diagonal of a figure is a segment that connects two nonconsecutive vertices of the figure.

Diagonal La diagonal de una figura es un segmento que conecta dos vértices no consecutivos de la figura.

Diameter A diameter is a segment that passes through the center of a circle and has both endpoints on the circle. The term diameter can also mean the length of this segment.

Diámetro Un diámetro es un segmento que atraviesa el centro de un círculo y tiene sus dos extremos en el círculo. El término diámetro también puede referirse a la longitud de este segmento.

English/Spanish Glossary

Difference The difference is the answer you get when subtracting two numbers.

Diferencia La diferencia es la respuesta que obtienes cuando restas dos números.

Dilation A dilation is a transformation that moves each point along the ray through the point, starting from a fixed center, and multiplies distances from the center by a common scale factor. If a vertex of a figure is the center of dilation, then the vertex and its image after the dilation are the same point.

Dilatación Una dilatación es una transformación que mueve cada punto a lo largo de la semirrecta a través del punto, a partir de un centro fijo, y multiplica las distancias desde el centro por un factor de escala común. Si un vértice de una figura es el centro de dilatación, entonces el vértice y su imagen después de la dilatación son el mismo punto.

Direct variation A linear relationship that can be represented by an equation in the form $y = kx$, where $x \neq 0$.

Dirija variación Una relación lineal que puede ser representada por una ecuación en la forma $y = kx$, donde x no iguale 0.

Distribution (of a data set) The distribution of a data set describes the way that its data values are spread out over all possible values. This includes describing the frequencies of each data value. The shape of a data display shows the distribution of a data set.

Distribución (de un conjunto de datos) La distribución de un conjunto de datos describe la manera en que sus valores se esparcen sobre todos los valores posibles. Eso incluye la descripción de las frecuencias de cada valor. La forma de una exhibición de datos muestra la distribución de un conjunto de datos.

Distributive Property Multiplying a number by a sum or difference gives the same result as multiplying that number by each term in the sum or difference and then adding or subtracting the corresponding products.
$a \cdot (b + c) = a \cdot b + a \cdot c$ and
$a \cdot (b - c) = a \cdot b - a \cdot c$

Propiedad distributiva Multiplicar un número por una suma o una diferencia da el mismo resultado que multiplicar ese mismo número por cada uno de los términos de la suma o la diferencia y después sumar o restar los productos obtenidos.
$a \cdot (b + c) = a \cdot b + a \cdot c$ and
$a \cdot (b - c) = a \cdot b - a \cdot c$

Dividend The dividend is the number to be divided.

Dividendo El dividendo es el número que se divide.

English/Spanish Glossary

Divisible A number is divisible by another number if there is no remainder after dividing.

Divisible Un número es divisible por otro número si no hay residuo después de dividir.

Divisor The divisor is the number used to divide another number.

Divisor El divisor es el número por el cual se divide otro número.

Dot plot A dot plot is a statistical graph that shows the shape of a data set with stacked dots above each data value on a number line. Each dot represents one data value.

Diagrama de puntos Un diagrama de puntos es una gráfica estadística que muestra la forma de un conjunto de datos con puntos marcados sobre cada valor de una recta numérica. Cada punto representa un valor.

E

Earned wages Earned wages are the income you receive from an employer for doing a job. Earned wages are also called gross pay.

Sueldos ganados Los sueldos ganados son los ingresos que usted recibe de un empleador para hacer un trabajo. Los sueldos ganados también son llamados la paga bruta.

Easy-access loan The term easy-access loan refers to a wide variety of loans with a streamlined application process. Many easy-access loans are short-term loans of relatively small amounts of money. They often have high interest rates.

Préstamo de fácil-acceso El préstamo del fácil-acceso del término se refiere a una gran variedad de préstamos con un proceso simplificado de aplicación. Muchos préstamos del fácil-acceso son préstamos a corto plazo de cantidades relativamente pequeñas de dinero. Ellos a menudo tienen los tipos de interés altos.

Edge of a three-dimensional figure An edge of a three-dimensional figure is a segment formed by the intersection of two faces.

Arista de una figura tridimensional Una arista de una figura tridimensional es un segmento formado por la intersección de dos caras.

English/Spanish Glossary

Enlargement An enlargement is a dilation with a scale factor greater than 1. After an enlargement, the image is bigger than the original figure.

Aumento Un aumento es una dilatación con un factor de escala mayor que 1. Después de un aumento, la imagen es más grande que la figura original.

Equation An equation is a mathematical sentence that includes an equals sign to compare two expressions.

Ecuación Una ecuación es una oración matemática que incluye un signo igual para comparar dos expresiones.

Equilateral triangle An equilateral triangle is a triangle whose sides are all the same length.

Triángulo equilátero Un triángulo equilátero es un triángulo que tiene todos sus lados de la misma longitud.

Equivalent equations Equivalent equations are equations that have exactly the same solutions.

Ecuaciones equivalentes Las ecuaciones equivalentes son ecuaciones que tienen exactamente la misma solución.

Equivalent expressions Equivalent expressions are expressions that always have the same value.

Expresiones equivalentes Las expresiones equivalentes son expresiones que siempre tienen el mismo valor.

Equivalent fractions Equivalent fractions are fractions that name the same number.

Fracciones equivalentes Las fracciones equivalentes son fracciones que representan el mismo número.

Equivalent inequalities Equivalent inequalities are inequalities that have the same solution.

Desigualdades equivalentes Las desigualdades equivalentes son desigualdades que tienen la misma solución.

Equivalent ratios Equivalent ratios are ratios that express the same relationship.

Razones equivalentes Las razones equivalentes son razones que expresan la misma relación.

Estimate To estimate is to find a number that is close to an exact answer.

Estimar Estimar es hallar un número cercano a una respuesta exacta.

English/Spanish Glossary

Evaluate a numerical expression To evaluate a numerical expression is to follow the order of operations.

Evaluar una expresión numérica Evaluar una expresión numérica es seguir el orden de las operaciones.

Evaluate an algebraic expression To evaluate an algebraic expression, replace each variable with a number, and then follow the order of operations.

Evaluar una expresión algebraica Para evaluar una expresión algebraica, reemplaza cada variable con un número y luego sigue el orden de las operaciones.

Event An event is a single outcome or group of outcomes from a sample space.

Evento Un evento es un resultado simple o un grupo de resultados de un espacio muestral.

Expand an algebraic expression To expand an algebraic expression, use the Distributive Property to rewrite a product as a sum or difference of terms.

Desarrollar una expresión algebraica Para desarrollar una expresión algebraica, usa la propiedad distributiva para reescribir el producto como una suma o diferencia de términos.

Expected family contribution The amount of money a student's family is expected to contribute towards the student's cost of attendance for school.

Contribución familiar esperado La cantidad de dinero que la familia de un estudiante es esperada contribuir hacia el estudiante es costado de asistencia para la escuela.

Expense Money that a business or a person needs to spend to pay for or buy something.

Gasto El dinero que un negocio o una persona debe gastar para pagar por o comprar algo.

Experiment To experiment is to try to gather information in several ways.

Experimentar Experimentar es intentar reunir información de varias maneras.

English/Spanish Glossary

Experimental probability You find the experimental probability of an event by repeating an experiment many times and using this ratio: $P(\text{event}) = \dfrac{\text{number of times event occurs}}{\text{total number of trials}}$

Probabilidad experimental Para hallar la probabilidad experimental de un evento, debes repetir un experimento muchas veces y usar esta razón: $P(\text{evento}) = \dfrac{\text{número de veces que sucede el evento}}{\text{número total de pruebas}}$

Explain To explain is to give facts and details that make an idea easier to understand. Explaining can involve a written summary supported by a diagram, chart, table, or a combination of these.

Explicar Explicar es brindar datos y detalles para que una idea sea más fácil de comprender. Para explicar algo se puede usar un resumen escrito sustentado por un diagrama, una tabla o una combinación de esos elementos.

Exponent An exponent is a number that shows how many times a base is used as a factor.

Exponente Un exponente es un número que muestra cuántas veces se usa una base como factor.

Expression An expression is a mathematical phrase that can involve variables, numbers, and operations. See algebraic expression or numerical expression.

Expresión Una expresión es una frase matemática que puede tener variables, números y operaciones. Ver expresión algebraica o expresión numérica.

Exterior angle of a triangle An exterior angle of a triangle is an angle formed by a side and an extension of an adjacent side.

Ángulo externo de un triángulo Un ángulo externo de un triángulo es un ángulo formado por un lado y una extensión de un lado adyacente.

F

Face of a three-dimensional figure A face of a three-dimensional figure is a flat surface shaped like a polygon.

Cara de una figura tridimensional La cara de una figura tridimensional es una superficie plana con forma de polígono.

English/Spanish Glossary

Factor an algebraic expression To factor an algebraic expression, write the expression as a product.

Descomponer una expresión algebraica en factores Para descomponer una expresión algebraica en factores, escribe la expresión como un producto.

Factors Factors are numbers that are multiplied to give a product.

Factores Los factores son los números que se multiplican para obtener un producto.

False equation A false equation has values that do not equal each other on each side of the equals sign.

Ecuación falsa Una ecuación falsa tiene valores a cada lado del signo igual que no son iguales entre sí.

Financial aid Financial aid is any money offered to a student to assist with the cost of attendance.

Ayuda financiera La ayuda financiera es cualquier dinero ofreció a un estudiante para ayudar con el costo de asistencia.

Financial need A student's financial need is the difference between the student's cost of attendance and the student's expected family contribution.

Necesidad financiera Una necesidad financiera del estudiante es la diferencia entre el estudiante es costada de asistencia y la contribución esperado de familia de estudiante.

Find To find is to calculate or determine.

Hallar Hallar es calcular o determinar.

First quartile For an ordered set of data, the first quartile is the median of the lower half of the data set.

Primer cuartil Para un conjunto ordenado de datos, el primer cuartil es la mediana de la mitad inferior del conjunto de datos.

Fixed expenses Fixed expenses are expenses that do not change from one budget period to the next.

Gastos fijos Los gastos fijos son los gastos que no cambian de un período económico al próximo.

English/Spanish Glossary

Fraction A fraction is a number that can be written in the form $\frac{a}{b}$, where a is a whole number and b is a positive whole number. A fraction is formed by a parts of size $\frac{1}{b}$.

Fracción Una fracción es un número que puede expresarse de forma $\frac{a}{b}$, donde a es un entero y b es un número entero positivo. La fracción está formada por a partes de tamaño $\frac{1}{b}$.

Frequency Frequency describes the number of times a specific value occurs in a data set.

Frecuencia La frecuencia describe el número de veces que aparece un valor específico en un conjunto de datos.

Function A function is a rule for taking each input value and producing exactly one output value.

Función Una función es una regla por la cual se toma cada valor de entrada y se produce exactamente un valor de salida.

G

Gap A gap is an area of a graph that contains no data points.

Espacio vacío o brecha Un espacio vacío o brecha es un área de una gráfica que no contiene ningún valor.

Grant A type of monetary award a student can use to pay for his or her education. The student does not need to repay this money.

Grant Un tipo de premio monetario que un estudiante puede utilizar para pagar por su educación. El estudiante no debe devolver este dinero.

Greater than > The greater-than symbol shows a comparison of two numbers with the number of greater value shown first, or on the left.

Mayor que > El símbolo de mayor que muestra una comparación de dos números con el número de mayor valor que aparece primero, o a la izquierda.

Greatest common factor The greatest common factor (GCF) of two or more whole numbers is the greatest number that is a factor of all of the numbers.

Máximo común divisor El máximo común divisor (M.C.D.) de dos o más números enteros no negativos es el número mayor que es un factor de todos los números.

English/Spanish Glossary

H

Height of a cone The height of a cone, *h*, is the length of a segment perpendicular to the base that joins the vertex and the base.

Altura de un cono La altura de un cono, *h*, es la longitud de un segmento perpendicular a la base que une el vértice y la base.

Height of a cylinder The height of a cylinder is the length of a perpendicular segment that joins the planes of the bases.

Altura de un cilindro La altura de un cilindro es la longitud de un segmento perpendicular que une los planos de las bases.

Height of a parallelogram A height of a parallelogram is the perpendicular distance between opposite bases.

Altura de un paralelogramo La altura de un paralelogramo es la distancia perpendicular que existe entre las bases opuestas.

Height of a prism The height of a prism is the length of a perpendicular segment that joins the bases.

Altura de un prisma La altura de un prisma es la longitud de un segmento perpendicular que une a las bases.

Height of a pyramid The height of a pyramid is the length of a segment perpendicular to the base that joins the vertex and the base.

Altura de una pirámide La altura de una pirámide es la longitud de un segmento perpendicular a la base que une al vértice con la base.

Height of a triangle The height of a triangle is the length of the perpendicular segment from a vertex to the base opposite that vertex.

Altura de un triángulo La altura de un triángulo es la longitud del segmento perpendicular desde un vértice hasta la base opuesta a ese vértice.

Hexagon A hexagon is a polygon with six sides.

Hexágono Un hexágono es un polígono de seis lados.

English/Spanish Glossary

Histogram A histogram is a statistical graph that shows the shape of a data set with vertical bars above intervals of values on a number line. The intervals are equal in size and do not overlap. The height of each bar shows the frequency of data within that interval.

Histograma Un histograma es una gráfica de estadísticas que muestra la forma de un conjunto de datos con barras verticales encima de intervalos de valores en una recta numérica. Los intervalos tienen el mismo tamaño y no se superponen. La altura de cada barra muestra la frecuencia de los datos dentro de ese intervalo.

Hundredths One hundredth is one part of 100 equal parts of a whole.

Centésima Una centésima es 1 de las 100 partes iguales de un todo.

Hypotenuse In a right triangle, the longest side, which is opposite the right angle, is the hypotenuse.

Hipotenusa En un triángulo rectángulo, el lado más largo, que es opuesto al ángulo recto, es la hipotenusa.

I

Identify To identify is to match a definition or description to an object or to recognize something and be able to name it.

Identificar Identificar es unir una definición o una descripción con un objeto, o reconocer algo y poder nombrarlo.

Identity Property of Addition The sum of 0 and any number is that number. For any number n, $n + 0 = n$ and $0 + n = n$.

Propiedad de identidad de la suma La suma de 0 y cualquier número es ese número. Para cualquier número n, $n + 0 = n$ and $0 + n = n$.

Identity Property of Multiplication The product of 1 and any number is that number. For any number n, $n \cdot 1 = n$ and $1 \cdot n = n$.

Propiedad de identidad de la multiplicación El producto de 1 y cualquier número es ese número. Para cualquier número n, $n \cdot 1 = n$ and $1 \cdot n = n$.

Illustrate To illustrate is to show or present information, usually as a drawing or a diagram. You can also illustrate a point using a written explanation.

Ilustrar Ilustrar es mostrar o presentar información, generalmente en forma de dibujo o diagrama. También puedes usar una explicación escrita para ilustrar un punto.

English/Spanish Glossary

Image An image is the result of a transformation of a point, line, or figure.

Imagen Una imagen es el resultado de una transformación de un punto, una recta o una figura.

Improper fraction An improper fraction is a fraction in which the numerator is greater than or equal to its denominator.

Fracción impropia Una fracción impropia es una fracción en la cual el numerador es mayor que o igual a su denominador.

Included angle An included angle is an angle that is between two sides.

Ángulo incluido Un ángulo incluido es un ángulo que está entre dos lados.

Included side An included side is a side that is between two angles.

Lado incluido Un lado incluido es un lado que está entre dos ángulos.

Income Money that a business receives. The money that a person earns from working is also called income.

Ingresos El dinero que un negocio recibe. El dinero que una persona gana de trabajar también es llamado los ingresos.

Income tax Income tax is money collected by the government based on how much you earn.

Impuesto de renta El impuesto de renta es dinero completo por el gobierno basado en cuánto gana.

Independent events Two events are independent events if the occurrence of one event does not affect the probability of the other event.

Eventos independientes Dos eventos son eventos independientes cuando el resultado de un evento no altera la probabilidad del otro.

Independent variable An independent variable is a variable whose value determines the value of another (dependent) variable.

Variable independiente Una variable independiente es una variable cuyo valor determina el valor de otra variable (dependiente).

Indicate To indicate is to point out or show.

Indicar Indicar es señalar o mostrar.

English/Spanish Glossary

Indirect measurement Indirect measurement uses proportions and similar triangles to measure distances that would be difficult to measure directly.

Medición indirecta La medición indirecta usa proporciones y triángulos semejantes para medir distancias que serían difíciles de medir de forma directa.

Inequality An inequality is a mathematical sentence that uses $<$, $\leq$, $>$, $\geq$, or $\neq$ to compare two quantities.

Desigualdad Una desigualdad es una oración matemática que usa $<$, $\leq$, $>$, $\geq$, o $\neq$ para comparar dos cantidades.

Inference An inference is a judgment made by interpreting data.

Inferencia Una inferencia es una opinión que se forma al interpretar datos.

Infinitely many solutions A linear equation in one variable has infinitely many solutions if any value of the variable makes the two sides of the equation equal.

Número infinito de soluciones Una ecuación lineal en una variable tiene un número infinito de soluciones si cualquier valor de la variable hace que los dos lados de la ecuación sean iguales.

Initial value The initial value of a linear function is the value of the output when the input is 0.

Valor inicial El valor inicial de una función lineal es el valor de salida cuando el valor de entrada es 0.

Integers Integers are the set of positive whole numbers, their opposites, and 0.

Enteros Los enteros son el conjunto de los números enteros positivos, sus opuestos y 0.

Interest When you deposit money in a bank account, the bank pays you interest for the right to use your money for a period of time.

Interés Cuando depositas dinero en una cuenta bancaria, el banco te paga un interés por el derecho a usar tu dinero por un período de tiempo.

Interest period The length of time on which compound interest is based. The total number of interest periods that you keep the money in the account is represented by the variable n.

Período de interés La cantidad de tiempo sobre la que se calcula el interés compuesto. El número total de períodos de interés que mantienes el dinero en la cuenta se representa con la variable n.

English/Spanish Glossary

Interest rate Interest is calculated based on a percent of the principal. That percent is called the interest rate (r).

Tasa de interés El interés se calcula con base en un porcentaje del capital. Ese porcentaje se llama tasa de interés, (r).

Interest rate for an interest period The interest rate for an interest period is the annual interest rate divided by the number of interest periods per year.

El tipo de interés por un período de interés El tipo de interés por un período de interés es el tipo de interés anual dividido por el número de períodos de interés por año.

Interquartile range The interquartile range (IQR) is the distance between the first and third quartiles of the data set. It represents the spread of the middle 50% of the data values.

Rango intercuartil El rango intercuartil es la distancia entre el primer y el tercer cuartil del conjunto de datos. Representa la ubicación del 50% del medio de los valores.

Interval An interval is a period of time between two points of time or events.

Intervalo Un intervalo es un período de tiempo entre dos puntos en el tiempo o entre dos sucesos.

Invalid inference An invalid inference is false about the population, or does not follow from the available data. A biased sample can lead to invalid inferences.

Inferencia inválida Una inferencia inválida es una inferencia falsa acerca de una población, o no se deduce a partir de los datos disponibles. Una muestra sesgada puede llevar a inferencias inválidas.

Inverse operations Inverse operations are operations that undo each other.

Operaciones inversas Las operaciones inversas son operaciones que se cancelan entre sí.

Inverse property of addition Every number has an additive inverse. The sum of a number and its additive inverse is zero.

Propiedad inversa de la suma Todos los números tienen un inverso de suma. La suma de un número y su inverso de suma es cero.

English/Spanish Glossary

Irrational numbers An irrational number is a number that cannot be written in the form $\frac{a}{b}$, where a and b are integers and $b \neq 0$. In decimal form, an irrational number cannot be written as a terminating or repeating decimal.

Números irracionales Un número irracional es un número que no se puede escribir en la forma $\frac{a}{b}$ donde a y b, son enteros y $b \neq 0$. Los números racionales en forma decimal no son finitos y no son periódicos.

Isolate a variable When solving equations, to isolate a variable means to get a variable with a coefficient of 1 alone on one side of an equation. Use the properties of equality and inverse operations to isolate a variable.

Aislar una variable Cuando resuelves ecuaciones, aislar una variable significa poner una variable con un coeficiente de 1 sola a un lado de la ecuación. Usa las propiedades de igualdad y las operaciones inversas para aislar una variable.

Isosceles triangle An isosceles triangle is a triangle with at least two sides that are the same length.

Triángulo isósceles Un triángulo isósceles es un triángulo que tiene al menos dos lados de la misma longitud.

J

Justify To justify is to support your answer with reasons or examples. A justification may include a written response, diagrams, charts, tables, or a combination of these.

Justificar Justificar es apoyar tu respuesta con razones o ejemplos. Una justificación puede incluir una respuesta escrita, diagramas, tablas o una combinación de esos elementos.

L

Lateral area of a cone The lateral area of a cone is the area of its lateral surface. The formula for the lateral area of a cone is L.A. = $\pi r \ell$, where r represents the radius of the base and ℓ represents the slant height of the cone.

Área lateral de un cono El área lateral de un cono es el área de su superficie lateral. La fórmula del área lateral de un cono es A.L. = $\pi r \ell$, donde r representa el radio de la base y ℓ representa la altura inclinada del cono.

English/Spanish Glossary

Lateral area of a cylinder The lateral area of a cylinder is the area of its lateral surface. The formula for the lateral area of a cylinder is L.A. $= 2\pi rh$, where r represents the radius of a base and h represents the height of the cylinder.

Área lateral de un cilindro El área lateral de un cilindro es el área de su superficie lateral. La fórmula del área lateral de un cilindro es A.L. $= 2\pi rh$, donde r representa el radio de una base y h representa la altura del cilindro.

Lateral area of a prism The lateral area of a prism is the sum of the areas of the lateral faces of the prism. The formula for the lateral area, L.A., of a prism is L.A. $= ph$, where p represents the perimeter of the base and h represents the height of the prism.

Área lateral de un prisma El área lateral de un prisma es la suma de las áreas de las caras laterales del prisma. La fórmula del área lateral, A.L., de un prisma es A.L. $= ph$, donde p representa el perímetro de la base y h representa la altura del prisma.

Lateral area of a pyramid The lateral area of a pyramid is the sum of the areas of the lateral faces of the pyramid. The formula for the lateral area, L.A., of a pyramid is L.A. $= \frac{1}{2}p\ell$ where p represents the perimeter of the base and ℓ represents the slant height of the pyramid.

Área lateral de una pirámide El área lateral de una pirámide es la suma de las áreas de las caras laterales de la pirámide. La fórmula del área lateral, A.L., de una pirámide es A.L. $= \frac{1}{2}p\ell$ donde p representa el perímetro de la base y ℓ representa la altura inclinada de la pirámide.

Lateral face of a prism A lateral face of a prism is a face that joins the bases of the prism.

Cara lateral de un prisma La cara lateral de un prisma es la cara que une a las bases del prisma.

Lateral face of a pyramid A lateral face of a pyramid is a triangular face that joins the base and the vertex.

Cara lateral de una pirámide La cara lateral de una pirámide es una cara lateral que une a la base con el vértice.

Lateral surface of a cone The lateral surface of a cone is the curved surface that is not included in the base.

Superficie lateral de un cono La superficie lateral de un cono es la superficie curva que no está incluida en la base.

English/Spanish Glossary

Lateral surface of a cylinder The lateral surface of a cylinder is the curved surface that is not included in the bases.

Superficie lateral de un cilindro La superficie lateral de un cilindro es la superficie curva que no está incluida en las bases.

Least common multiple The least common multiple (LCM) of two or more numbers is the least multiple shared by all of the numbers.

Mínimo común múltiplo El mínimo común múltiplo (MCM) de dos o más números es el múltiplo menor compartido por todos los números.

Leg of a right triangle In a right triangle, the two shortest sides are legs.

Cateto de un triángulo rectángulo En un triángulo rectángulo, los dos lados más cortos son los catetos.

Less than < The less-than symbol shows a comparison of two numbers with the number of lesser value shown first, or on the left.

Menor que < El símbolo de menor que muestra una comparación de dos números con el número de menor valor que aparece primero, o a la izquierda.

Liability A liability is money that you owe.

Obligación Una obligación es dinero que usted debe.

Lifetime income The amount of money earned over a lifetime of working.

Ingresos para toda la vida La cantidad de dinero ganó sobre una vida de trabajar.

Like terms Terms that have identical variable parts are like terms.

Términos semejantes Los términos que tienen partes variables idénticas son términos semejantes.

Line of reflection A line of reflection is a line across which a figure is reflected.

Eje de reflexión Un eje de reflexión es una línea a través de la cual se refleja una figura.

Linear equation An equation is a linear equation if the graph of all of its solutions is a line.

Ecuación lineal Una ecuación es lineal si la gráfica de todas sus soluciones es una línea recta.

English/Spanish Glossary

Linear function A linear function is a function whose graph is a straight line. The rate of change for a linear function is constant.

Función lineal Una función lineal es una función cuya gráfica es una línea recta. La tasa de cambio en una función lineal es constante.

Linear function rule A linear function rule is an equation that describes a linear function.

Regla de la función lineal La ecuación que describe una función lineal es la regla de la función lineal.

Loan A loan is an amount of money borrowed for a period of time with the promise of paying it back.

Préstamo Un préstamo es una cantidad de dinero pedido prestaddo por un espacio de tiempo con la promesa de pagarlo apoya.

Loan length Loan length is the period of time set to repay a loan.

Preste longitud La longitud del préstamo es el conjunto de espacio de tiempo de devolver un préstamo.

Loan term The term of a loan is the period of time set to repay the loan.

Preste término El término de un préstamo es el conjunto de espacio de tiempo de devolver el préstamo.

Locate To locate is to find or identify a value, usually on a number line or coordinate graph.

Ubicar Ubicar es hallar o identificar un valor, generalmente en una recta numérica o en una gráfica de coordenadas.

Loss When a business's expenses are greater than the business's income, there is a loss.

Pérdida Cuando los gastos de un negocio son más que los ingresos del negocio, hay una pérdida.

English/Spanish Glossary

M

Mapping diagram A mapping diagram describes a relation by linking the input values to the corresponding output values using arrows.

Diagrama de correspondencia Un diagrama de correspondencia describe una relación uniendo con flechas los valores de entrada con sus correspondientes valores de salida.

Markdown Markdown is the amount of decrease from the selling price to the sale price. The markdown as a percent decrease of the original selling price is called the percent markdown.

Rebaja La rebaja es la cantidad de disminución de un precio de venta a un precio rebajado. La rebaja como una disminución porcentual del precio de venta original se llama porcentaje de rebaja.

Markup Markup is the amount of increase from the cost to the selling price. The markup as a percent increase of the original cost is called the percent markup.

Margen de ganancia El margen de ganancia es la cantidad de aumento del costo al precio de venta. El margen de ganancia como un aumento porcentual del costo original se llama porcentaje del margen de ganancia.

Mean The mean represents the center of a numerical data set. To find the mean, sum the data values and then divide by the number of values in the data set.

Media La media representa el centro de un conjunto de datos numéricos. Para hallar la media, suma los valores y luego divide por el número de valores del conjunto de datos.

Mean absolute deviation The mean absolute deviation is a measure of variability that describes how much the data values are spread out from the mean of a data set. The mean absolute deviation is the average distance that the data values are spread around the mean.

$$\text{mean absolute deviation} = \frac{\text{sum of the absolute deviations of the data values}}{\text{total number of data values}}$$

Desviación absoluta media La desviación absoluta media es una medida de variabilidad que describe cuánto se alejan los valores de la media de un conjunto de datos. La desviación absoluta media es la distancia promedio que los valores se alejan de la media.

$$\text{desviación absoluta media} = \frac{\text{suma de las desviaciones absolutas de los valores}}{\text{número total de valores}}$$

English/Spanish Glossary

Measure of variability A measure of variability describes the spread of values in a data set. There may be more than one measure of variability for a data set.

Medida de variabilidad Una medida de variabilidad describe la distribución de los valores de un conjunto de datos. Puede haber más de una medida de variabilidad para un conjunto de datos.

Measurement data Measurement data consist of data that are measures.

Datos de mediciones Los datos de mediciones son datos que son medidas.

Measures of center A measure of center is a value that represents the middle of a data set. There may be more than one measure of center for a data set.

Medida de tendencia central Una medida de tendencia central es un valor que representa el centro de un conjunto de datos. Puede haber más de una medida de tendencia central para un conjunto de datos.

Median The median represents the center of a numerical data set. For an odd number of data values, the median is the middle value when the data values are arranged in numerical order. For an even number of data values, the median is the average of the two middle values when the data values are arranged in numerical order.

Mediana La mediana representa el centro de un conjunto de datos numéricos. Para un número impar de valores, la mediana es el valor del medio cuando los valores están organizados en orden numérico. Para un número par de valores, la mediana es el promedio de los dos valores del medio cuando los valores están organizados en orden numérico.

Median-median line The median-median line, or median trend line, is a method of finding a fit line for a scatter plot that suggests a linear association. This method involves dividing the data into three subgroups and using medians to find a summary point for each subgroup. The summary points are used to find the equation of the fit line.

Recta mediana-mediana La recta mediana-mediana es un método que se usa para hallar una línea de ajuste para un diagrama de dispersión que sugiere una asociación lineal. Este método implica dividir los datos en tres subgrupos y usar medianas para hallar un punto medio para cada subgrupo. Los puntos medios se usan para hallar la ecuación de la línea de ajuste.

Million Whole numbers in the millions have 7, 8, or 9 digits.

Millón Los números enteros no negativos que están en los millones tienen 7, 8 ó 9 dígitos.

English/Spanish Glossary

Mixed number A mixed number combines a whole number and a fraction.

Número mixto Un número mixto combina un número entero no negativo con una fracción.

Mode The item, or items, in a data set that occurs most frequently.

Modo El artículo, o los artículos, en un conjunto de datos que ocurre normalmente.

Model To model is to represent a situation using pictures, diagrams, or number sentences.

Demostrar Demostrar es usar ilustraciones, diagramas o enunciados numéricos para representar una situación.

Monetary incentive A monetary incentive is an offer that might encourage customers to buy a product.

Estímulo monetario Un estímulo monetario es una oferta que quizás favorezca a clientes para comprar un producto.

Multiple A multiple of a number is the product of the number and a whole number.

Múltiplo El múltiplo de un número es el producto del número y un número entero no negativo.

N

Natural numbers The natural numbers are the counting numbers.

Números naturales Los números naturales son los números que se usan para contar.

Negative exponent property For every nonzero number a and integer n, $a^{-n} = \frac{1}{a^n}$.

Propiedad del exponente negativo Para todo número distinto de cero a y entero n, $a^{-n} = \frac{1}{a^n}$.

Negative numbers Negative numbers are numbers less than zero.

Números negativos Los números negativos son números menores que cero.

English/Spanish Glossary

Net A net is a two-dimensional pattern that you can fold to form a three-dimensional figure. A net of a figure shows all of the surfaces of that figure in one view.

Modelo plano Un modelo plano es un diseño bidimensional que puedes doblar para formar una figura tridimensional. Un modelo plano de una figura muestra todas las superficies de la figura en una vista.

Net worth Net worth is the total value of all assets minus the total value of all liabilities.

Patrimonio neto El patrimonio neto es el valor total de todas las ventajas menos el valor total de todas las obligaciones.

Net worth statement Net worth is the total value of all assets minus the total value of all liabilities.

Declaración de patrimonio neto El patrimonio neto es el valor total de todas las ventajas menos el valor total de todas las obligaciones.

No solution A linear equation in one variable has no solution if no value of the variable makes the two sides of the equation equal.

Sin solución Una ecuación lineal en una variable no tiene solución si ningún valor de la variable hace que los dos lados de la ecuación sean iguales.

Nonlinear function A nonlinear function is a function that does not have a constant rate of change.

Función no lineal Una función no lineal es una función que no tiene una tasa de cambio constante.

Numerator The numerator is the number above the fraction bar in a fraction.

Numerador El numerador es el número que está arriba de la barra de fracción en una fracción.

Numerical expression A numerical expression is a mathematical phrase that consists of numbers and operation symbols.

Expresión numérica Una expresión numérica es una frase matemática que contiene números y símbolos de operaciones.

English/Spanish Glossary

O

Obtuse angle An obtuse angle is an angle with a measure greater than 90° and less than 180°.

Ángulo obtuso Un ángulo obtuso es un ángulo con una medida mayor que 90° y menor que 180°.

Obtuse triangle An obtuse triangle is a triangle with one obtuse angle.

Triángulo obtusángulo Un triángulo obtusángulo es un triángulo que tiene un ángulo obtuso.

Octagon An octagon is a polygon with eight sides.

Octágono Un octágono es un polígono de ocho lados.

Online payment system An online payment system allows money to be exchanged electronically between buyer and seller, usually using credit card or bank account information.

Sistema en línea de pago Un sistema en línea del pago permite dinero para ser cambiado electrónicamente entre comprador y vendedor, utilizando generalmente información de tarjeta de crédito o cuenta bancaria.

Open sentence An open sentence is an equation with one or more variables.

Enunciado abierto Un enunciado abierto es una ecuación con una o más variables.

Opposites Opposites are two numbers that are the same distance from 0 on a number line, but in opposite directions.

Opuestos Los opuestos son dos números que están a la misma distancia de 0 en la recta numérica, pero en direcciones opuestas.

Order of operations The order of operations is the order in which operations should be performed in an expression. Operations inside parentheses are done first, followed by exponents. Then, multiplication and division are done in order from left to right, and finally addition and subtraction are done in order from left to right.

Orden de las operaciones El orden de las operaciones es el orden en el que se deben resolver las operaciones de una expresión. Las operaciones que están entre paréntesis se resuelven primero, seguidas de los exponentes. Luego, se multiplica y se divide en orden de izquierda a derecha, y finalmente se suma y se resta en orden de izquierda a derecha.

English/Spanish Glossary

Ordered pair An ordered pair identifies the location of a point in the coordinate plane. The x-coordinate shows a point's position left or right of the y-axis. The y-coordinate shows a point's position up or down from the x-axis.

Par ordenado Un par ordenado identifica la ubicación de un punto en el plano de coordenadas. La coordenada x muestra la posición de un punto a la izquierda o a la derecha del eje de las y. La coordenada y muestra la posición de un punto arriba o abajo del eje de las x.

Origin The origin is the point of intersection of the x- and y-axes on a coordinate plane.

Origen El origen es el punto de intersección del eje de las x y el eje de las y en un plano de coordenadas.

Outcome An outcome is a possible result of an action.

Resultado Un resultado es un desenlace posible de una acción.

Outlier An outlier is a piece of data that doesn't seem to fit with the rest of a data set.

Valor extremo Un valor extremo es un valor que parece no ajustarse al resto de los datos de un conjunto.

P

Parallel lines Parallel lines are lines in the same plane that never intersect.

Rectas paralelas Las rectas paralelas son rectas que están en el mismo plano y nunca se intersecan.

Parallelogram A parallelogram is a quadrilateral with both pairs of opposite sides parallel.

Paralelogramo Un paralelogramo es un cuadrilátero en el cual los dos pares de lados opuestos son paralelos.

Partial product A partial product is part of the total product. A product is the sum of the partial products.

Producto parcial Un producto parcial es una parte del producto total. Un producto es la suma de los productos parciales.

English/Spanish Glossary

Pay period Wages for many jobs are paid at regular intervals, such a weekly, biweekly, semimonthly, or monthly. The interval of time is called a pay period.

Pague el período Los sueldos para muchos trabajos son pagados con regularidad, tal semanal, quincenal, quincenal, o mensual. El intervalo de tiempo es llamado un período de la paga.

Payroll deductions Your employer can deduct your income taxes from your wages before you receive your paycheck. The amounts deducted are called payroll deductions.

Deducciones de nómina Su empleador puede descontar sus impuestos de renta de sus sueldos antes que reciba su cheque de pago. Las cantidades descontadas son llamadas nómina deducciones.

Percent A percent is a ratio that compares a number to 100.

Porcentaje Un porcentaje es una razón que compara un número con 100.

Percent bar graph A percent bar graph is a bar graph that shows each category as a percent of the total number of data items.

Gráfico de barras de por ciento Un gráfico de barras del por ciento es un gráfico de barras que muestra cada categoría como un por ciento del número total de artículos de datos.

Percent decrease When a quantity decreases, the percent of change is called a percent decrease. percent decrease = $\frac{\text{amount of decrease}}{\text{original quantity}}$

Disminución porcentual Cuando una cantidad disminuye, el porcentaje de cambio se llama disminución porcentual. disminución porcentual = $\frac{\text{cantidad de disminución}}{\text{cantidad original}}$

Percent equation The percent equation describes the relationship between a part and a whole. You can use the percent equation to solve percent problems. part = percent · whole

Ecuación de porcentaje La ecuación de porcentaje describe la relación entre una parte y un todo. Puedes usar la ecuación de porcentaje para resolver problemas de porcentaje. parte = por ciento · todo

Percent error Percent error describes the accuracy of a measured or estimated value compared to an actual or accepted value.

Error porcentual El error porcentual describe la exactitud de un valor medido o estimado en comparación con un valor real o aceptado.

English/Spanish Glossary

Percent increase When a quantity increases, the percent of change is called a percent increase.

Aumento porcentual Cuando una cantidad aumenta, el porcentaje de cambio se llama aumento porcentual.

Percent of change Percent of change is the percent something increases or decreases from its original measure or amount. You can find the percent of change by using the equation: percent of change = amount of change original quantity

Porcentaje de cambio El porcentaje de cambio es el porcentaje en que algo aumenta o disminuye en relación a la medida o cantidad original. Puedes hallar el porcentaje de cambio con la siguiente ecuación: porcentaje de cambio = cantidad de cambio cantidad original

Perfect cube A perfect cube is the cube of an integer.

Cubo perfecto Un cubo perfecto es el cubo de un entero.

Perfect square A perfect square is a number that is the square of an integer.

Cuadrado perfecto Un cuadrado perfecto es un número que es el cuadrado de un entero.

Perimeter Perimeter is the distance around a figure.

Perímetro El perímetro es la distancia alrededor de una figura.

Period A period is a group of 3 digits in a number. Periods are separated by a comma and start from the right of a number.

Período Un período es un grupo de 3 dígitos en un número. Los períodos están separados por una coma y empiezan a la derecha del número.

Periodic savings plan A periodic savings plan is a method of saving that involves making deposits on a regular basis.

Plan de ahorros periódico Un plan de ahorros periódico es un método de guardar que implica depósitos que hace con regularidad.

Perpendicular lines Perpendicular lines intersect to form right angles.

Rectas perpendiculares Las rectas perpendiculares se intersecan para formar ángulos rectos.

English/Spanish Glossary

Pi Pi (π) is the ratio of a circle's circumference, C, to its diameter, d.

Pi Pi (π) es la razón de la circunferencia de un círculo, C, a su diámetro, d.

Place value Place value is the value given to an individual digit based on its position within a number.

Valor posicional El valor posicional es el valor asignado a determinado dígito según su posición en un número.

Plane A plane is a flat surface that extends indefinitely in all directions.

Plano Un plano es una superficie plana que se extiende indefinidamente en todas direcciones.

Polygon A polygon is a closed figure formed by three or more line segments that do not cross.

Polígono Un polígono es una figura cerrada compuesta por tres o más segmentos que no se cruzan.

Population A population is the complete set of items being studied.

Población Una población es todo el conjunto de elementos que se estudian.

Positive numbers Positive numbers are numbers greater than zero.

Números positivos Los números positivos son números mayores que cero.

Power A power is a number expressed using an exponent.

Potencia Una potencia es un número expresado con un exponente.

Predict To predict is to make an educated guess based on the analysis of real data.

Predecir Predecir es hacer una estimación informada según el análisis de datos reales.

Prime factorization The prime factorization of a composite number is the expression of the number as a product of its prime factors.

Descomposición en factores primos La descomposición en factores primos de un número compuesto es la expresión del número como un producto de sus factores primos.

English/Spanish Glossary

Prime number A prime number is a whole number greater than 1 with exactly two factors, 1 and the number itself.

Número primo Un número primo es un número entero mayor que 1 con exactamente dos factores, 1 y el número mismo.

Principal The original amount of money deposited or borrowed in an account.

Capital La cantidad original de dinero que se deposita o se pide prestada en una cuenta.

Prism A prism is a three-dimensional figure with two parallel polygonal faces that are the same size and shape.

Prisma Un prisma es una figura tridimensional con dos caras poligonales paralelas que tienen el mismo tamaño y la misma forma.

Probability model A probability model consists of an action, its sample space, and a list of events with their probabilities. The events and probabilities in the list have these characteristics: each outcome in the sample space is in exactly one event, and the sum of all of the probabilities must be 1.

Modelo de probabilidad Un modelo de probabilidad consiste en una acción, su espacio muestral y una lista de eventos con sus probabilidades. Los eventos y las probabilidades de la lista tienen estas características: cada resultado del espacio muestral está exactamente en un evento, y la suma de todas las probabilidades debe ser 1.

Probability of an event The probability of an event is a number from 0 to 1 that measures the likelihood that the event will occur. The closer the probability is to 0, the less likely it is that the event will happen. The closer the probability is to 1, the more likely it is that the event will happen. You can express probability as a fraction, decimal, or percent.

Probabilidad de un evento La probabilidad de un evento es un número de 0 a 1 que mide la probabilidad de que suceda el evento. Cuanto más se acerca la probabilidad a 0, menos probable es que suceda el evento. Cuanto más se acerca la probabilidad a 1, más probable es que suceda el evento. Puedes expresar la probabilidad como una fracción, un decimal o un porcentaje.

Product A product is the value of a multiplication or an expression showing multiplication.

Producto Un producto es el valor de una multiplicación o una expresión que representa la multiplicación.

English/Spanish Glossary

Profit When a business's expenses are less than the business's income, there is a profit.

Ganancia Cuando los gastos de un negocio son menos que los ingresos del negocio, hay una ganancia.

Proof A proof is a logical, deductive argument in which every statement of fact is supported by a reason.

Comprobación Una comprobación es un argumento lógico y deductivo en el que cada enunciado de un hecho está apoyado por una razón.

Proper fraction A proper fraction has a numerator that is less than its denominator.

Fracción propia Una fracción propia tiene un numerador que es menor que su denominador.

Proportion A proportion is an equation stating that two ratios are equal.

Proporción Una proporción es una ecuación que establece que dos razones son iguales.

Proportional relationship Two quantities x and y have a proportional relationship if y is always a constant multiple of x. A relationship is proportional if it can be described by equivalent ratios.

Relación de proporción Dos cantidades x y y tienen una relación de proporción si y es siempre un múltiplo constante de x. Una relación es de proporción si se puede describir con razones equivalentes.

Pyramid A pyramid is a three-dimensional figure with a base that is a polygon and triangular faces that meet at a vertex. A pyramid is named for the shape of its base.

Pirámide Una pirámide es una figura tridimensional con una base que es un polígono y caras triangulares que se unen en un vértice. El nombre de la pirámide depende de la forma de su base.

English/Spanish Glossary

Pythagorean Theorem In any right triangle, the sum of the squares of the lengths of the legs equals the square of the length of the hypotenuse. If a triangle is a right triangle, then $a^2 + b^2 = c^2$, where a and b represent the lengths of the legs, and c represents the length of the hypotenuse.

Teorema de Pitágoras En cualquier triángulo rectángulo, la suma del cuadrado de la longitud de los catetos es igual al cuadrado de la longitud de la hipotenusa. Si un triángulo es un triángulo rectángulo, entonces $a^2 + b^2 = c^2$, donde a y b representan la longitud de los catetos, y c representa la longitud de la hipotenusa.

Q

Quadrant The x- and y-axes divide the coordinate plane into four regions called quadrants.

Cuadrante Los ejes de las x y de las y dividen el plano de coordenadas en cuatro regiones llamadas cuadrantes.

Quadrilateral A quadrilateral is a polygon with four sides.

Cuadrilátero Un cuadrilátero es un polígono de cuatro lados.

Quarter circle A quarter circle is one fourth of a circle.

Círculo cuarto Un círculo cuarto es la cuarta parte de un círculo.

Quartile The quartiles of a data set divide the data set into four parts with the same number of data values in each part.

Cuartil Los cuartiles de un conjunto de datos dividen el conjunto de datos en cuatro partes que tienen el mismo número de valores cada una.

Quotient The quotient is the answer to a division problem. When there is a remainder, "quotient" sometimes refers to the whole-number portion of the answer.

Cociente El cociente es el resultado de una división. Cuando queda un residuo, "cociente" a veces se refiere a la parte de la solución que es un número entero.

English/Spanish Glossary

R

Radius A radius of a circle is a segment that has one endpoint at the center and the other endpoint on the circle. The term radius can also mean the length of this segment.

Radio Un radio de un círculo es un segmento que tiene un extremo en el centro y el otro extremo en el círculo. El término radio también puede referirse a la longitud de este segmento.

Radius of a sphere The radius of a sphere, r, is a segment that has one endpoint at the center and the other endpoint on the sphere.

Radio de una esfera El radio de una esfera, r, es un segmento que tiene un extremo en el centro y el otro extremo en la esfera.

Random sample In a random sample, each member in the population has an equal chance of being selected.

Muestra aleatoria En una muestra aleatoria, cada miembro en la población tiene una oportunidad igual de ser seleccionado.

Range The range is a measure of variability of a numerical data set. The range of a data set is the difference between the greatest and least values in a data set.

Rango El rango es una medida de la variabilidad de un conjunto de datos numéricos. El rango de un conjunto de datos es la diferencia que existe entre el mayor y el menor valor del conjunto.

Rate A rate is a ratio involving two quantities measured in different units.

Tasa Una tasa es una razón que relaciona dos cantidades medidas con unidades diferentes.

Rate of change The rate of change of a linear function is the ratio vertical change horizontal change between any two points on the graph of the function.

Tasa de cambio La tasa de cambio de una función lineal es la razón del cambio vertical cambio horizontal que existe entre dos puntos cualesquiera de la gráfica de la función.

Ratio A ratio is a relationship in which for every x units of one quantity there are y units of another quantity.

Razón Una razón es una relación en la cual por cada x unidades de una cantidad hay y unidades de otra cantidad.

English/Spanish Glossary

Rational numbers A rational number is a number that can be written in the form $\frac{a}{b}$ or $-\frac{a}{b}$, where a is a whole number and b is a positive whole number. The rational numbers include the integers.

Números racionales Un número racional es un número que se puede escribir como $\frac{a}{b}$ or $-\frac{a}{b}$, donde a es un número entero no negativo y b es un número entero positivo. Los números racionales incluyen los enteros.

Real numbers The real numbers are the set of rational and irrational numbers.

Números reales Los números reales son el conjunto de los números racionales e irracionales.

Reason To reason is to think through a problem using facts and information.

Razonar Razonar es usar hechos e información para estudiar detenidamente un problema.

Rebate A rebate returns part of the purchase price of an item after the buyer provides proof of purchase through a mail-in or online form.

Reembolso Un reembolso regresa la parte del precio de compra de un artículo después de que el comprador proporcione comprobante de compra por un correo-en o forma en línea.

Recall To recall is to remember a fact quickly.

Recordar Recordar es traer a la memoria un hecho rápidamente.

Reciprocals Two numbers are reciprocals if their product is 1. If a nonzero number is named as a fraction, , then its reciprocal is .

Recíprocos Dos números son recíprocos si su producto es 1. Si un número distinto de cero se expresa como una fracción, , entonces su recíproco es .

Rectangle A rectangle is a quadrilateral with four right angles.

Rectángulo Un rectángulo es un cuadrilátero que tiene cuatro ángulos rectos.

Rectangular prism A rectangular prism is a prism with bases in the shape of a rectangle.

Prisma rectangular Un prisma rectangular es un prisma cuyas bases tienen la forma de un rectángulo.

English/Spanish Glossary

Reduction A reduction is a dilation with a scale factor less than 1. After a reduction, the image is smaller than the original figure.

Reducción Una reducción es una dilatación con un factor de escala menor que 1. Después de una reducción, la imagen es más pequeña que la figura original.

Reflection A reflection, or flip, is a transformation that flips a figure across a line of reflection.

Reflexión Una reflexión, o inversión, es una transformación que invierte una figura a través de un eje de reflexión.

Regular polygon A regular polygon is a polygon with all sides of equal length and all angles of equal measure.

Polígono regular Un polígono regular es un polígono que tiene todos los lados de la misma longitud y todos los ángulos de la misma medida.

Relate To relate two different things, find a connection between them.

Relacionar Para relacionar dos cosas diferentes, halla una conexión entre ellas.

Relation Any set of ordered pairs is called a relation.

Relación Todo conjunto de pares ordenados se llama relación.

Relative frequency relative frequency

$$\text{of an event} = \frac{\text{number of times event occurs}}{\text{total number of trials}}$$

Frecuencia relativa frecuencia relativa de un evento $=$

$$\frac{\text{número de veces que sucede el evento}}{\text{número total de pruebas}}$$

Relative frequency table A relative frequency table shows the ratio of the number of data in each category to the total number of data items. The ratio can be expressed as a fraction, decimal, or percent.

Mesa relativa de frecuencia Una mesa relativa de la frecuencia muestra la proporción del número de datos en cada categoría al número total de artículos de datos. La proporción puede ser expresada como una fracción, el decimal, o el por ciento.

Remainder In division, the remainder is the number that is left after the division is complete.

Residuo En una división, el residuo es el número que queda después de terminar la operación.

English/Spanish Glossary

Remote interior angles Remote interior angles are the two nonadjacent interior angles corresponding to each exterior angle of a triangle.

Ángulos internos no adyacentes Los ángulos internos no adyacentes son los dos ángulos internos de un triángulo que se corresponden con el ángulo externo que está más alejado de ellos.

Repeating decimal A repeating decimal has a decimal expansion that repeats the same digit, or block of digits, without end.

Decimal periódico Un decimal periódico tiene una expansión decimal que repite el mismo dígito, o grupo de dígitos, sin fin.

Represent To represent is to stand for or take the place of something else. Symbols, equations, charts, and tables are often used to represent particular situations.

Representar Representar es sustituir u ocupar el lugar de otra cosa. A menudo se usan símbolos, ecuaciones y tablas para representar determinadas situaciones.

Representative sample A representative sample is a sample of a population in which the number of subjects in the sample with the trait that you are studying is proportional to the number of members in the population with that trait. A representative sample accurately represents the population and does not have bias.

Muestra representativa Una muestra representativa es una muestra de una población en la que el número de sujetos de la muestra que tiene la característica que se estudia es proporcional al número de miembros de la población que tienen esa característica. Una muestra representativa representa la población con exactitud y no está sesgada.

Rhombus A rhombus is a parallelogram whose sides are all the same length.

Rombo Un rombo es un paralelogramo que tiene todos sus lados de la misma longitud.

Right angle A right angle is an angle with a measure of 90°.

Ángulo recto Un ángulo recto es un ángulo que mide 90°.

Right cone A right cone is a cone in which the segment representing the height connects the vertex and the center of the base.

Cono recto Un cono recto es un cono en el que el segmento que representa la altura une el vértice y el centro de la base.

English/Spanish Glossary

Right cylinder A right cylinder is a cylinder in which the height joins the centers of the bases.

Cilindro recto Un cilindro recto es un cilindro en el que la altura une los centros de las bases.

Right prism In a right prism, all lateral faces are rectangles.

Prisma recto En un prisma recto, todas las caras laterales son rectángulos.

Right pyramid In a right pyramid, the segment that represents the height intersects the base at its center.

Pirámide recta En una pirámide recta, el segmento que representa la altura interseca la base en el centro.

Right triangle A right triangle is a triangle with one right angle.

Triángulo rectángulo Un triángulo rectángulo es un triángulo que tiene un ángulo recto.

Rigid motion A rigid motion is a transformation that changes only the position of a figure.

Movimiento rígido Un movimiento rígido es una transformación que sólo cambia la posición de una figura.

Rotation A rotation is a rigid motion that turns a figure around a fixed point, called the center of rotation.

Rotación Una rotación es un movimiento rígido que hace girar una figura alrededor de un punto fijo, llamado centro de rotación.

Rounding Rounding a number means replacing the number with a number that tells about how much or how many.

Redondear Redondear un número significa reemplazar ese número por un número que indica más o menos cuánto o cuántos.

S

Sale A sale is a discount offered by a store. A sale does not require the customer to have a coupon.

Venta Una venta es un descuento ofreció por una tienda. Una venta no requiere al cliente a tener un cupón.

English/Spanish Glossary

Sales tax A tax added to the price of goods and services.

Las ventas tasan Un impuesto añadió al precio de bienes y servicios.

Sample of a population A sample of a population is part of the population. A sample is useful when you want to find out about a population but you do not have the resources to study every member of the population.

Muestra de una población Una muestra de una población es una parte de la población. Una muestra es útil cuando quieres saber algo acerca de una población, pero no tienes los recursos para estudiar a cada miembro de esa población.

Sample space The sample space for an action is the set of all possible outcomes of that action.

Espacio muestral El espacio muestral de una acción es el conjunto de todos los resultados posibles de esa acción.

Sampling method A sampling method is the method by which you choose members of a population to sample.

Método de muestreo Un método de muestreo es el método por el cual escoges miembros de una población para muestrear.

Savings Savings is money that a person puts away for use at a later date.

Ahorros Los ahorros son dinero que una persona guarda para el uso en una fecha posterior.

Scale A scale is a ratio that compares a length in a scale drawing to the corresponding length in the actual object.

Escala Una escala es una razón que compara una longitud en un dibujo a escala con la longitud correspondiente en el objeto real.

Scale drawing A scale drawing is an enlarged or reduced drawing of an object that is proportional to the actual object.

Dibujo a escala Un dibujo a escala es un dibujo ampliado o reducido de un objeto que es proporcional al objeto real.

English/Spanish Glossary

Scale factor The scale factor is the ratio of a length in the image to the corresponding length in the original figure.

Factor de escala El factor de escala es la razón de una longitud de la imagen a la longitud correspondiente en la figura original.

Scalene triangle A scalene triangle is a triangle in which no sides have the same length.

Triángulo escaleno Un triángulo escaleno es un triángulo que no tiene lados de la misma longitud.

Scatter plot A scatter plot is a graph that uses points to display the relationship between two different sets of data. Each point can be represented by an ordered pair.

Diagrama de dispersión Un diagrama de dispersión es una gráfica que usa puntos para mostrar la relación entre dos conjuntos de datos diferentes. Cada punto se puede representar con un par ordenado.

Scholarship A type of monetary award a student can use to pay for his or her education. The student does not need to repay this money.

Beca Un tipo de premio monetario que un estudiante puede utilizar para pagar por su educación. El estudiante no debe devolver este dinero.

Scientific notation A number in scientific notation is written as the product of two factors, one greater than or equal to 1 and less than 10, and the other a power of 10.

Notación científica Un número en notación científica está escrito como el producto de dos factores, uno mayor que o igual a 1 y menor que 10, y el otro una potencia de 10.

Segment A segment is part of a line. It consists of two endpoints and all of the points on the line between the endpoints.

Segmento Un segmento es una parte de una recta. Está formado por dos extremos y todos los puntos de la recta que están entre los extremos.

Semicircle A semicircle is one half of a circle.

Semicírculo Un semicírculo es la mitad de un círculo.

English/Spanish Glossary

Similar figures A two-dimensional figure is similar to another two-dimensional figure if you can map one figure to the other by a sequence of rotations, reflections, translations, and dilations.

Figuras semejantes Una figura bidimensional es semejante a otra figura bidimensional si puedes hacer corresponder una figura con otra mediante una secuencia de rotaciones, reflexiones, traslaciones y dilataciones.

Simple interest Simple interest is interest paid only on an original deposit. To calculate simple interest, use the formula where I is the simple interest, p is the principal, r is the annual interest rate, and t is the number of years that the account earns interest.

Interés simple El interés simple es el interés que se paga sobre un depósito original solamente. Para calcular el interés simple, usa la fórmula donde I es el interés simple, c es el capital, r es la tasa de interés anual y t es el número de años en que la cuenta obtiene un interés.

Simple random sampling Simple random sampling is a sampling method in which every member of the population has an equal chance of being chosen for the sample.

Muestreo aleatorio simple El muestreo aleatorio simple es un método de muestreo en el que cada miembro de la población tiene la misma probabilidad de ser seleccionado para la muestra.

Simpler form A fraction is in simpler form when it is equivalent to a given fraction and has smaller numbers in the numerator and denominator.

Forma simplificada Una fracción está en su forma simplificada cuando es equivalente a otra fracción dada, pero tiene números más pequeños en el numerador y el denominador.

Simplest form A fraction is in simplest form when the only common factor of the numerator and denominator is one.

Mínima expresión Una fracción está en su mínima expresión cuando el único factor común del numerador y el denominador es 1.

Simplify an algebraic expression To simplify an algebraic expression, combine the like terms of the expression.

Simplificar una expresión algebraica Para simplificar una expresión algebraica, combina los términos semejantes de la expresión.

English/Spanish Glossary

Simulation A simulation is a model of a real-world situation that is used to find probabilities.

Simulación Una simulación es un modelo de una situación de la vida diaria que se usa para hallar probabilidades.

Sketch To sketch a figure, draw a rough outline. When a sketch is asked for, it means that a drawing needs to be included in your response.

Bosquejo Para hacer un bosquejo, dibuja un esquema simple. Si se pide un bosquejo, tu respuesta debe incluir un dibujo.

Slant height of a cone The slant height of a cone, ℓ, is the length of its lateral surface from base to vertex.

Altura inclinada de un cono La altura inclinada de un cono, ℓ, es la longitud de su superficie lateral desde la base hasta el vértice.

Slant height of a pyramid The slant height of a pyramid is the height of a lateral face.

Altura inclinada de una pirámide La altura inclinada de una pirámide es la altura de una cara lateral.

Slope Slope is a ratio that describes steepness.

$$\text{slope} = \frac{\text{vertical change}}{\text{horizontal change}} = \frac{\text{rise}}{\text{run}}$$

Pendiente La pendiente es una razón que describe la inclinación.

$$\text{pendiente} = \frac{\text{cambio vertical}}{\text{cambio horizontal}}$$
$$= \frac{\text{distancia vertical}}{\text{distancia horizontal}}$$

Slope of a line slope =
$$\frac{\text{change in } y\text{-coordinates}}{\text{change in } x\text{-coordinates}} = \frac{\text{rise}}{\text{run}}$$

Pendiente de una recta pendiente =
$$\frac{\text{cambio en las coordenadas } y}{\text{cambio en las coordenadas } x}$$
$$= \frac{\text{distancia vertical}}{\text{distancia horizontal}}$$

Slope-intercept form An equation written in the form $y = mx + b$ is in slope-intercept form. The graph is a line with slope m and y-intercept b.

Forma pendiente-intercepto Una ecuación escrita en la forma $y = mx + b$ está en forma de pendiente-intercepto. La gráfica es una línea recta con pendiente m e intercepto en y b.

English/Spanish Glossary

Solution of a system of linear equations A solution of a system of linear equations is any ordered pair that makes all the equations of that system true.

Solución de un sistema de ecuaciones lineales Una solución de un sistema de ecuaciones lineales es cualquier par ordenado que hace que todas las ecuaciones de ese sistema sean verdaderas.

Solution of an equation A solution of an equation is a value of the variable that makes the equation true.

Solución de una ecuación Una solución de una ecuación es un valor de la variable que hace que la ecuación sea verdadera.

Solution of an inequality The solutions of an inequality are the values of the variable that make the inequality true.

Solución de una desigualdad Las soluciones de una desigualdad son los valores de la variable que hacen que la desigualdad sea verdadera.

Solution set A solution set contains all of the numbers that satisfy an equation or inequality.

Conjunto solución Un conjunto solución contiene todos los números que satisfacen una ecuación o desigualdad.

Solve To solve a given statement, determine the value or values that make the statement true. Several methods and strategies can be used to solve a problem, including estimating, isolating the variable, drawing a graph, or using a table of values.

Resolver Para resolver un enunciado dado, determina el valor o los valores que hacen que ese enunciado sea verdadero. Para resolver un problema se pueden usar varios métodos y estrategias, como estimar, aislar la variable, dibujar una gráfica o usar una tabla de valores.

Sphere A sphere is the set of all points in space that are the same distance from a center point.

Esfera Una esfera es el conjunto de todos los puntos en el espacio que están a la misma distancia de un punto central.

Square A square is a quadrilateral with four right angles and all sides the same length.

Cuadrado Un cuadrado es un cuadrilátero que tiene cuatro ángulos rectos y todos los lados de la misma longitud.

English/Spanish Glossary

Square root A square root of a number is a number that, when multiplied by itself, equals the original number.

Raíz cuadrada La raíz cuadrada de un número es un número que, cuando se multiplica por sí mismo, es igual al número original.

Square unit A square unit is the area of a square that has sides that are 1 unit long.

Unidad cuadrada Una unidad cuadrada es el área de un cuadrado en el que cada lado mide 1 unidad de longitud.

Standard form A number written using digits and place value is in standard form.

Forma estándar Un número escrito con dígitos y valor posicional está escrito en forma estándar.

Statistical question A statistical question is a question that investigates an aspect of the real world and can have variety in the responses.

Pregunta estadística Una pregunta estadística es una pregunta que investiga un aspecto de la vida diaria y puede tener varias respuestas.

Statistics Statistics is the study of collecting, organizing, graphing, and analyzing data to draw conclusions about the real world.

Estadística La estadística es el estudio de la recolección, organización, representación gráfica y análisis de datos para sacar conclusiones sobre la vida diaria.

Stem-and-leaf plot A stem-and-leaf plot is a graph that uses the digits of each number to show the data distribution. Each data item is broken into a stem and into a leaf. The leaf is the last digit of the data value. The stem is the other digit or digits of the data value.

Complot de tallo y hoja Un complot del tallo y la hoja es un gráfico que utiliza los dígitos de cada número para mostrar la distribución de datos. Cada artículo de datos es roto en un tallo y en una hoja. La hoja es el último dígito de los datos valora. El tallo es el otro dígito o los dígitos de los datos valoran.

Stored-value card A stored-value card is a prepaid card electronically coded to be worth a specified amount of money.

Tarjeta de almacenado-valor Una tarjeta del almacenado-valor es una tarjeta pagada por adelantado codificó electrónicamente valer una cantidad especificado de dinero.

English/Spanish Glossary

Straight angle A straight angle is an angle with a measure of 180°.

Ángulo llano Un ángulo llano es un ángulo que mide 180°.

Student Loan A student loan provides money to a student to pay for college. The student needs to repay the loan after leaving college. Often the student will need to pay interest on the amount of the loan.

Crédito personal para estudiantes Un crédito personal para estudiantes le proporciona dinero a un estudiante para pagar por el colegio. El estudiante debe devolver el préstamo después de dejar el colegio. A menudo el estudiante deberá pagar interés en la cantidad del préstamo.

Subject Each member in a sample is a subject.

Sujeto Cada miembro de una muestra es un sujeto.

Sum The sum is the answer to an addition problem.

Suma o total La suma o total es el resultado de una operación de suma.

Summarize To summarize an explanation or solution, go over or review the most important points.

Resumir Para resumir una explicación o solución, revisa o repasa los puntos más importantes.

Supplementary angles Two angles are supplementary angles if the sum of their measures is 180°. Supplementary angles that are adjacent form a straight angle.

Ángulos suplementarios Dos ángulos son suplementarios si la suma de sus medidas es 180°. Los ángulos suplementarios que son adyacentes forman un ángulo llano.

Surface area of a cone The surface area of a cone is the sum of the lateral area and the area of the base. The formula for the surface area of a cone is S.A. L.A. *B*.

Área total de un cono El área total de un cono es la suma del área lateral y el área de la base. La fórmula del área total de un cono es A.T. A.L. *B*.

English/Spanish Glossary

Surface area of a cube The surface area of a cube is the sum of the areas of the faces of the cube. The formula for the surface area, S.A., of a cube is S.A. , where s represents the length of an edge of the cube.

Área total de un cubo El área total de un cubo es la suma de las áreas de las caras del cubo. La fórmula del área total, A.T., de un cubo es A.T. , donde s representa la longitud de una arista del cubo.

Surface area of a cylinder The surface area of a cylinder is the sum of the lateral area and the areas of the two circular bases. The formula for the surface area of a cylinder is S.A. L.A. 2B, where L.A. represents the lateral area of the cylinder and B represents the area of a base of the cylinder.

Área total de un cilindro El área total de un cilindro es la suma del área lateral y las áreas de las dos bases circulares. La fórmula del área total de un cilindro es A.T. A.L. 2B, donde A.L. representa el área lateral del cilindro y B representa el área de una base del cilindro.

Surface area of a pyramid The surface area of a pyramid is the sum of the areas of the faces of the pyramid. The formula for the surface area, S.A., of a pyramid is S.A. = L.A. + B, where L.A. represents the lateral area of the pyramid and B represents the area of the base of the pyramid.

Área total de una pirámide El área total de una pirámide es la suma de las áreas de las caras de la pirámide. La fórmula del área total, A.T., de una pirámide es A.T. = A.L. + B, donde A.L. representa el área lateral de la pirámide y B representa el área de la base de la pirámide.

Surface area of a sphere The surface area of a sphere is equal to the lateral area of a cylinder that has the same radius, r, and height 2r. The formula for the surface area of a sphere is S.A. = $4\pi r^2$, where r represents the radius of the sphere.

Área total de una esfera El área total de una esfera es igual al área lateral de un cilindro que tiene el mismo radio, r, y una altura de 2r. La fórmula del área total de una esfera es A.T. = $4\pi r^2$, donde r representa el radio de la esfera.

Surface area of a three-dimensional figure The surface area of a three-dimensional figure is the sum of the areas of its faces. You can find the surface area by finding the area of the net of the three-dimensional figure.

Área total de una figura tridimensional El área total de una figura tridimensional es la suma de las áreas de sus caras. Puedes hallar el área total si hallas el área del modelo plano de la figura tridimensional.

English/Spanish Glossary

System of linear equations A system of linear equations is formed by two or more linear equations that use the same variables.

Sistema de ecuaciones lineales Un sistema de ecuaciones lineales está formado por dos o más ecuaciones lineales que usan las mismas variables.

Systematic sampling Systematic sampling is a sampling method in which you choose every nth member of the population, where n is a predetermined number. A systematic sample is useful when the researcher is able to approach the population in a systematic, or methodical, way.

Muestreo sistemático El muestreo sistemático es un método de muestreo en el que se escoge cada enésimo miembro de la población, donde n es un número predeterminado. Una muestra sistemática es útil cuando el investigador puede enfocarse en la población de manera sistemática o metódica.

T

Taxable wages For federal income tax purposes, your taxable wages are the difference between your earned wages and your withholding allowance. Your employer divides your withholding allowance equally among the pay periods of one year.

Sueldos imponibles Para propósitos federales de impuesto de renta, sus sueldos imponibles son la diferencia entre sus sueldos ganados y su concesión que retienen. Su empleador divide su concesión que retiene igualmente entre los períodos de paga de un año.

Tenths One tenth is one out of ten equal parts of a whole.

Décimas Una décima es 1 de 10 partes iguales de un todo.

Term A term is a number, a variable, or the product of a number and one or more variables.

Término Un término es un número, una variable o el producto de un número y una o más variables.

Terminating decimal A terminating decimal has a decimal expansion that terminates in 0.

Decimal finito Un decimal finito tiene una expansión decimal que termina en 0.

English/Spanish Glossary

Terms of a ratio The terms of a ratio are the quantities *x* and *y* in the ratio.

Términos de una razón Los términos de una razón son la cantidad *x* y la cantidad *y* de la razón.

Theorem A theorem is a conjecture that is proven.

Teorema Un teorema es una conjetura que se ha comprobado.

Theoretical probability When all outcomes of an action are equally likely,

$$P(\text{event}) = \frac{\text{number of favourable outcomes}}{\text{number of possible outcomes}}.$$

Probabilidad teórica Cuando todos los resultados de una acción son igualmente probables, $P(\text{evento}) =$

$$\frac{\text{número de resultados favorables}}{\text{número de resultados posibles}}.$$

Third quartile For an ordered set of data, the third quartile is the median of the upper half of the data set.

Tercer cuartil Para un conjunto de datos ordenados, el tercer cuartil es la mediana de la mitad superior del conjunto de datos.

Thousandths One thousandth is one part of 1,000 equal parts of a whole.

Milésimas Una milésima es 1 de 1,000 partes iguales de un todo.

Three-dimensional figure A three-dimensional (3-D) figure is a figure that does not lie in a plane.

Figura tridimensional Una figura tridimensional es una figura que no está en un plano.

Total cost of a loan The total cost of a loan is the total amount spent to repay the loan. Total cost includes the principal and all interest paid over the length of the loan. Total cost also includes any fees charged.

El coste total de un préstamo El coste total de un préstamo es el cantidad total que es gastado para devolver el préstamo. El coste total incluye al director y todo el interés pagó sobre la longitud del préstamo. El coste total también incluye cualquier honorario cargado.

Transaction A banking transaction moves money into or out of a bank account.

Transacción Una transacción bancaria mueve dinero en o fuera de una cuenta bancaria.

English/Spanish Glossary

Transfer A transaction that moves money from one bank account to another is a transfer. The balance of one account increases by the same amount the other account decreases.

Transferencia Una transacción que mueve dinero de una cuenta bancaria a otro es una transferencia. El equilibrio de un aumentos de cuenta por la misma cantidad que la otra cuenta disminuye.

Transformation A transformation is a change in position, shape, or size of a figure. Three types of transformations that change position only are translations, reflections, and rotations.

Transformación Una transformación es un cambio en la posición, la forma o el tamaño de una figura. Tres tipos de transformaciones que cambian sólo la posición son las traslaciones, las reflexiones y las rotaciones.

Translation A translation, or slide, is a rigid motion that moves every point of a figure the same distance and in the same direction.

Traslación Una traslación, o deslizamiento, es un movimiento rígido que mueve cada punto de una figura a la misma distancia y en la misma dirección.

Transversal A transversal is a line that intersects two or more lines at different points.

Transversal o secante Una transversal o secante es una línea que interseca dos o más líneas en distintos puntos.

Trapezoid A trapezoid is a quadrilateral with exactly one pair of parallel sides.

Trapecio Un trapecio es un cuadrilátero que tiene exactamente un par de lados paralelos.

Trend line A trend line is a line on a scatter plot, drawn near the points, that approximates the association between the data sets.

Línea de tendencia Una línea de tendencia es una línea en un diagrama de dispersión, trazada cerca de los puntos, que se aproxima a la relación entre los conjuntos de datos.

Trial In a probability experiment, you carry out or observe an action repeatedly. Each observation of the action is a trial.

Prueba En un experimento de probabilidad, realizas u observas una acción varias veces. Cada observación de la acción es una prueba.

Triangle A triangle is a polygon with three sides.

Triángulo Un triángulo es un polígono de tres lados.

English/Spanish Glossary

Triangular prism A triangular prism is a prism with bases in the shape of a triangle.

Prisma triangular Un prisma triangular es un prisma cuyas bases tienen la forma de un triángulo.

True equation A true equation has equal values on each side of the equals sign.

Ecuación verdadera En una ecuación verdadera, los valores a ambos lados del signo igual son iguales.

Two-way frequency table A two-way frequency table displays the counts of the data in each group.

Tabla de frecuencia con dos variables Una tabla de frecuencia con dos variables muestra el conteo de los datos de cada grupo.

Two-way relative frequency table A two-way relative frequency table shows the ratio of the number of data in each group to the size of the population. The relative frequencies can be calculated with respect to the entire population, the row populations, or the column populations. The relative frequencies can be expressed as fractions, decimals, or percents.

Tabla de frecuencias relativas con dos variables Una tabla de frecuencias relativas con dos variables muestra la razón del número de datos de cada grupo al tamaño de la población. Las frecuencias relativas se pueden calcular respecto de la población entera, las poblaciones de las filas o las poblaciones de las columnas. Las frecuencias relativas se pueden expresar como fracciones, decimales o porcentajes.

Two-way table A two-way table shows bivariate categorical data for a population.

Tabla con dos variables Una tabla con dos variables muestra datos bivariados por categorías de una población.

U

Uniform probability model A uniform probability model is a probability model based on using the theoretical probability of equally likely outcomes.

Modelo de probabilidad uniforme Un modelo de probabilidad uniforme es un modelo de probabilidad que se basa en el uso de la probabilidad teórica de resultados igualmente probables.

English/Spanish Glossary

Unit fraction A unit fraction is a fraction with a numerator of 1 and a denominator that is a whole number greater than 1.

Fracción unitaria Una fracción unitaria es una fracción con un numerador 1 y un denominador que es un número entero mayor que 1.

Unit price A unit price is a unit rate that gives the price of one item.

Precio por unidad El precio por unidad es una tasa por unidad que muestra el precio de un artículo.

Unit rate The rate for one unit of a given quantity is called the unit rate.

Tasa por unidad Se llama tasa por unidad a la tasa que corresponde a 1 unidad de una cantidad dada.

Use To use given information, draw on it to help you determine something else.

Usar Para usar una información dada, apóyate en ella para determinar otra cosa.

V

Valid inference A valid inference is an inference that is true about the population. Valid inferences can be made when they are based on data from a representative sample.

Inferencia válida Una inferencia válida es una inferencia verdadera acerca de una población. Se pueden hacer inferencias válidas si están basadas en los datos de una muestra representativa.

Variability Variability describes how much the items in a data set differ (or vary) from each other. On a data display, variability is shown by how much the data on the horizontal scale are spread out.

Variabilidad La variabilidad describe qué diferencia (o variación) existe entre los elementos de un conjunto de datos. Al exhibir datos, la variabilidad queda representada por la distancia que separa los datos en la escala horizontal.

Variable A variable is a letter that represents an unknown value.

Variable Una variable es una letra que representa un valor desconocido.

Variable expenses Variable expenses are expenses that change from one budget period to the next.

Gastos variables Los gastos variables son los gastos que cambian de un período económico al próximo.

English/Spanish Glossary

Vertex of a cone The vertex of a cone is the point farthest from the base.

Vértice de un cono El vértice de un cono es el punto más alejado de la base.

Vertex of a polygon The vertex of a polygon is any point where two sides of a polygon meet.

Vértice de un polígono El vértice de un polígono es cualquier punto donde se encuentran dos lados de un polígono.

Vertex of a three-dimensional figure A vertex of a three-dimensional figure is a point where three or more edges meet.

Vértice de una figura tridimensional El vértice de una figura tridimensional es un punto donde se unen tres o más aristas.

Vertex of an angle The vertex of an angle is the point of intersection of the rays that make up the sides of the angle.

Vértice de un ángulo El vértice de un ángulo es el punto de intersección de las semirrectas que forman los lados del ángulo.

Vertical angles Vertical angles are formed by two intersecting lines and are opposite each other. Vertical angles have equal measures.

Ángulos opuestos por el vértice Los ángulos opuestos por el vértice están formados por dos rectas secantes y están uno frente a otro. Los ángulos opuestos por el vértice tienen la misma medida.

Vertical-line test The vertical-line test is a method used to determine if a relation is a function or not. If a vertical line passes through a graph more than once, the graph is not the graph of a function.

Prueba de recta vertical La prueba de recta vertical es un método que se usa para determinar si una relación es una función o no. Si una recta vertical atraviesa la gráfica más de una vez, la gráfica no es la gráfica de una función.

Volume Volume is the number of cubic units needed to fill a solid figure.

Volumen El volumen es el número de unidades cúbicas que se necesitan para llenar un cuerpo geométrico.

English/Spanish Glossary

Volume of a cone The volume of a cone is the number of unit cubes, or cubic units, needed to fill the cone. The formula for the volume of a cone is $V = \frac{1}{3}Bh$, where B represents the area of the base and h represents the height of the cone.

Volumen de un cono El volumen de un cono es el número de bloques de unidades, o unidades cúbicas, que se necesitan para llenar el cono. La fórmula del volumen de un cono $V = \frac{1}{3}Bh$, donde B representa el área de la base y h representa la altura del cono.

Volume of a cube The volume of a cube is the number of unit cubes, or cubic units, needed to fill the cube. The formula for the volume V of a cube is $V = s^3$, where s represents the length of an edge of the cube.

Volumen de un cubo El volumen de un cubo es el número de bloques de unidades, o unidades cúbicas, que se necesitan para llenar el cubo. La fórmula del volumen, V, de un cubo es $V = s^3$, donde s representa la longitud de una arista del cubo.

Volume of a cylinder The volume of a cylinder is the number of unit cubes, or cubic units, needed to fill the cylinder. The formula for the volume of a cylinder is $V = \pi r^2 h$, where r represents the radius of a base and h represents the height of the cylinder.

Volumen de un cilindro El volumen de un cilindro es el número de bloques de unidades, o unidades cúbicas, que se necesitan para llenar el cilindro. La fórmula del volumen de un cilindro es $V = \pi r^2 h$, donde r representa el radio de una base y h representa la altura del cilindro.

Volume of a prism The volume of a prism is the number of unit cubes, or cubic units, needed to fill the prism. The formula for the volume V of a prism is $V = Bh$, where B represents the area of a base and h represents the height of the prism.

Volumen de un prisma El volumen de un prisma es el número de bloques de unidades, o unidades cúbicas, que se necesitan para llenar el prisma. La fórmula del volumen, V, de un prisma $V = Bh$, donde B representa el área de una base y h representa la altura del prisma.

Volume of a pyramid The volume of a pyramid is the number of unit cubes needed to fill the pyramid. The formula for the volume V of a pyramid is $V = \frac{1}{3}Bh$, where B represents the area of the base and h represents the height of the pyramid.

Volumen de una pirámide El volumen de una pirámide es el número de bloques de unidades, o unidades cúbicas, que se necesitan para llenar la pirámide. La fórmula del volumen, V, de una pirámide es $V = \frac{1}{3}Bh$, donde B representa el área de la base y h representa la altura de la pirámide.

English/Spanish Glossary

Volume of a sphere The volume of a sphere is the number of unit cubes, or cubic units, needed to fill the sphere. The formula for the volume of a sphere is $V = \frac{4}{3}\pi r^3$.

Volumen de una esfera El volumen de una esfera es el número de bloques de unidades, o unidades cúbicas, que se necesitan para llenar la esfera. La fórmula del volumen de una esfera es $V = \frac{4}{3}\pi r^3$.

W

Whole numbers The whole numbers consist of the number 0 and all of the natural numbers.

Números enteros no negativos Los números enteros no negativos son el número 0 y todos los números naturales.

Withdrawal A transaction that takes money out of a bank account is a withdrawal.

Retirada Una transacción que toma dinero fuera de una cuenta bancaria es una retirada.

Withholding allowance You can exclude a portion of your earned wages, called a withholding allowance, from federal income tax. You can claim one withholding allowance for yourself and one for each person dependent upon your income.

Retener concesión Puede excluir una porción de sus sueldos ganados, llamó una concesión que retiene, del impuesto de renta federal. Puede reclamar una concesión que retiene para usted mismo y para uno para cada dependiente de persona sobre sus ingresos.

Word form of a number The word form of a number is the number written in words.

Número en palabras Un número en palabras es un número escrito con palabras en lugar de dígitos.

Work-Study Work-study is a type of need-based aid that schools might offer to a student. A student must earn work-study money by working certain jobs.

Práctica estudiantil La práctica estudiantil es un tipo de ayuda necesidad-basado que escuelas quizás ofrezcan a un estudiante. Un estudiante debe ganar dinero de práctica estudiantil por ciertos trabajos de trabajo.

English/Spanish Glossary

X

x-axis The x-axis is the horizontal number line that, together with the y-axis, forms the coordinate plane.

Eje de las x El eje de las x es la recta numérica horizontal que, junto con el eje de las y, forma el plano de coordenadas.

x-coordinate The x-coordinate is the first number in an ordered pair. It tells the number of horizontal units a point is from 0.

Coordenada x La coordenada x (abscisa) es el primer número de un par ordenado. Indica cuántas unidades horizontales hay entre un punto y 0.

Y

y-axis The y-axis is the vertical number line that, together with the x-axis, forms the coordinate plane.

Eje de las y El eje de las y es la recta numérica vertical que, junto con el eje de las x, forma el plano de coordenadas.

y-coordinate The y-coordinate is the second number in an ordered pair. It tells the number of vertical units a point is from 0.

Coordenada y La coordenada y (ordenada) es el segundo número de un par ordenado. Indica cuántas unidades verticales hay entre un punto y 0.

y-intercept The y-intercept of a line is the y-coordinate of the point where the line crosses the y-axis.

Intercepto en y El intercepto en y de una recta es la coordenada y del punto por donde la recta cruza el eje de las y.

Z

Zero exponent property For any nonzero number a, $a^0 = 1$.

Propiedad del exponente cero Para cualquier número distinto de cero a, $a^0 = 1$.

Zero Property of Multiplication The product of 0 and any number is 0. For any number n, $n \cdot 0 = 0$ and $0 \cdot n = 0$.

Propiedad del cero en la multiplicación El producto de 0 y cualquier número es 0. Para cualquier número n, $n \cdot 0 = 0$ and $0 \cdot n = 0$.

Formulas

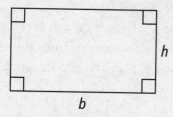

$$P = 2b + 2h$$
$$A = bh$$

Rectangle

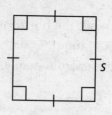

$$P = 4s$$
$$A = s^2$$

Square

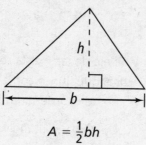

$$A = \frac{1}{2}bh$$

Triangle

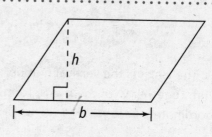

$$A = bh$$

Parallelogram

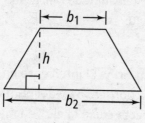

$$A = \frac{1}{2}h(b_1 + b_2)$$

Trapezoid

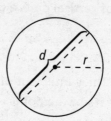

$$C = 2\pi r \text{ or } C = \pi d$$
$$A = \pi r^2$$

Circle

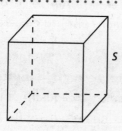

$$S.A. = 6s^2$$
$$V = s^3$$

Cube

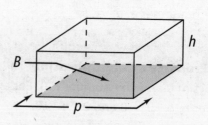

$$V = Bh$$
$$L.A. = ph$$
$$S.A. = L.A. + 2B$$

Rectangular Prism

Formulas

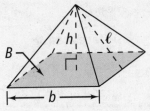

$V = \frac{1}{3}Bh$

L.A. $= 2b\ell$

S.A. $=$ L.A. $+ B$

Square Pyramid

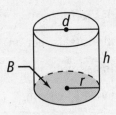

$V = Bh$

L.A. $= 2\pi rh$

S.A. $=$ L.A. $+ 2B$

Cylinder

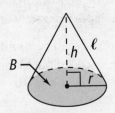

$V = \frac{1}{3}Bh$

L.A. $= \pi r\ell$

S.A. $=$ L.A. $+ B$

Cone

$V = \frac{4}{3}\pi r^3$

S.A. $= 4\pi r^2$

Sphere

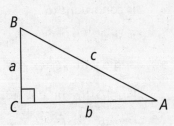

$a^2 + b^2 = c^2$

Pythagorean Theorem

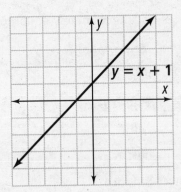

$y = mx + b$, where
$m =$ slope and
$b = y$-intercept

Equation of Line

Math Symbols

$+$	plus (addition)		r	radius
$-$	minus (subtraction)		S.A.	surface area
$\times$, $\cdot$	times (multiplication)		B	area of base
$\div$, $\overline{)}$, $\frac{a}{b}$	divide (division)		L.A.	lateral area
$=$	is equal to		ℓ	slant height
$<$	is less than		V	volume
$>$	is greater than		a^n	nth power of a
$\leq$	is less than or equal to		$\sqrt{x}$	nonnegative square root of x
$\geq$	is greater than or equal to		π	pi, an irrational number approximately equal to 3.14
$\neq$	is not equal to			
$(\ )$	parentheses for grouping		(a, b)	ordered pair with x-coordinate a and y-coordinate b
$[\ ]$	brackets for grouping			
$-a$	opposite of a		$\overline{AB}$	segment AB
$\ldots$	and so on		A'	image of A, A prime
$^{\circ}$	degrees		$\triangle ABC$	triangle with vertices A, B, and C
$|a|$	absolute value of a			
$\stackrel{?}{=}, \stackrel{?}{<}, \stackrel{?}{>}$	Is the statement true?		$\rightarrow$	arrow notation
$\approx$	is approximately equal to		$a : b, \frac{a}{b}$	ratio of a to b
$\frac{b}{a}$	reciprocal of $\frac{a}{b}$		$\cong$	is congruent to
A	area		$\sim$	is similar to
ℓ	length		$\angle A$	angle with vertex A
w	width		AB	length of segment $\overline{AB}$
h	height		$\overrightarrow{AB}$	ray AB
d	distance		$\angle ABC$	angle formed by $\overrightarrow{BA}$ and $\overrightarrow{BC}$
r	rate		$m\angle ABC$	measure of angle ABC
t	time		$\perp$	is perpendicular to
P	perimeter		$\overleftrightarrow{AB}$	line AB
b	base length		$\parallel$	is parallel to
C	circumference		$\%$	percent
d	diameter		P (event)	probability of an event

Measures

Customary	Metric
Length	**Length**
1 foot (ft) = 12 inches (in.) 1 yard (yd) = 36 in. 1 yd = 3 ft 1 mile (mi) = 5,280 ft 1 mi = 1,760 yd	1 centimeter (cm) = 10 millimeters (mm) 1 meter (m) = 100 cm 1 kilometer (km) = 1,000 m 1 mm = 0.001 m
Area	**Area**
1 square foot (ft^2) = 144 square inches ($in.^2$) 1 square yard (yd^2) = 9 ft^2 1 square mile (mi^2) = 640 acres	1 square centimeter (cm^2) = 100 square millimeters (mm^2) 1 square meter (m^2) = 10,000 cm^2
Volume	**Volume**
1 cubic foot (ft^3) = 1,728 cubic inches ($in.^3$) 1 cubic yard (yd^3) = 27 ft^3	1 cubic centimeter (cm^3) = 1,000 cubic millimeters (mm^3) 1 cubic meter (m^3) = 1,000,000 cm^3
Mass	**Mass**
1 pound (lb) = 16 ounces (oz) 1 ton (t) = 2,000 lb	1 gram (g) = 1,000 milligrams (mg) 1 kilogram (kg) = 1,000 g
Capacity	**Capacity**
1 cup (c) = 8 fluid ounces (fl oz) 1 pint (pt) = 2 c 1 quart (qt) = 2 pt 1 gallon (gal) = 4 qt	1 liter (L) = 1,000 milliliters (mL) 1000 liters = 1 kiloliter (kL)

Customary Units and Metric Units	
Length	1 in. = 2.54 cm 1 mi ≈ 1.61 km 1 ft ≈ 0.3 m
Capacity	1 qt ≈ 0.94 L
Weight and Mass	1 oz ≈ 28.3 g 1 lb ≈ 0.45 kg

Properties

Unless otherwise stated, the variables *a*, *b*, *c*, *m*, and *n* used in these properties can be replaced with any number represented on a number line.

Identity Properties

Addition $\quad n + 0 = n$ and $0 + n = n$

Multiplication $\quad n \cdot 1 = n$ and $1 \cdot n = n$

Commutative Properties

Addition $\quad a + b = b + a$

Multiplication $\quad a \cdot b = b \cdot a$

Associative Properties

Addition $\quad (a + b) + c = a + (b + c)$

Multiplication $\quad (a \cdot b) \cdot c = a \cdot (b \cdot c)$

Inverse Properties

Addition

$a + (-a) = 0$ and $-a + a = 0$

Multiplication

$a \cdot \frac{1}{a} = 1$ and $\frac{1}{a} \cdot a = 1$, $(a \neq 0)$

Distributive Properties

$a(b + c) = ab + ac \quad (b + c)a = ba + ca$

$a(b - c) = ab - ac \quad (b - c)a = ba - ca$

Properties of Equality

Addition $\quad$ If $a = b$,

then $a + c = b + c$.

Subtraction $\quad$ If $a = b$,

then $a - c = b - c$.

Multiplication $\quad$ If $a = b$,

then $a \cdot c = b \cdot c$.

Division $\quad$ If $a = b$, and $c \neq 0$,

then $\frac{a}{c} = \frac{b}{c}$.

Substitution $\quad$ If $a = b$, then b can

replace a in any

expression.

Zero Property

$a \cdot 0 = 0$ and $0 \cdot a = 0$.

Properties of Inequality

Addition $\quad$ If $a > b$,

then $a + c > b + c$.

If $a < b$,

then $a + c < b + c$.

Subtraction $\quad$ If $a > b$,

then $a - c > b - c$.

If $a < b$,

then $a - c < b - c$.

Multiplication

If $a > b$ and $c > 0$, then $ac > bc$.

If $a < b$ and $c > 0$, then $ac < bc$.

If $a > b$ and $c < 0$, then $ac < bc$.

If $a < b$ and $c < 0$, then $ac > bc$.

Division

If $a > b$ and $c > 0$, then $\frac{a}{c} > \frac{b}{c}$.

If $a < b$ and $c > 0$, then $\frac{a}{c} < \frac{b}{c}$.

If $a > b$ and $c < 0$, then $\frac{a}{c} < \frac{b}{c}$.

If $a < b$ and $c < 0$, then $\frac{a}{c} > \frac{b}{c}$.

Properties of Exponents

For any nonzero number *n* and any integers *m* and *n*:

Zero Exponent $\quad a^0 = 1$

Negative Exponent $\quad a^{-n} = \frac{1}{a^n}$

Product of Powers $\quad a^m \cdot a^n = a^{m+n}$

Power of a Product $\quad (ab)^n = a^n b^n$

Quotient of Powers $\quad \frac{a^m}{a^n} = a^{m-n}$

Power of a Quotient $\quad \left(\frac{a}{b}\right)^n = \frac{a^n}{b^n}$

Power of a Power $\quad (a^m)^n = a^{mn}$